SCM STUDYGUIDE TO CHRISTIAN SPIRITUALITY

Ross Thompson
with Gareth Williams

scm press

Scripture quotations are from the New Revised Standard Version of
the Bible, copyright 1989 by the Division of Christian Education of
the National Council of the Churches of Christ in the USA. Used by
permission. All rights reserved.

British Library Cataloguing in Publication data

A catalogue record for this book is available
from the British Library

978 0 334 04093 4

First published in 2008 by SCM Press
13–17 Long Lane,
London EC1A 9PN

www.scm-canterburypress.co.uk

SCM Press is a division of
SCM-Canterbury Press Ltd

Typeset by Regent Typesetting, London
Printed and bound in Great Britain by
Biddles Ltd, King's Lynn, Norfolk

Contents

Introduction

So you have decided to study Christian spirituality. You are not alone. From being thought of as a quirky sideshow of something – maybe philosophy, maybe theology, maybe psychology, nobody was quite sure – spirituality has over the last couple of decades become a focus of great interest, both to people generally, and academically. This book aims to respond to this groundswell of interest, and present Christian spirituality in a way that motivates and engages, and provides a way in to exploring it that is academically sound and rigorous, without presupposing previous study of the subject. It is suitable for Level One students and the equivalent, and the second half might well help provide a foundation for exploration at Level Two. It is equally suitable for the private reader as an introduction covering the ground and offering pointers for reflection and further exploration.

Why are People Studying Spirituality?

But first, let us see what it is we have to tap into; where is all this new interest coming from? It seems to be coming from four different places simultaneously.

Groundswell at the Grassroots

Recent years have seen a growing interest in religious practices and experiences – from the Enneagram to the I Ching, from Ignatian retreats to Zen meditation – in detachment from specific religious commitment. It is commonplace in

Western Europe, at least, that fewer and fewer people identify themselves with religious worship, creeds and institutions, but more and more claim to have their own 'spirituality'. In this sense 'mystics' are increasing, at the expense of 'theists' (Roof, 1993). Books on all kinds of spirituality jostle together on the shelves of even quite small bookshops. People are willing to try anything and to pick and mix in a thoroughly eclectic manner, which some joyfully hail as a liberating 'virtual faith' (Beaudoin, 1998), while others condemn as part of an ominous 'New Age'.

Part of the challenge of a book such as this is to welcome what for many will be their primary motive for studying spirituality, and to harness the associated energy, but to reconcile this with the disciplined respect for the integrity of distinctive faith systems (in this case, Christianity) on the one hand, and the demands of academic study on the other.

Awareness of the Mystical Side of Theology

Meanwhile, there has been a growing interest in the mystical dimension of Christian theology. For many of the neo-orthodox theologians of the twentieth century, mysticism was anathema, and serious theology concerned itself with the supposedly more objective dimensions of scripture, doctrine, faith and revelation. Conversely psychologists such as James, and philosophers of religion, like Otto, Stace and Zaehner (see Chapter 7) were arguing that 'mystical experience' might be studied objectively, independently of theology or confessional belief.

However, as we shall see, this latter approach underwent severe challenges in the face of a growing understanding of how all experience, and spiritual experience in particular, is always linked with the concepts, beliefs and practices of a society. At the same time there were moves to reclaim mysticism for theology (e.g. Lossky, 1957; McIntosh, 1998). Such writers noted the fact that the 'mystics' of the first 12 centuries of Christianity largely coincided with the theologians, and urged the retrieval of a 'mystical theology' in which spirituality and theology are inextricably intertwined.

Though the jury is still out on this issue, there are many today who would say that doctrine without spirituality is barren, and spirituality without doctrine, or at least, without some coherent shared tradition of expression, is subjective and escapist. Of course there are many caught up in the popular groundswell just mentioned who might resent such an appropriation of spirituality by theology, seeing spirituality as a universal human phenomenon which different religions express – and distort – in different ways.

The Political Resurgence of Faith

Until the collapse of Soviet communism around 1990, many shared a paradigm of the world as dominated by two secular ideologies, communism and liberal capitalism. Faiths were assumed to be on the wane, already irrelevant as geo-political powers, and probably destined to die out as personal belief systems too. As today we witness a titanic struggle between an America increasingly influenced by Christian neoconservatism, and an Islamic Middle East, as militant Hinduism gains strength in India and Orthodoxy in the new Russia, and as even vast, atheist China proves unable to overwhelm the Buddhism of the tiny population of Tibet, it has become obvious that this theory of universal secularization represents a projection on the world at large of the parochial experience of Western Europe. To understand the wider world – for better or for worse – it has become essential again to understand the faiths and spiritualities that continue to motivate the majority of its inhabitants.

The 'Postmodern' Academy

And this need has been served by factors making the academy more amenable to the study of spirituality, not as a sideshow of philosophy or theology, but as a stand-alone subject in its own right. In the 'modern' academy, dominated by scientific and philosophical understandings of objectivity, spirituality seemed to most far too subjective to be worthy of study. But with what is often called 'postmodernism', the academy, or at least the 'humanities' branch of it, has become dominated instead by anthropological and cultural studies. This has meant that spirituality has come to be studied as an anthropological phenomenon, in a manner carefully pioneered by the likes of Sandra Schneiders. At the same time, cultural studies has also made possible a deconstructive approach, in which spirituality is studied to be unmasked as a part of the religious ideologies used to control people.

Possible Tensions

All these factors make for exciting possibilities and a growing demand for the study of spirituality. But the factors are not all in harmony; they are rather like waves that clash and form vortices as they contest for the mainstream. In these turbulent waters, there are several instances of 'Scylla and Charybdis', hazards which, as we negotiate the rapids of the contemporary study of the subject, we have to steer carefully between.

Academic Versus Popular, or 'Outsider' Versus 'Insider'

As you come to study the subject the most obvious tension may be between studying spirituality as an academic subject and practising it as part of your life. As the tender plant of spiritual growth and awareness is subjected to the cold gaze of academic scrutiny, is there a danger it will wither and die? Conversely, if you come without any specific faith commitment, are you going to be somehow pressured to have one?

This links with a distinction that could be described as an 'outside' versus an 'inside' stance. At one extreme, some would argue that to be properly academic, the study of spirituality needs to be as objective and detached as possible, such that a Buddhist or humanist could study Christian spirituality as well as or perhaps better than a Christian. On such an understanding, you have at least to imagine yourself to be an outsider in order to study spirituality objectively. It is necessary to profess neutrality regarding the core ideas about God and reality contained in the tradition or writer being studied. At the other extreme, some argue (e.g. Lindbeck, 1984, discussed on pp. 118–19) that only participants in a culture can truly understand it. You need an 'insider view', so that only Buddhists can understand Buddhist spirituality, and only Christians Christian. The study of spirituality is as confessional by nature as spirituality itself.

However, between these extremes there is a third possibility, according to which you do not need actually to profess or practise the beliefs you are study-ing, but you do need to enter imaginatively into those beliefs, and suspend dis-belief or the desire to contradict them with your own different beliefs. So though a Christian student of Buddhist spirituality, say, would not have temporarily to become a Buddhist, she would need – according to this stance – to take seriously the reality of Buddhist spirituality for Buddhists. Otherwise she would not be able to understand what Buddhist belief systems and ritual and moral practices were all about. And that might come more easily if she took seriously the reality of her own Christian spirituality.

So Mary Frohlich and Sandra Schneiders (in Dreyer and Burrows, 2005, pp. 65–78 and pp. 17–18) make a strong case that the study of spirituality can and should be 'self-implicating' without being confessional. Such self-implication involves not narcissistic introspection in a quest for special inner experiences, Frohlich argues, but interiority, a sense of oneself as a person standing before the ultimate.

And we might add, self-implication is quite compatible with a degree of academic scepticism. As we shall see, the mystics were always ready to be sceptical about themselves, and to cast aside infantile or delusory spirituality in the search for the living God. And they could be challengingly sceptical of the orthodoxies of their day, ready to treat doctrines with a liberating playfulness that sometimes found them on the wrong side of the authorities. As you go through this book we hope that, if you bring a personal spirituality to your studies (and it is not presupposed that you do), you will find it enhanced rather than diminished by this scepticism and playfulness, which are integral to the spiritual journey itself.

'Above' Versus 'Below'

Another tension comes from the difference between the revival in 'mystical theology' and the anthropological and cultural approach of the postmodern university. Is one studying great 'mystics' for their theological ideas, or looking at the spirituality implicit in cultural traditions and practices of ordinary people? Sandra Schneiders (in Dreyer and Burrows, 2005, p. 56ff) called these approaches theological and anthropological respectively; or 'from above' and 'from below'. However, she argues for a 'both/and' approach. Because it studies *Christian* experience, the study of spirituality will have to engage with theology, biblical studies and Christian history. But because it studies Christian *experience*, it will equally need psychology, anthropology and the other tools for the study of experience. Meanwhile Bernard McGinn in his monumental study (1991–) takes a slightly different but equally balanced approach, exploring Christian spirituality 'from below' as a human historical phenomenon in which the presence of God 'above' is disclosed.

Mysticism Versus Spirituality

This divergence is not unrelated to another: whether we should think of what we are studying as 'mysticism' or 'spirituality'. The words have somewhat different connotations (cf. McGrath, 1999, pp. 5–7).

- **'Mysticism'**, unlike 'spirituality', has corresponding terms for its practitioner, the 'mystic', and its object, the 'mysteries': *ta musteria*, the things about which one had to *muo*, close the mouth and keep quiet, the ineffable truths and sacraments of Christian faith, from which 'mysticism' takes its name (Thompson, 2006, pp. 12–14). Mysticism relates much more specifically than spirituality to a particular kind of people – one might say an elite – and their secret or ineffable experience. Not many people, and very few non-religious people, would call themselves 'mystics'.
- **'Spirituality'** has no corresponding name either for the people who practise it or for its object. As used in the sense relevant to this book – from the fifth century (McGinn, in Dreyer and Burrows, p. 26) but rarely until the twentieth – it relates to a noun, 'spirit', which denotes generally the non-material animating principle of life (Hebrew *ruach*, Geek *pneuma*, originally 'wind' or 'breath'). In Christian spirituality this has the specific connotation of life inspired by the Holy Spirit, understood as the third person of the divine Trinity. More widely, however, the term relates to what is vaguely regarded as a whole 'spiritual' dimension of experience or life. As noted, an increasing number of people, including many who profess no religious faith, would claim they have a 'spirituality' or are a 'spiritual person'.

Both terms have strengths and weaknesses for our purposes. 'Mysticism' has the problem of sounding somewhat old fashioned, narrow, elitist and irrelevant to ordinary people's faith. 'Spirituality' has the opposite problem of being all too fashionable, and so broad and varied – as is manifest in McGinn's excellent short history of the term (Dreyer and Burrows, pp. 26–9) – as to defy coherent understanding.

This book will follow the main trends and predominantly use the 'spirituality' set of terms. But we shall be using the word 'mystic', as there is no other convenient term for the practitioner of spirituality, not all of whom were 'spiritual writers'. And we will not offer our own definition, but rather, let the above notions of mysticism and spirituality serve as an indication, and then, in the conclusion, explore whether we have come to a clearer idea of the elusive, many-sided phenomenon we have been chasing.

This Book's Stance and Structure

This book, then, represents a 'middle way' approach: self-implicating rather than either confessional or detached, and looking at spirituality from both 'above' and 'below'. Such an approach is probably best suited to a book designed both for Christian ministerial and lay education, and for university students and general readers of all persuasions. And it is the approach for which the authors are best equipped. Evangelical conversion, work as Anglo-Catholic parish priests, experience of Eastern Orthodoxy – to which one of us is particularly drawn – and teaching of spirituality and other subjects to people with a variety of life experience and faith commitments, have given us an 'insider' empathy with many spiritualities, combined with a need to pose questions 'from outside'. Ambivalent about developments in our own denomination, and not wanting to promote any confessional stance, we remain 'self-implicated' in what we study. And one of the main ways we approach God is through delight in the diverse spiritualities of God's people.

So this book will first emphasize the 'above' approach by studying, in the first part, the great mystics in their theological and historical contexts. In this part we will try to present an encyclopaedic spectrum of the amazing range of Christian mystics, leaving it to the reader to decide what to follow up in greater detail through the recommended 'further' reading at the end of each chapter, and the wider range of references and suggestions for further study at the back of the book. At this stage we will not offer too much by way of interconnecting themes, and the result may be a little like a firework display in which one focuses on the amazing explosion of ideas, knowing there are connections but not seeing them in clear focus.

In the second half of the book we will turn to the 'below' approach, tracing the connections and setting Christianity in a multiplicity of contexts in human life – experience, science, the human body and mind, ethics and human difference – while not letting go of the theological perspective on the way.

At the beginning of Part 2 you will find a table to help you correlate the two approaches. And at the end of each chapter there will be questions to help you reflect in a 'self-implicating' way on issues raised.

Thanks

It is only right to give thanks to those without whom this book would not have been possible: to Barbara Laing of SCM Press, who bravely engaged us to write this book; to the great mystics themselves, studying whom has brought home how much more of them there is yet to understand and delight in; to the great scholars of spirituality whose vast work we have mined for wisdom and insight, among whom we would like to single out the broad perspectives of Louis Bouyer, Bernard McGinn and the specific challenging insights of Denys Turner; and last but by no means least, to Judith, whose hard work and patient love materially and spiritually sustained the main author while writing this book.

Feedback

Finally, comment and feedback on the book would be much appreciated, and can be channelled through Ross Thompson's website, www.holydust.org.

Part 1

History

This first part of the book investigates how Christian spirituality has developed and defined itself in response to a succession of historical challenges. In a book of this size, the chapters cannot contain full historical analysis or exhaustive treatments. Rather they offer a series of sketch maps or half-pictures, to stir you to explore further and complete the picture for yourself.

Table 1 offers a timeline summarizing the main writers and teachers discussed, together with some key events cited in the text as changing the spiritual landscape in some radical way. The line is segmented into strict three-century segments, and within each segment the writers are indented according to the century in which they were mainly active. In this way it is possible to see the fascinating coming and going of the mystics in relation to one another. You may like to reflect on the periods of intense creativity, and the periods of leanness, that emerge from the table much more clearly than from the text.

The text itself is divided historically, but not strictly chronologically. To tell a coherent historical narrative it is often necessary to transgress chronological boundaries. This is most evident between Chapters 2 and 3, which overlap chronologically, but narrate, as will be apparent and as the chapter headings make clear, different aspects of the development of Christian spirituality. It also applies in Chapter 4, where it seemed logical, as will be explained, to carry the story of Eastern Orthodox spirituality through to the present day.

Table 1: Timeline, in 300 year periods (many earlier dates are approximate – see text)

Date	before 300BC	300BC⇒	AD0⇒
People	18th c? Abraham 13th c? Moses 10th c. on: Prophets 630–535 Zoroaster 604–? Lao Tzu 581–497 Pythagoras 551–479 Confucius 550–480 Gautama Buddha 6th c. 'Second Isaiah' 427–347 Plato 5th c. on: Wisdom writers	c.165 Book of Daniel Rise of chariot mysticism and apocalyptic	10BC–50AD Philo of Alexandria 4BC–30AD Jesus of Nazareth AD10–65 Paul of Tarsus 35–107 Ignatius of Antioch 110–160 Marcion 130–200 Irenaeus 150–215 Clement of Alexandria 160–225 Tertullian 185–254 Origen 204–270 Plotinus
Events	587 Jerusalem conquered	167-4 Maccabean revolt	70 Temple destroyed, Jews dispersed

Date	300AD⇒	600⇒	900⇒
People	251–356 Anthony of Egypt 300–391 Makarios the Great 306–373 Ephrem the Syrian 335–394 Gregory of Nyssa 346–399 Evagrius of Pontus 354–450 Augustine of Hippo 5th century: 'Denys' ?–493 Patrick 480–547 Benedict 521–597 Columba 540–604 Gregory the Great	570–632 Mohammed 580–662 Maximus the Confessor c.750 Book of Kells 810–877 John the Scot	949–1042 Symeon the New Theologian 1033–1109 Anselm of Canterbury 1077–1148 William of St Thierry 1090–1153 Bernard of Clairvaux ?–1173 Richard of St Victor 1098–1179 Hildegard of Bingen
Events	312 Constantine converted		1054 Schism of East and West churches

1200 ⇒	1500 ⇒	1800 ⇒
1181–1226 Francis of Assisi	1483–1546 Martin Luther	1770–1831 Friedrich Hegel
1210–1285 Mechthild of Magdeburg	1491–1556 Ignatius of Loyola	1772–1834 S. T. Coleridge
1221–1274 Bonaventure	1509–1564 John Calvin	1792–1866 John Keble
1224–1274 Thomas Aquinas	1515–1582 Teresa of Avila	1797–1883 Sojourner Truth
13th century Hadewijch of Brabant	1542–1591 John of the Cross	1801–1890 John Henry
?–1310 Marguerite Porete	1555–1621 Johann Arndt	Newman
1260–1328 Meister Eckhart	1561–1622 Francis de Sales	1813–1855 Søren Kierkegaard
1265–1321 Dante Alighieri	1564–1616 William Shakespeare	1844–1889 G. M. Hopkins
1293–1381 John Ruusbroec	1575–1624 Jacob Boehme	1870–1922 William Seymour
1296–1359 Gregory Palamas	1593–1633 George Herbert	1873–1897 Thérèse de Lisieux
1322–1392 Sergius of Radonezh	1623–1662 Blaise Pascal	1886–1968 Karl Barth
1330–1387 William Langland	1624–1691 George Fox	1906–1945 D. Bonhoeffer
1340–1380 Catherine of Siena	1633–1705 Jakob Spener	1909–1943 Simone Weil
1342–1417 Julian of Norwich	1637–1674 Thomas Traherne	1929–1968 Martin Luther
1380–1471 Thomas à Kempis	1668–1761 William Law	King
1401–1464 Nicholas of Cusa	1675–1751 J.–P. de Caussade	1915–1968 Thomas Merton
1433–1508 Nil Sorsky	1697–1769 Gerhard Tersteegen	1915–2005 Brother Roger
1439–1515 Joseph of Volokolamsk	1700–1760 N.–L. von Zinzendorf	of Taizé
	1703–1758 Jonathan Edwards	
	1703–1791 John Wesley	
	1724–1827 Immanuel Kant	
	1725–1807 John Newton	
	1757–1827 William Blake	
	1759–1833 Seraphim of Sarov	
	1759–1836 Charles Simeon	
	1768–1834 F. Schleiermacher	
1310 Marguerite Porete burned	**1518** Luther refuses to recant	**1968** 'Student revolution'
	1789 French Revolution	

1

Appearance and Abandonment: Biblical Spirituality

Has any people ever heard the voice of a god speaking out of a fire, as you have heard, and lived? Or has any god ever attempted to go and take a nation for himself from the midst of another nation, by trials, by signs and wonders, by war . . .? To you it was shown so that you would acknowledge that the Lord is God; there is no other besides him. From heaven he made you hear his voice to discipline you. On earth he showed you his great fire, while you heard his words coming out of the fire. (Deut. 4.33–34a, 35–36)

This passage epitomizes several vital characteristics of the prophetic strand of spirituality to be found in the Hebrew Bible, characteristics we could summarize as

- **Experiential** – based on sights like fire, sounds like a voice heard, and events like the exodus from Egypt and the conquest of Canaan. These are 'theophanies' – events believed to manifest God.
- **Awestruck** – these events are exceptional, wonder-inspiring and miraculous.
- **Relational** – the vision, and still more the voice, establishes a relationship between God and the hearers.
- **Corporate** – though it was actually Moses who was described as receiving these visions, they are addressed to the whole people of Israel.

- **Ethical** – the experience conveys commandments and challenges the people to live faithfully to these as expressions of their relationship with God.
- **Theological** – the experience establishes God as the one and only effective God.
- **Imperial** – conquest of other peoples and victory in war are undeniably part of this spirituality. The people are not imperialistic about their faith, but their conquests are seen as tokens of God's faithful presence with them.

The writer of Deuteronomy, and the prophets, were of course not Christians. It may seem strange to begin a book on Christian spirituality by studying spirituality that is not Christian. But Christianity, along with Judaism and Islam, inherited many characteristics of Hebrew spirituality. The founders of what would become Christianity – Jesus, Paul, the other apostles – would have all been steeped in it, and Christian spirituality has always sought its roots in the Bible, including – perhaps especially – the Hebrew Bible, which became the Christian 'Old Testament'.

So in this chapter we will look at the prophetic tradition, and then at the two traditions that arose after its decline. Then we will turn to consider two spiritualities that can only be decisive for Christian spirituality – the spirituality of Jesus himself – so far as we can discern this – and the spirituality of the experience of Jesus Christ by those who formed the earliest Church.

Theophany

The Old Testament narrates many theophanies or appearances of God. These are not straightforward descriptions, but include regular stylized features. Sometimes, for instance, an angel, rather than God, appears and utters God's message – reflecting belief that to see God unmediated means death (e.g. Ex. 33.20; Deut. 18.16; Judg. 13.22; contrast Deut. 5.24). Many theophanies involve the 'presence' or 'radiance' (*shekinah*) that clouds or shrouds, as well as reveals, God. And the narratives were recorded – after a long oral and fragmentary written tradition – extremely long after they were presumed to have taken place: thus Abraham is often dated around the eighteenth century BC, and Moses around the thirteenth, whereas the final textual editing of their stories was around 500. Nevertheless, whatever the original experience, these theophanies were firmly believed to have taken place, and were constitutive of Hebrew spirituality.

Here are some examples to read and ponder:

1   Noah and the Rainbow: Genesis 8.20—9.17.
2   Abraham and the three Angels: Genesis 18.1–15.
3   Jacob's Ladder: Genesis 28.10–18.
4   Jacob wrestling with God: Genesis 32.22–31.
5   Moses and the Burning Bush: Exodus 3.1–14.
6   The fire and the cloud: Exodus 13.20–22.
7   Moses and the Elders on the Mountain: Exodus 24.1–18.
8   Moses in the Tent of Meeting: Exodus 33.7–11.
9   Moses in the Mountain Cleft: Exodus 33.18–23.
10 Elijah and the Still Small Voice: 1 Kings 19.4–15.
11 Elijah and the Chariot of Fire: 2 Kings 2.6–14.
12 Isaiah and the *shekinah* in the Temple: Isaiah 6.1–8.
13 Ezekiel's Chariot Vision: Ezekiel 1.4—3.3.

Law, Prophets and Holiness

The Hebrew scriptures initially consisted of 'the law and the prophets'. Though later commentators have sometimes contrasted the ritual and priestly stance of the former with the ethical and charismatic orientation of the latter, for the early Jews, including Jesus, the two formed a unity of revelation. At the heart of the law was the call expressed in the holiness code to 'be holy, for I the Lord your God am holy' (Lev. 11.45). Holiness here meant separation from other peoples and traditions in imitation of the Hebrew God through adherence to law and right sacrifice, which were in due course focused on the Temple on the 'mountain' at Jerusalem. Prophecy was always a recall to this initial call to holiness; and as time went on, theophanies became more and more closely linked to the experience of God in his holiness on the mountain or in the Temple. The developments considered next, and Jesus himself, would both intensify and transcend this call to holiness and separation, which has remained a deep and consistent trend in Christian spirituality.

The Departure of God

Soon after his chariot vision (13 above) Ezekiel narrates a haunting vision of the chariot of God's presence forsaking the Temple where God had been believed to dwell (Ezek. 9.9—10.22). In 586 BC, indeed, the Temple was destroyed and the Israelites forced into exile in Babylon. God seemed to have forsaken his people.

Events such as these may lie behind the psalmist's questioning:

Will the Lord spurn for ever
and never again be favourable?
Has his steadfast love for ever ceased?
Are his promises at an end for all time?
Has God forgotten to be gracious?
Has he in anger shut up his compassion?
And I say, 'It is my grief
that the right hand of the Most High has changed.
I will call to mind the deeds of the Lord.' (Ps. 77.7–10)

This sounds a note familiar to us today, hovering as it does between a celebration of the rich experience of God in the past, and the lament that such experiences no longer seem to happen. The time of vision seems to be over, leaving a bereaved sense of God's absence. To use Evelyn Underhill's analogy (p. 112) the orchestra has left, leaving the audience with only the scores in their hands. The signposts and the road remain, but the destination has become unreachable, or vanished.

This was a decisive time for spirituality, seeing the origins of many traditions of thought still current. In these same decades, the Greek thinkers Pythagoras and Anaximander were born, as probably were the Buddha, Confucius and Lao Tzu, and Zoroaster was teaching. And it was in exile that, through the teacher known as 'second Isaiah', and through the beginning of the compilation of the creation story and a great deal of the Old Testament, a new understanding of God began to develop, not only as Israel's personal deity, but as the transcendent Creator of the cosmos and Lord and judge of all peoples and all time. Monotheism as we have it now – the notion of one holy and transcendent sovereign God, shared by Jews, Christians and Muslims – arose out of the *end* of theophany. The absence of God opened the way to thoughts of a wider presence.

And this led to the two forms of biblical spirituality that largely replaced the prophetic: wisdom and apocalyptic.

Wisdom

The Wisdom tradition is to be found in some of the Psalms, Proverbs, Ecclesiastes, Job and the Song of Songs, and apocryphal books such as Ecclesiasticus and Wisdom. In it, the whole person (Ps. 139) or the whole creation (Pss. 19, 104, 147) is seen as theophany in a new sense, expressing God's wisdom. Reflection on the laws of creation, in parallel with the revealed law now gives access to God.

The Greek word for wisdom, *sophia* and the Hebrew *hokhma* both convey an essentially practical know-how, even cunning and cleverness, rather than the armchair ruminations we have perhaps come to understand by 'philosophy'. Wisdom is personified (Wisd. 7.22b—8.2) as a female figure who emanates from God. She cries out to be heard (Prov. 8.1–36) and before and in the creation she was God's delight, playing or rejoicing with God (v.30).

Wisdom in the Old Testament takes other forms, however, like the pithy, practical worldly wisdom expressed in the Proverbs, the radical, angry theological questioning of Job, and the sometimes dark and cynical broodings of Ecclesiastes. What is common to all these is the deep interest in observing the way the world works, for good or ill, as a basis for faith and ethics. It is not that the great Jewish revelations of the law and the prophets are forgotten, but they are recast in terms of the great understanding of creation that had been forged in the time of the Jewish exile. It is now Lady Wisdom who is seen to guide the Jewish people through the time of the patriarchs and the exodus (Wisd. 10), while reflection on the laws of nature and on the laws of Moses have become inseparable (Pss. 19 and 119).

Significantly, while the prophets typically saw God as the faithful bridegroom, seeking his people as the (generally unfaithful) bride, now it is the wise man who seeks God as the elusive but ever-present and ever-lovely bride, Lady Wisdom.

Finally, the book of Job concludes with what is perhaps the most dazzling theophany in the whole of scripture (Job 38—41). Here the whole creation, manifests a glory we cannot fathom. If we follow the order of the Hebrew Bible (where the wisdom writings come after the prophets) this is in fact the last theophany. As God declaims from the whirlwind, though it is Job who first seems reduced to silence, it is God who never speaks again (Miles, 1996, p. 329). His revelation seems to have passed over and consumed itself in the whole of creation, in its riches and beauties, but also its terrors.

Apocalypse and Mystery

If wisdom literature represents the experience of God generalized to a presence in the whole creation, apocalyptic writing represents it hidden, rendered secret and deferred to the deep future.

Apocalyptic literature developed in the context of long and painful struggles, first Persian, then Greek (overcome in the Maccabean revolt of 167–64 BC) and finally Roman. In it the history of the nations is, as for wisdom, in the hands of God. But God's working is a secret – *raz*, a mystery – waiting to be revealed (apocalypse actually means 'revelation') in God's coming vindication of his people against their oppressors. Indeed the subversive meanings of apocalyptic had to be kept secret and coded partly to escape suspicion. The secret meaning is revealed only in the dreams of seers like Daniel, who decodes their often bizarre workings through allegories in which the dream figures stand for political-cum-spiritual realities. The book of the Apocalypse that ends the Christian scriptures is a case in point.

So the notion arose that scripture contained, underneath its obvious meaning, a hidden or 'mystical' meaning. One root of Judaeo-Christian mysticism lies in the widening to all scripture of the apocalyptic approach of extracting esoteric meanings. The *merkhbar, chariot mysticism* took this approach to the chariot visions of Elijah and Ezekiel (11 and 13 in the list on p. 6). In the latter, God is seen 'in the form of a human being' on his chariot throne. Later seers described amazing chariot journeys through the heavenly realms.

The Jewish scholar Alan Segal contends that 'apocalypticism and mysticism . . . refer to two different, easily distinguishable types of literature. But they are not unrelated experiences' (1990, p. 38). Certainly, along with wisdom, such experience was undeniably part of the soil in which Christianity grew.

The Spirituality of Jesus

If spirituality were a private affair between a believer and God, it would be impossible for us to know anything about Jesus' spirituality, since he left no record of his thoughts. Whether or not he was a 'mystic', he was certainly no 'spiritual writer'. But if spirituality is something embodied in what we say or do, it is as possible to know about it as it is to know anything of Jesus' life and teaching. However, the spirituality Jesus himself had and shared with others needs to be disentangled from the spiritual experience others had – and many believe they still have – of Jesus. The Christian tradition has tended to fuse the two, but we shall consider the latter separately in the following section, 'Christ in Spirituality'.

Prophecy

Jesus undoubtedly shows many prophetic features. A challenge to repent of hypocrisy and injustice was integral to his message. Nevertheless his own prophetic call was not a straightforward theophany. The theophany at his baptism *included* him; he was, at times, described as a theophany in his own person (see below). So while some (Sanders, 1985) regard him as a Hebrew prophet born out of time, others (Wright, 1996) argue that Jesus saw himself as the God of the prophets appearing decisively to his people.

Wisdom

Meanwhile, a recent, controversial study of Jesus (Crossan, 1992) unearths someone closer to a wandering philosopher or sage than the conventional prophet. Whether or not Elisabeth Schüssler Fiorenza (1995) is right about him regarding himself as the child and prophet of Lady Wisdom (Luke 7.35), the style of most sayings ascribed to Jesus tempers (yet in a way sharpens) prophetic challenge with sagelike wit. This wisdom strand in Jesus' spirituality may be less familiar, so we will say a little more about it.

Jesus' parables and pithy sayings paint vivid and sometimes humorous pictures of the ways of human society – kings, parents, stewards, vineyard owners, neighbours – or nature – crops, mustard bushes, fish and nets, sheep and shepherds. They are full of observations of how things can happen – or don't – in real life: the different things that can happen to sown corn (Matt. 13.1–9); the different responses of characters like the father and his two sons (Luke 15.11–32); or the real life feelings of vineyard labourers (Matt. 20.1–16).

If the approach – drawing ethics from close observation of society and nature – is close to that of the wisdom proverbs, the style and intent are different. Jesus' *parables* are more extended than proverbs, and the trajectory of their thought is not a straight inference from society to ethic, but something like a *parabola* (same Greek word) that ploughs our experience of the world deeply only to take off for somewhere else. They point to a kingdom or reign of God where mustard bushes grow into vast trees (Matt. 13.31–32; Mark 4.30–32), farmers waste seed on rocks (Matt. 13.1–9), and vineyard owners pay a flat rate irrespective of hours worked (Matt. 20.1–16).

So parables raise more questions than they answer, inviting us to imagine our way towards the kind of society where God reigns, which is a strange world with 'quite different things going on' (R. S. Thomas, 'The Kingdom', written in 1995, p. 233 – a poem worth reading in full).

Embodiment

Wisdom was not only something Jesus taught. His life, dedicated to gathering the outcasts, shows him doing the unifying and reconciling work of Wisdom. It is possible that his sharing of bread and wine is intended to do exactly what Lady Wisdom does in Proverbs 9.5, setting up her table to share bread and wine with everyone. Schüssler Fiorenza (1994, p. 11) contrasts the Wisdom of the Old Testament and Jesus' teaching with the narrower perspectives of the later Church:

> Her dwelling of cosmic dimensions has no walls; she permeates the whole world. Her inviting table, with the bread of sustenance and the wine of celebration, is set between seven cosmic pillars that allow the spirit of fresh air to blow where it will.

From all this it is clear that Jesus did not only teach, but embodied and personified Wisdom (just as, according to Wright, he embodied the God of the prophets). So much so that when the early Christians sang hymns about him, they applied the kind of language the Old Testament ascribed to Lady Wisdom to Jesus. He is praised as emanating from God as his perfect image, altogether beautiful and adorable, enlightening all people, filling the universe and holding it together, and reconciling all things into his peace (Col. 1.15–20; Eph. 1.3–14; John 1.1–14).

Christ in Spirituality

Jesus was therefore not only, for his followers, someone who shared his spiritual experience; for the New Testament writers he clearly *was* himself a shared spiritual experience, as Christians believe he has gone on being. It is to this we now briefly turn as we conclude this chapter with some of the threads that will be taken up throughout the story of Christian spirituality. We consider Paul's experience of Jesus, then that expressed by the canonical Gospels, and finally that expressed in writings that were not included in the New Testament.

Jesus and the Chariot

St Paul is certainly decisive for the way Jesus' spirituality and teaching became formational of a new, international community – the Church. And decisive for Paul was his conversion from the orthodox, Pharisaic Judaism of his day.

Segal argues (1990, p. 58) that behind Paul's social and ethical concerns lay a mysticism. He was converted by a mystical insight into Jesus provided by the chariot mysticism with which as a Pharisaic rabbi he would have been familiar. Paul came to believe that the chariot-enthroned 'Son of man' or human likeness of God was in fact the Jesus of Nazareth whom he had been persecuting. 'Paul's conversion experience involved his identification of Jesus as the image and Glory of God, as the human figure in heaven, and thereafter as Christ, son and saviour' (Segal, 1990, p. 61, referring to 2 Cor. 4.6).

So 'Son of man' language came to be applied to Jesus along with the Wisdom concepts we have just noted, feeding the spiritual roots of the later doctrine of the incarnation, which in the rather different and more 'masculine' terms of Greek metaphysics, identifies Christ with the Son of the Father within the divine Trinity.

Theophany in the New Testament

However, it was not only Paul who encountered something awesome in Jesus. Whatever the balance of wisdom, prophecy and apocalyptic in Jesus' teaching – and it is hard at this distance to be precise – he was certainly understood by the Gospel writers in terms that include prophetic theophany. This is most apparent at certain decisive points, like the following:

1 His conception by Mary: Luke 1.26–38.
2 His baptism (called 'The Theophany' in the Orthodox Church): Mark 1.1, 9–11; Matthew 3.13–17; Luke 3.21–22.
3 His transfiguration: Matthew 17.1–9; Mark 9.2–10; Luke 9.28–36.
4 His resurrection: Matthew 28.1–10; Mark 16.1–8; Luke 24.1–11; John 20.1–18. (One account here seems more theophanic than the others.)
5 His appearance to Paul: Acts 9.3–9 and elsewhere.
6 His appearance in Revelation 1.10–19.

Participation in Christ

Alongside these descriptions of *encounter* with Christ, in the writings of John and Paul we find traditions of *participation* in him. For Paul at least this sharing was focused often on baptism and the Eucharist, and always on the cross: 'With Christ I am concrucified; no longer I, but Christ in me' (Gal. 2.20 – my literal translation).

The phrase 'in Christ' recurs throughout Paul, whereas the notion of Christ in us – found here – is much rarer. In the farewell discourses in John the two ideas are balanced, Christ being in us and we in him (e.g. 14.20). Both themes are equally vital for the development of Christian spirituality, though we shall see that the theme of mutual indwelling with Christ tended to give way to that of participation in the divine nature (*theosis*) or sharing in the life of the Trinity. Sharing in the crucifixion was a constant theme of the martyrs, which would return to centre stage in the medieval West.

Extra-canonical writings

Many early writings about Jesus did not find acceptance when the canon of the New Testament was defined in the fourth century, often because their Gnostic theology (see pp. 19–20) was rejected by the mainstream Church. Whether or not they represent a suppressed strand of Jesus' teaching (Pagels, 1979), they certainly represent Christ as experienced in a significant part of early Christian spirituality.

Perhaps the most valuable part of this literature is that which continues and radicalizes the wisdom themes we have been exploring, themes which later theology tended to drop as Jesus moved from being (Lady?) Wisdom incarnate to God's Word incarnate and then God the Son incarnate. A poem written in the feminine gender called 'Thunder perfect Mind' declares in riddles:

> It is I who am the first: and the last.
> It is I who am the revered: and the despised.
> It is I who am the harlot: and the holy.
> It is I who am the wife: and the virgin.
> It is I who am the mother: and the daughter . . .
> It is I who am incomprehensible silence . . .
> It is I who am the voice whose sounds are so numerous . . .
> It is I who am the speaking of my (own) name. (in Layton, 1987, p. 80)

Such sayings may echo Jesus' own identification with the whores and outcasts, while the 'I am' form is reminiscent of the Johannine writings (compare Rev. 1.11, 17; 2.8; 22.13). You might like to compare them with Charles Causley's poem, 'Written on a Normandy Crucifix', which begins, 'I am the great sun' (1975).

Meanwhile, well-known lines from the Gospel of Thomas (v. 77) actually identify Jesus with the kind of omnipresent creative figure we have seen Wisdom to be:

> I am the light that is above them all. I am all things: all things came forth from me, and all things attained to me. Split a piece of wood, I am there; lift up the stone, and you will find me there.

Conclusion

We have explored three trajectories which run from the Hebrew Bible through Jesus into the spirituality of the early Church.

1 **Prophecy**: arising from *theophany*, experience of God in awe and dread leading to ethical challenge to change society. It is clear that Jesus, even if distinct in style from the prophets, was prophetic in his ministry as a whole. Mark's Gospel especially portrays Jesus as an awe-inspiring theophany, while John's portrays him as a living embodiment of God's prophetic Word.
2 **Wisdom**: a more philosophical *contemplation* of creation and humanity leading to virtuous life in society. Jesus was in style a witty sage, but his sayings carry more prophetic challenge than conventional wisdom. Later tradition, including Luke's Gospel – if not Jesus himself – identified him with a gentle and open wisdom that reconciles the outcast.
3 **Apocalyptic**: revolutionary hopes encoded in dreamlike *mysteries*. Early Jewish mysticism sought to decode scripture and seek out hidden meanings. The amount of apocalyptic in Jesus' original teaching is controversial, but Paul's experience of Jesus was apocalyptic or mystical in a certain sense, and apocalyptic certainly colours a great deal of the synoptic Gospels, especially Matthew.

All three strands – encounter, contemplation and mystery – fed into later Christian spirituality, though in proportions that have varied through history.

For Reflection and Discussion

1 In the passages cited on p. 13
   • What does the writer see?
   • (and/or not see?)
   • What does he hear?
   • What does he learn about God?
   • How is he changed?
2 Read Wisdom 7.22b—8.2 carefully and reflectively. Try and imagine the 'wisdom' described – does it/she/he correspond to anything in your own experience? Write in your own terms six key sentences summarizing what this passage says about wisdom.

3 Which of the bullet points noted on pp. 4–5 do you think apply to Jesus? And which of the characteristics of theophany you noted in question (1) apply to him in your view?

4 In which ways do you think later Christian spiritual tradition has continued to set forth Wisdom's open table for all, or not? In what ways do you think the doctrine of the incarnation of God in Christ develops, or obscures, the original wisdom Jesus taught and embodied?

5 Read the passages listed on p. 13 and compare. In what ways are they like and unlike the Old Testament theophanies? Why do you think Jesus is presented as a theophany at these particular moments?

6 In what ways (if any) do you feel the two extra-canonical quotations on p. 14 enrich your understanding of Jesus, and in what ways do you feel they distort it?

Further Reading

Stephen Barton, 1992, *The Spirituality of the Gospels,* London: DLT.

Walter Brueggemann, 1986, *Hopeful Imagination: Prophetic Voices in Exile,* Philadelphia: Fortress Press.

Bentey Layton, tr., 1987, *The Gnostic Scriptures, a New Translation*, London: SCM Press.

Elisabeth Schüssler Fiorenza, 1995, *Jesus: Miriam's Child, Sophia's Prophet: Issues in Feminist Christology*, London: SCM Press.

John Holdsworth, 2003, *Dwelling in a Strange Land: Exile in the Bible and the Church*, Norwich: Canterbury Press.

Bernard McGinn, 1991, *The Foundations of Mysticism: Origins to the Fifth Century*, New York: Crossroad.

M. A. Powell, 1998, *The Jesus Debate*, Oxford: Lion Books.

Gerd Theissen, 1987, *The Shadow of the Galilean: The Quest of the Historical Jesus in Narrative Form*, London: SCM Press.

2

Struggle and Synthesis: Patristic Spirituality

In AD 64 the first persecution of Christians had begun under Nero, with Peter being executed in 67, while in 70 the Romans destroyed Jerusalem and its Temple, forcing the Jews – including the Christians of Jerusalem, who kept Jewish law – into diaspora from their homeland. In a world that was generally sceptical and frequently hostile and persecutory, the early Christians, who were beginning to be more than a Jewish sect, confronted two opposing problems.

- They needed a language with which to speak to this world. Their own native 'tongues' were the various prophetic, apocalyptic, wisdom and mystical strands of Judaism. But this language could seem unintelligible or unsophisticated in the Hellenistic and Roman world in which Christianity was now rapidly advancing.
- Having jettisoned the distinctive marks of their early Jewish status – circumcision, Sabbath and other legal observances – Christians needed their own marks of identity, to make it clear what a convert might be joining, and to maintain cohesion and loyalty under persecution.

Each problem generated a vital aspect of early Christian spirituality. The second led to specific practices, liturgies, procedures of initiation that gave the new faith the kind of permeable boundary it needed. It led to a rigorous and world-defying spirituality whose fruit was the monastic and the liturgical spiritualities we shall discuss in Chapter 3. The first led to the developments discussed in this chapter, which 'inculturated' the gospel into the framework provided by Greek philosophy. Because we are dealing with parallel, interacting themes, these chapters will overlap in terms of time.

Mountain and Cave

The Greek philosophers were concerned above all to discover the ultimate enduring substance behind the changing appearances of the world. For some this consisted in material atoms, and for others an indivisible unity, and for others again, incessant flux like fire. It was natural, when early Christians sought a language to make themselves intelligible, that they turned to the philosopher for whom the ultimate substance was eternal and in some sense divine: Plato.

> You could extract [the] building blocks [of the Western Christian tradi-
> tion] from two stories, each foundational in the intellectual and religious
> cultures of its respective tradition: the 'Allegory of the Cave' in Book 7 of
> Plato's *Republic*, and the story in Exodus of Moses' encounter with Yahweh
> on Mount Sinai.

So Denys Turner (1995, p. 1) contends that the Western Christian spiritual tradition derives from a marriage of two specific stories, one from Plato,
the other from Exodus. As a historical thesis this is somewhat overstated, but
Turner carefully presents it as a possible way of conceptualizing the tradition,
rather than historical cause and effect. He is arguing that when spiritual writers
refer to ascent, contemplation, vision and darkness, they are best understood as
having these two stories superimposed in their minds.

The *exodus* story in question is that of the Jews from Egypt, led by Moses,
who is seen as the original mystic. Moses' encounters with God in the bush and
on the mountain (items 5–9 on p. 6) are especially important.

Plato's *Allegory of the Cave*, from *The Republic*, compares us all to prisoners in
a cave fastened so that we can only see shadows of things cast by a fire behind us
on the wall of the cave. We take these shadows to be the reality. But one day the
philosopher manages to break free, turn round and see the fire, the true cause of
those shadows. He then sees the entrance to the cave, climbs out, and finally, by
much training, learns to gaze (the Greek term is *theoreia*, most often translated
'contemplate', but also the origin of our word 'theory') on the sun, which at first

seems like darkness, it is so dazzling. After much gazing he decides to return to the cave to lead out his fellow humans. But as he enters the cave, he staggers in the darkness, and the people consider him mad. They reject his crazy talk about the true reality, since reality for them is what they can see, the shadow-play on the wall. This is how the allegory is explained:

> The visible realm corresponds to the prison . . . And you won't go wrong if you connect an ascent into the upper world and the sight of the objects there with the upward progress of the mind into the intelligible realm . . . The final thing to be perceived in the intelligible realm . . . is the absolute form of Good; once seen, it is inferred to be responsible for everything right and good . . . the controlling source of reality and intelligence. (Plato, 1955, pp. 281–2: Book 7, 517)

Early Struggles

Early Christianity was tempted to a subtle, reflective yet ritualized kind of Platonism.

Gnosticism

Gnosticism refers specifically to the arcane systems of Valentinus (second century), Marcion (*c*.110–160) and others, but is also a rather vaguer description of a trend in spirituality from which Christianity has found it extremely difficult to extricate itself, marked by these features:

- Plato had distinguished the ultimate Good from the Creator of the universe, or demiurge. Gnostics, noting the evil and suffering in the universe, ascribed it to an *evil* demiurge, which they identified with the harsh judge, the false God of the Old Testament, and contrasted with the true God of Christ.
- Christ revealed God but only *appeared* in human form, since he could not be truly embodied in flawed matter. Christ showed the way whereby the pure spark of the soul could release itself from the shackles of matter and return to the true God.

- Weaker Christians need the material expressions of faith found in the sacraments and the literal meaning of the Bible. The truly spiritual, however, recognize that it is the soul that matters, not the body. Actions of the body – like burning incense to worship the Emperor – do no harm to a soul whose intention is pure. So Gnostics saw no point in martyrdom, or the institutional structures and sacraments of the developing Catholic Church.

Irenaeus of Lyons (c.130–200)

Irenaeus was one of an early group of 'apologists' – including also *Ignatius of Antioch* (*c.*35–107) and *Justin Martyr* (*c.*100–65) – who countered the Gnostics with a strong understanding of creation, incarnation, the sacraments and the Church, as well as trying to establish the intellectual credentials of the Christian faith. He developed a very different and more down-to-earth and historical understanding of salvation.

In his view, Adam was not an originally perfect being who fell into sin, but was created like a spiritual child with the capacity to grow towards God. He gave way to sin and failed, but the various stages of Christ's life restored what Adam lost, and enabled humankind once more to grow towards the restoration (*apokatastasis*) of all things to their divine vocation. The latter involved the resurrection of the body on a restored earth, rather than the timeless, spiritual destiny of the gnostics.

Irenaeus offers a very dynamic, time-oriented view of salvation, in which sin is taken seriously, but as part of the long story of transformation in Christ, rather than the dark shadow of the flesh which it became for Augustine (Hick, 2007). He shows, perhaps, what theology might have become, and how spirituality might have developed, without significant Platonic influence.

Tertullian (c.160–225)

Tertullian, from Carthage, vehemently rejected the assimilation of Neoplatonist philosophy, asking 'what has Athens to do with Jerusalem?' – opposing the place of reason to the place of faith. The clause ascribed to him, '*credo quia impossibile*' well describes his position: 'I believe it because it is impossible,' not because it is reasonable. He later became a Montanist, believing that the Holy Spirit continued the divine revelation in the Church through visions and spiritual experiences.

The divergence between Tertullian's spirituality – which made the Church a place of experiential revelation over against the deluded rationalism of the world – and the more accommodating Alexandrian approach considered next, continued to feature in Christian spirituality, and is still with us in the tension between pietists, evangelicals and charismatics on the one hand, and liberals on the other.

The Alexandrian Synthesis

Whether Plato was a mystic is much debated. His 'forms' were the eternal patterns and laws which geometry and science were beginning to discover lying underneath the ever-shifting appearances of things. So his 'upward progress of the mind into the intelligible realm' is primarily a philosophical search for underlying order, which we will understand better through the 'mathematical taster' in Chapter 8. However, in the quote above Plato did not separate this progress from the ethical search for the 'form of the Good . . . the controlling source of reality and intelligence'. Later Christians, not unreasonably, identified this source of all goodness, reality and truth with God, and Plato's scientific-cum-ethical search came to be seen as a kind of spiritual search.

That process of identification had, however, an intervening step, which was the work of the Neoplatonists of the early Christian centuries. *Philo of Alexandria (c.10 BC– c.AD 50)* strove to reconcile Platonism with his Jewish monotheism, while the pagans *Plotinus* (AD 204–70), and *Proclus* (412–85) created a mystical cosmology of emanations from the original One, down through the *Logos* (rational order or Word) and the World Soul, to the cosmos. The mystic sought to ascend by corresponding stages from contemplation of the cosmos to unity with the One. Such notions form a component of the 'perennial philosophy' discussed in Chapter 7.

Clement of Alexandria (150–215)

The term *logos* – the 'Word' of John 1 – arguably combines the Hebrew Wisdom and prophetic Word of God with the Neoplatonic emanation just noted. Clement believed that though Plato and other non-Christian philosophers did not know the revelation of the *logos* made flesh in Christ, they were able to contemplate God through the *logos spermatikos* (seedlike word) sown in the rational minds of all human beings. Christians were free therefore to gather the wisdom strewn throughout the surrounding Greco-Roman culture. Clement's own spirituality owed a lot to the classical Greek ethic of moderation and the ideal of *gnosis* or spiritual knowledge, as well as the Platonic demotion of the physical (see pp. 156–7).

Origen (c.185–254)

Origen took these trajectories of Clement to greater heights and depths. His Neoplatonism led him to see the entire universe as a visible expression of an eternal divine reality, and the human soul as likewise eternal, pre-existing birth and destined, after a series of reincarnations, for *theosis* (next). His consequent universalism – believing everyone would ultimately come to salvation – was later condemned by the Church. Nevertheless, alongside Augustine, Origen ranks as perhaps the greatest individual post-biblical influence on Christian spirituality.

- He systematized the tradition – originating in Jewish scriptural reading (p. 9) – of looking behind the surface *literal* meaning of a biblical text for its *ethical* and *mystical* meanings. He elucidated this by reference to the Platonic process of seeking the eternal forms beneath the surface appearances. The discernment of mystical or spiritual meanings in the sacred texts remained central to Christian spirituality, until the Reformation shifted the focus to the plain literal meaning.
- He originated the notion of *three stages* of the mystical journey, purgation, illumination and union with God. His mystical exegesis associated these stages with the three wisdom books of the Bible. Proverbs – in his scheme – dealt with moral purity, Ecclesiastes with enlightenment in the nature

of the universe, and the Song of Songs with loving union with God. This last parallel was to have immense consequences for the development of an understanding of the goal of the Christian life, and spiritual writers would return time and again to the Song.

* The *spiritual senses*. Plato saw the five senses, which merely convey images of the material world, as inferior to the mind, which accesses the underlying realities. But noting the way the Bible addresses all five senses, Origen saw the outward senses as prototypes of the way the mind and spirit work. So mystics access the eternal forms by something analogous to sight – as is implied in Plato's cave analogy – but also discern the Word of God by an inward hearing. They taste the nourishing goodness of God in the scriptures, smell the sweet fragrance of Christ, and in the imagery of the Song of Songs, touch, embrace and are aroused by the love of Christ.

Godding

All the Christian 'fathers' considered in this chapter used the terms *theosis* and *theopoiesis* to describe the transformation of the believer into a partaker of the divine nature. The terms have continued in the Orthodox East to this day, but in the West dwindled, and died out completely after the Reformation.

The latter term, literally 'god-making', originally referred to the making of idols, and was used to refer to the ceremony whereby the Roman emperors were made into 'gods', but the former term is unique to Christian writers (Bouyer 1990, p. 227). It is simply a verb invented to correspond to the noun *theos*, God. The term usually used to translate it, divinization – sharing in an abstract divine quality – does not quite capture it, but nor of course would the notion of being made individually into 'a god'. A verb like 'godding' is better, suggesting the dynamic process of coming to share personally in the life of the Trinity.

After Constantine's Conversion

The conversion of Constantine in 312 and the beginnings of a Christian empire in many ways eased the problem of intelligibility, since Christianity itself became by stages the cultural *lingua franca* of the empire. But it intensified the problem of Christian identity. There was pressure for Christian theology to serve the cohesion of the empire, and this was the period when the emperors convened the great ecumenical councils such as Nicaea (325) and Chalcedon (451) to hammer out what was to count as orthodox Christian faith.

The period saw a shift in the centre of theology from the academy – as represented by the Alexandrians and others – to the monastery: for many centuries thereafter theology would be rooted in the contemplative religious life. The monks would often prove staunch defenders of orthodoxy. Intimidation by armed bands of Egyptian monks was one (regrettable) factor at the Council of Chalcedon, and later they fought doggedly for the use of icons.

There was an ominous side to the new marriage between Christianity and imperial power. In 385 the purist Christian ascetic Priscillian and his followers were executed by the Emperor as heretics, the first of a long series of Christians to be shamefully martyred by their fellow Christians. And in Alexandria in 415 a Christian mob, encouraged by Patriarch Cyril, murdered the female pagan philosopher Hypatia.

Athanasius (c.296–373)

Athanasius, in the Alexandrian tradition, fiercely defended the notion that Christ was 'one in being with the Father', rather than merely like the Father, as his powerful Arian opponents suggested. His argument was based on the logic of *theosis*. 'God became human that humanity might become divine,' he declared. Put more literally, if barbarically, 'God humaned that humans might God.'

If Jesus was not fully human, Athanasius argued, he could not bring divinity *to humans*; but if he was not fully divine, he could not bring the fullness of *divinity* to humans. Thus the doctrine of the incarnation was originally developed to preserve the spiritual experience of salvation through sharing in the divinity of Christ, and it has been questioned whether it really makes sense outside that context (Hick, 1977).

Ephrem the Syrian (306–73)

While understanding and incorporating Greek philosophy, and defending Athanasian orthodoxy, Ephrem represents a long Syrian tradition of spirituality framed not in Greek but in Aramaic derived from the very language Jesus had spoken. His many poems employ mystical imagery in the manner then widespread in rabbinic Judaism and the wider Semitic worlds, rather than the more systematic and metaphysical mode of the Greeks.

Ephrem's poetry draws rich parallels between the mountain of paradise, Mount Sinai, the Jerusalem Temple, the liturgy and architecture of the Church, and the inner ascent of the soul. In due course Denys, probably a fellow Syrian, would synthesize these features with Neoplatonic philosophy with remarkable results.

The Cappadocians

The orthodoxy that was being hammered out at the councils found spiritual expression in the 'Cappadocian Fathers' who have proven definitive for Eastern Orthodox spirituality: the great bishop and organizer *Basil the Great* (*c.*330–79), the lyrical orator *Gregory Nazianzen* (*c.*329–91) and *Gregory of Nyssa*, of whom more below.

Athanasius had convinced the Church that Christ, the Son of God, was God the Son, equal to and one with God the Father. The Cappadocians argued the same for the Holy Spirit, formulating the notion of the *Trinity* as an interpenetrating dance ('*perichoresis*') of three 'persons' sharing a single 'being'. The roots of this often arcane sounding doctrine lie, once again, in Christian spirituality. If Christ's equality with the Father ensured the divinization of human nature in general, the equality of the Spirit who dwells in people ensures their personal adoption as equal children in the life of the Triune God (Lossky, 1957, Chapter 8).

Gregory of Nyssa (c.335–94)

Gregory made explicit the marriage noted by Turner, between Plato's Cave and the story of Moses, creating many of the sparks of inter-illumination that have been so central to the Christian spiritual tradition ever since. But Gregory thereby stood Platonism on its head in three ways.

- In Plato, the ascent is from the dark obscurity of the cave to the intense clarity and light of the Good. Moses, on the contrary, journeys (eventually) from a bush radiant with light to the dark cloud on the mountain, and finds God there.
- Change was negative for Plato, but for Gregory 'the soul's only security is in change' (Williams, 1979, p. 62) and transformation in Christ.
- For Plato the Good was a 'form', by definition finite, bounded and clear. For Gregory God is boundless (*apeiron*), and the seeker reaches out (*epektasis*) ever deeper, eternally, into God's unknowability. The rational search for clarity is replaced by the journey described in the strand of spirituality that came to be known as 'apophatic' or negating. According to Gregory of Nyssa (1987, p. 40):

> Moses' vision of God began with light; afterwards God spoke to him in a cloud. But when Moses rose higher and became more perfect he saw God in the darkness . . . Our initial withdrawal from wrong and erroneous ideas of God is a transition from darkness to light. Next comes a closer awareness of hidden things, and by this the soul is guided through sense phenomena to the world of the invisible. And this awareness is a kind of cloud, which overshadows all appearances, and slowly guides and accustoms the soul to look towards what is hidden. Next the soul . . . enters within the secret chamber of the divine knowledge, and here she is cut off on all sides by the divine darkness. Now she leaves outside all that can be grasped by sense or by reason, and the only thing left for her contemplation is the invisible and the incomprehensible. And here God is, as the Scriptures tell us in connection with Moses: 'But Moses went to the dark cloud wherein God was' (Ex. 20.21).

Augustine of Hippo (354–450)

If the Cappadocians were foundational for what became Eastern Orthodoxy, Augustine has proven an equally decisive influence on Christian spirituality in the West, where in many ways both Catholicism and Protestantism take their cue from him.

Before his conversion to Christianity, Augustine was a Manichaean (seeing the universe in Zoroastrian terms as a conflict between equal forces of good and evil) and then a Neoplatonist. He retained many aspects of both. Positively, he emphasized the soul's affinity to, and restless desire (*eros*) for, its true home in God. But negatively, he disparaged the material world, and emphasized the barrier sin places between people and God.

Sin for Augustine is not simply – as the Eastern fathers as well as Augustine's rival, the British Pelagius, tended to see it – a free choice to do wrong. Rather it was Adam's 'original sin' sexually propagating itself throughout humankind (see Chapter 10), a contagion destroying our free will, until we are freed and restored by God's grace

Augustine developed the Cappadocian Trinity in a way that became normative in the West, seeing the Spirit as the loving bond between Father and Son. He added a psychological analogy: humans – comprising memory, knowledge, and love or will – are images of the Trinity, 'comprising' Father, Son and Spirit respectively. Crudely, if the Orthodox Trinity consists of three persons united in one relationship, Augustine's is essentially modelled on one being expressed in three different relationships. The difference is subtle, but the Orthodox have since tended to give the Spirit a more 'independent' role in the spiritual life, and always to see God in Trinitarian terms, while Western spirituality (with exceptions like William of St Thierry, p. 48) has been more drawn to the unity of the Godhead.

With Augustine, spirituality became an inward mystery, hidden from the outward flesh. As with the Alexandrians, the stories and parables of the Bible were used as analogies for the spiritual life, but this now became an *inner* life. The soul became an 'inner person' with a biography, a story to tell, all of its own. Augustine's *Confessions* (1997) are simultaneously a philosophical investigation of God, time and all the mysteries, and an autobiography describing Augustine's own journey to God (Turner, 1998).

'Denys the Areopagite' (fifth to sixth century)

'Denys' or 'pseudo-Dionysius' was a monk who ascribed his work to the Dionysius who was converted by Paul. Formerly regarded by many as a thinly disguised Neoplatonist, recent work (e.g. Golitzin in Kessler, 2003) has emphasized Syrian Christian roots.

Like Ephrem the Syrian, Denys drew deep analogies between the liturgy, the cosmos and the spiritual journey. All three involved participation in a hierarchy or 'great chain of being' (Lovejoy, 1972) ascending from the mundane through the human, the celestial and the angelic to God. God's ecstatic love cascaded down to all creatures through these levels.

This hierarchy derived, for Denys, from the nature of language in relation to the divine. Words or names relate to God in three ways. (It is tempting to relate them to Father, Word and Spirit respectively, but Denys does not seem to take this step.)

1 **Apophatic**: nothing truly expresses God – not even words like Good and Being – because God is *hyperousios*, beyond all being. In the ultimate stillness of union with God, nothing needs to be said or can usefully be said. God's own *essence* or being is beyond all comprehension.
2 **Symbolic**: all things in some non literal way express God because of God's descent, incarnation and self-expression in revelation and liturgy.
3 **Kataphatic** or affirming: everything expresses God just as it is because of God's presence in all creatures, whereby all things participate in, praise and return to God. The *energies* (inward working) of God fill the creation.

Denys's hierarchy provided a useful ideology for feudal society and the hierarchical Church, especially as creatures do not rise from one level to another, but receive God's grace from within their allotted level. Yet quite unlike Plato, for whom ultimate reality is the static, eternal form of the Good, Denys's God creates through an ecstasy of longing, *eros*, which draws him out beyond himself.

Maximus the Confessor (c.580–662)

Maximus synthesized the apophatic trends in Gregory and Denys with a sense of the redeeming work of Christ, especially as expressed in the liturgy that was then becoming standardized (Lossky, 1984, p. 105). This synthesis was to become the basis of what is now known as Eastern Orthodoxy. Thus

1 The **incarnation** and the material body of Christ is linked to the six days of created being, and the contemplation of it in science. The incarnation would have been necessary even if humankind had not sinned, as the fulfilment of the creation.
2 The **cross** and the soul of Christ, and his seventh day rest in the tomb, are linked to well-being and questions of ethics, will and the inner nature of things.
3 The **resurrection** is linked to the mysteries of the 'eighth day', the eternal day of the new creation and the divine nature of Christ. This is linked in turn with the contemplative vision of God in the human face of Christ, and the reaching out to the divinity of Christ in the darkness of unknowing.

Maximus was mutilated, and later died, for his belief that Christ had both human and divine wills. The belief that our human will is overwhelmed or annihilated in the divine was to recur in different ways in Calvinism and in Quietism, but for Maximus (and later Orthodoxy) the spiritual life never overcomes an element of temptation and struggle. In Christ, however, it is the human will that is a struggle to achieve, whereas for us it is conforming ourselves to the divine will, that is costly.[1]

Icons: the Divine in Person

In the eighth and ninth century a conflict raged which was to prove decisive for the definition of Orthodoxy. Perhaps in the wake of Islam, a wave of iconoclasm swept the Eastern Church, partly on the biblical basis that images are forbidden in the ten commandments, but also on the Platonic basis that material things could not represent the spiritual. Either an icon of Christ was trying idolatrously

---

1 I owe this point to Fr Maximus Lavriotes.

to depict his divinity – it was argued – or it was merely representing his human-ity, so that to venerate it would be idolatrous.

In the West the retort has tended to be that art and imagery can indeed only represent the humanity of Christ and the saints, so while they can be edifying examples, they should not be adored. But in the East icons had become an inte-gral part of the worship. John of Damascus, Theodore the Studite and others defended this – in the end successfully – on the grounds that the icon of Christ represents neither the divine nature, nor the historical human Jesus (whose looks are after all unknown!). Rather they represent the divine person of the Word that was incarnate in him (Lossky, 1984, pp. 111–12).

This is a subtle point, but it explains the way icons pare away the bodily and fleshly nature of Christ or the saint, and emphasize the face – the almost caricatured persona – and especially the eyes and their gaze. Rather than depict-ing them and bringing them bodily into the gaze of the worshipper – as an idol does – icons serve to bring the worshipper into the personal gaze, judging and loving, of Christ and the saints (Marion, see p. 210). This relationship – often misunderstood in the West – lies at the heart of Orthodox spirituality of the icon, which is integral to a liturgy that strives to take the worshipper up into the communion of Christ and the saints.

Christian Mysticism a Platonic Intrusion?

So had the 'fathers' sold the theological pass to Neoplatonic philosophy, and was mysticism therefore the result of a betrayal?

Albert Ritschl ('History of Pietism' in 2005) famously argued that mysticism represented a Hellenic intrusion, perpetuated by the Catholic Church, into the Jewish purity of the original gospel. In the same German Protestant tradition, Friedrich Heiler (1997) contrasted *mystical* prayer of absorption in the eternal with the *prophetic* prayer of co-operation with God's work in the world. And Anders Nygren (1953) contrasted Platonic *eros*, as an essentially selfish desire of the soul to possess beauty and goodness, with New Testament *agapé*, the self-giving love of God for us and our self-giving in response. He argued

the entire structure of Platonic eros is egocentric . . . All that matters from first to last is the soul that is aflame with eros. The aim of [such] love is to gain possession of an object which is regarded as valuable . . . 'It is by the acquisition of good things,' [Plato] says, 'that the happy are made happy.' (pp. 179–80)

On the other hand von Hügel and Underhill (see Chapter 7) and W. R. Inge (1959) welcomed the Platonic influence as enabling the Pauline and Johannine mysticism of participation to find a fuller expression, while K. E. Kirk (1931) criticized Heiler's contrast.

Most of these polarizations now seem overstated, and a more careful view is possible. For while it is true that many key concepts of the Christian spiritual tradition derive from Plato, the tradition we have been exploring transformed the meaning of key concepts like

1 **Aporia**, a state of resourcelessness, confusion or lack, which according to Socrates and Plato precedes all genuine wisdom. For Gregory and subsequent writers, the experience of Moses *ends*, as well as beginning, with *aporia*.
2 **Eros** or desire, in God. Love could not be attributed to Plato's Good, because it is an eternal form, not a person. But though *eros* and its equivalents are seldom used in the Bible, God's love for his people is certainly depicted there as costly. In Isaiah and Hosea it is compared with the love of a husband for his bride, and Dionysius saw creation and redemption as arising out of God's ecstatic love, as it were taking God out of Godself as the blessed Trinity.
3 **Theoria**. Whereas for Plato this was the kind of intellectual, abstracting process suggested by our word 'theory', for the Christian tradition it includes contemplative prayer and adoration.
4 **Participation**. Platonic participation in the form of the Good was based on an affinity between the eternal, spiritual soul and the eternal world of forms. The philosopher ascended from the material world as from the cave to find his true home in the eternal light. But the developing Christian doctrine of *creation out of nothing* placed the great gulf, not between the eternal and spiritual and the temporal and material, but between the whole creation, spiritual *and* material, and the uncreated or divine.

> The drama of the alien soul flying from the bondage of the senses is replaced by the very different 'drama' of soul and senses together struggling to live into and assimilate a truth greater than themselves. (Williams 1979, p. 62)

5 In this process **time and change** are not opposed to the eternity of God. In Augustine God's eternity is not a static timelessness, but the co-presence of all time in God's 'eternal moment' of creation and redemption, seen as a single act of love (Taylor, 2007, p. 56).

6 The Neoplatonic descending hierarchy of the One, the Logos and the World Soul becomes a **Trinity** of equals. The Spirit or grace of God does not (even in Denys's hierarchy) admit of degrees of participation, but invites all who respond to it to equal friendship with God

7 **Icons**. Plato allowed us to ascend from contemplation of material things to see – intellectually – the eternal forms. But in doing so we pass from the shadow to the reality, the unreal to the wholly real. With the resolution of the iconoclast controversy, this was reversed. Matter was no unreal shadow, but God's good creation, through which God's incarnate presence reaches out to us. The Orthodox suspect that behind the Western rejection of icons, a hidden Platonism lurks, privileging intellectual over bodily and material participation.

Notwithstanding (5), however, Neoplatonism set its seal on a shift from *eschatology* to *eternity*. The parables of Jesus related to a kingdom that was in some sense beginning now, and was to be consummated historically at the close of the age. The same could be said of the other Judaic spiritualities like apocalyptic: they related to changing, historical or in some cases cosmological realities. With Origen the mystical meaning of texts and parables was transferred to the eternal and unchanging world of forms. Parables were read as allegories; and everything in scripture became a type of something eternal.

So spirituality began to separate from science, matter, history and politics and to align itself with the contemplation of eternal verities. In Chapter 8 we will consider the division, increasingly apparent in modern times, between spirituality and science, and in Chapter 10 we shall see if the sundering of spirituality from our material bodies can be repaired. But now we turn to developments that overlap with those considered in this chapter, developments which in many ways exacerbated this division.

For Reflection and Discussion

1 What similarities do you notice between the stories of the mountain and the cave? What images and journeys feature in both? What differences, in these images or the way in which one thing leads to another? Do both make the same use of light and darkness, ascent and descent, illusion and reality, and gazing or contemplation?
2 Which aspects of (a) your experience of Christian faith or its exponents and (b) the contemporary vogue for 'spirituality', are closer to the understanding of the Gnostics, and which closer to Irenaeus?
3 Does Origen's notion of 'spiritual senses' make sense to you? Do you regard some senses as more spiritual than others, and if so, which and why?
4 What elements of clarity and *'aporia'* do you find in your own spiritual journey or experience of God?
5 What, if anything, do you think is the right place for icons in (a) worship and (b) personal spirituality?
6 Consider the ways listed at the end of the chapter in which Christian spirituality has differed from Platonism. Do you think some forms of Christian spirituality have remained closer to Platonism? If so, which forms, in which ways?

Further Reading

Augustine, tr. M. Boulding, 1997, *The Confessions*, London, Sydney, Auckland: Hodder and Stoughton.

Olivier Clément, 1993, *The Roots of Christian Mysticism, Texts from the Patristic Era with Commentary*, London, Dublin, Edinburgh: New City.

Vladimir Lossky, 1984, *The Vision of God*, New York: St Vladimir's Seminary Press.

Andrew Louth, 1981, *The Origins of the Christian Mystical Tradition: From Plato to Denys.* Oxford: Clarendon Press.

Bernard McGinn, 1991, *The Foundations of Mysticism: Origins to the Fifth Century*, New York: Crossroad.

Gregory of Nyssa, tr. 1987, *Commentary on the Song of Songs*, Brookline, MA: Hellenic College Press.

Rowan Williams, 1979, *The Wound of Knowledge*, London: DLT.

3

Monastery and Mystery: Spirituality through the 'Dark Ages'

In the first chapter we looked at spirituality in terms of the biblical challenge to articulate an *experience* of God even in the absence of God. In the second we looked at it in terms of the early Christian concern for God's *intelligibility*, even in his mystery. In this chapter the focus shifts to spirituality as manifest in *practice*, even in his exacting ethical judgement upon the human 'world', through commitments, styles and rules of life, and the repeated actions involved in liturgies and sacraments.

For many, spirituality is really a matter not of what we experience or think, but how a faith commitment expresses and develops itself in action. This is what came to matter as Christian spirituality sought to define itself in a world in which Christian belief was in many ways becoming the norm, especially as the classical world collapsed and values needed protecting in an age that has since come to be called 'dark'.

The Challenge to Integrity

Of course, in the early centuries, in which Christianity was a minority, often-persecuted faith, practice was far from being regarded as unimportant. But at this stage the differences in Christian practice were very clear and obvious, for example:

- **pacifism**, and the refusal to serve in the army, viewed as idolizing the state and contrary to Christ's teaching;
- strict **monotheism** and the refusal to idolize the Emperor or other pagan gods;
- a readiness for **martyrdom**, which had huge long-term impact on the course of Christian spirituality;
- very distinctive, often esoteric rites (Stroumsa, 2005, see next) including the **'mysteries'** (sacraments) and the increasingly complex and secret ceremonies involved in Christian initiation.

The problem at this stage, as we have seen, was to present this isolated and eccentric-seeming minority as a reasonable and credible option for the majority.

After 312, when the Emperor Constantine converted to Christianity, the latter moved fast from being an illegal and suspect minority faith to being the ideology of the Empire. Idolatry ceased to be mandatory and eventually became prohibited; martyrdom ceased to be a risk; there was no longer any need for secrecy; and finally, Christians lost their pacifism and came to serve in an army that was seen as defending and propagating Christian values. The problem now became how to develop, within a new ideology of 'Christendom', ways of life and worship that expressed the integrity and difference of God's kingdom within a society that at least nominally accepted its values.

Christian practice was led in two directions, both of which had profound and lasting effects on the development of Christian spirituality. One, in a movement sweeping outward from the cities and towns where the new cathedrals and churches were first built, was the development of rich and beautiful liturgies for initiation, worship and the sacraments. By this means existing society was adorned, enriched, sanctified and as it were pointed in a godward direction. The other, moving in from the wild fringes of the Empire (Egypt, Syria, Ireland), was the attempt to live out pure, uncorrupted kingdom values in isolated monastic communities and hermitages.

These developments were not opposed. Out of the cross-fertilization between them there emerged a distinctive practice for those who wished for a spirituality that possessed Christian integrity within a world that broadly acknowledged the Christian faith.

From Esotericism to Mysticism

In Chapter 2 we discussed the origins of Christian mysticism in the interaction between biblical and Neoplatonic wisdoms – 'mountain' and 'cave' – which gave rise to what we could term a Christian mystery *of belief*. But the *lived* Christian mystery – as expressed in the liturgical and monastic practices that are the theme of this chapter – had other sources also. Guy Stroumsa (2005) has identified the existence of esoteric traditions – that is, teachings passed on secretly by word of mouth rather than in publicly accessible written form – within the earliest phases of Christianity.

Of course Jesus' own teachings were passed on orally at first, the first surviving written records originating at least 30 years after his death. The complex mythologies of Gnosticism owed much to such esoteric teachings, which continued to be a major feature of Judaism and, later, Islam. Origen followed Judaism in identifying 'the discipline of your father' (Prov. 1.8) with written tradition and 'the instruction of your mother' with oral tradition. He considered them equally important.

However, by the end of the second century a shift had taken place in favour of the written tradition, which was just beginning to be defined. When the Empire became Christian, the need for secrecy gave way to the need for control. Written traditions were much easier to censor and control than oral ones. And Christianity was anxious to establish itself as a publicly available religion for everyone rather than a secretive elite.

At the same time, Stroumsa notes, deep changes were taking place in the understanding of personhood, with the generation of the notion of an inner life. (The development of the notion of the 'person' in Trinitarian and incarnational theology probably both capitalized upon, and assisted this change.) As a result, Stroumsa argues, *the esoteric became the mystical*. Secret teaching about the outward cosmos became open teaching inwardly applied to the soul. And – as we note next – the secret rite became the mystery, or to use the Western term, the sacrament, a public outward rite with an inner meaning for the soul. Such developments are among the many deep roots of the Christian mystical tradition.

Initiation and the Sacraments

It was once widely believed, particularly among Protestant commentators, that Christian sacramental participation in the death and resurrection of Christ followed a pattern established by the pagan mystery cults. But Bouyer contends (1990) that the existence of these cults was wildly exaggerated by contemporary poets and philosophers. Only the Eleusinian mysteries – which centred on the lament over Persephone's descent into the underworld in winter, and the celebration of her return with the new corn in the spring – had a real following. None of the mysteries involved participation in the life of a god through a sacramental initiation or meal. Many of the so-called mysteries in any case developed later than Christianity and could have been influenced by it rather than vice versa. The roots of the Christian mysteries – or sacraments – lay with Jesus himself and the practice of the Church. Baptism and the Eucharist were well established by the time St Paul wrote around the middle of the first century, where the real participation in the dying and rising Christ is cited as an existing tradition (Rom. 6.3–5; 1 Cor. 10.16, 11.23–25).

What concerns us now is the relation of mysticism to these mysteries, or spirituality to the sacramental life. While for many today the latter belongs to the institutional rather than spiritual life of the Church, for early Christianity each was unthinkable without the other. According to Blondel and Garrigou-Lagrange, 'the whole of authentic mysticism is present in germ even in baptismal experience' (Bouyer, 1990, p. 286). The mystical life developed as the life of participation in Christ through the mysteries. The systematization, elaboration and proliferation of eucharistic liturgies from the fourth century onward went hand in hand with the development of the mystical tradition, as mystical meanings were increasingly found or expressed in public worship. And though the sense of spirituality as a *corporate* journey undertaken in *public* worship has largely vanished from the West, it remains almost tangible at times in the Orthodox liturgy.

Thus the three stages of the mystical 'ascent' described from Origen onward were related in some patristic thought to what was believed about the sacramental process of initiation and the three stages of the Eucharist: see Table 2.

The other Catholic sacraments – reconciliation, healing, marriage and ordination – may equally be seen as relating to the spiritual journey (Thompson, 2006, pp. 104–6). Matthew Ashley even *identifies* mysticism with 'mystagogy'

Table 2: The Mystical Stages, Initiation and the Eucharist

Spirituality	Christian Initiation	Eucharist
Purification: repentance and ascetic purification from sin	**Baptism:** turning to Christ and cleansing of sin	**Preparation:** Confession of sin, sometimes sprinkling with water
Illumination: encounter with God through the spiritual senses	**Chrismation or Confirmation:** anointing of the senses	**Ministry of Word:** illumination through teaching
Union with God: loving mutual indwelling or theosis	**Holy Communion:** participation in Christ through bread and wine	**Ministry of Sacrament:** Eucharistic Prayer, Holy Communion, and Dismissal

(the initiation into the Christian mysteries following baptism), proposing that 'a spirituality is a classic constellation of practices which forms a mystagogy into a life of Christian discipleship' (in Dreyer and Burrows, 2005, p. 160). Though there is much more to be said about the development of Christian spirituality, this captures a core aspect that is often forgotten.

Spirituality, Space and Saints

The Christianization of the Empire certainly enabled, and perhaps demanded, many more concrete outward signs of faith than had been possible before. Space acquired a new spiritual significance, as churches were built in every town and city; while now they were free to express their faith in public acts, Christians went on pilgrimage to the Holy Land, and later, other sacred places. No longer martyred (unless, alas, by other Christians!) the cult of the martyrs and their relics blossomed into a cult of saints.

Pre-eminent among these was Mary, venerated from the fourth century onwards as *Theotokos*, the Birth-Giver – or more loosely, 'Mother' – of God. Some (Graves, 1999) argue that, in a Mediterranean world used to honouring female as well as male divinities, the Mother of God compensated for the lack of the feminine in the Christian Trinity. But theologians from Cyril of Alexandria onward urged the title as a touchstone of Christian orthodoxy, arguing that it cannot be denied without denying the Godhood of Christ.

Meanwhile the veneration of the saints was based on the doctrine of *theosis*. If saints are people in whom the white light of God is refracted in many human colours, contemplating their lives and personalities is appropriate on the path to God. In any event, Marian devotion, saints and pilgrimages became universal aspects of Christian spirituality, until challenged at the Reformation.

Spirituality and Time

Meanwhile Christians began to revive Jewish traditions of celebrating God's action in history through the natural cycles of time.

The *week* had been linked by the priestly writings in Judaism with the creation of the world, with the Sabbath representing the day on which God rested and on which God's people should likewise abstain from work and focus on worship. For Christians the following day, Sunday, on which Jesus rose from the dead (having himself rested in the tomb on the Sabbath) became the focal day of worship, with Friday, the day of the crucifixion, often a fast day.

As we shall see, from Benedict onward the monastic life in its various forms has centred around the Divine Office: the *daily* rhythms of the hours, each linked with a specific stage of Christ's passion, interlaced with times for study, work and conviviality.

Meanwhile, the liturgical *year* has become more and more enriched. The early celebrations of the resurrection at Easter and the coming of the Holy Spirit at Pentecost framed a 50-day season of joy. This was preceded by Lent, a time of preparation, originally for baptism candidates, and later for the whole church, culminating in the Holy Week remembrance of the supper and crucifixion of Christ. Later, Roman midwinter festivals became the chosen times to celebrate Christ's birth and Epiphany (which celebrated his baptism in the East, and the visit of the wise men in the West). In the West this was preceded by the preparatory fast of Advent. In time a host of other festivals and saints' days were added

Many Protestant traditions later curtailed the observance of these seasons, seeing any focus on specific times and places as possible occasions for trusting in 'works', observances designed to earn salvation. On the other hand, they transferred the Jewish piety of the seventh day to Sunday, the first day of the week. If the year meant less for them, the week meant more.

The Desert and Eastern Monasticism

The Christians were not the first to develop monastic communities. The practice had long been intrinsic to Buddhism, while within Judaism from *c*.150 BC–100 AD the *Essenes* had formed an ascetic, celibate community of men and women sharing goods in common, dedicated to a holy life of virtue, rejecting Temple worship but otherwise adhering to Jewish Law, adding many rites of bathing in water for cleansing from sin, and awaiting the coming kingdom of God. Many have speculated that John the Baptist may have been an Essene. Though Jesus was reputedly contrasted with him as not at all ascetic (Matt. 11.19; Luke 7.34), he himself did not marry, and seems to have sympathized with radical celibacy (Matt. 19.12) and to have shared many of the Essene ideals and hopes.

It was in nearby Egypt and Syria that the first Christians began to leave the cities to live in monastic communities or in solitude in the desert. The movement was characterized by

- A profound sense of **darkness within**. The desert fathers sought to quell the passions and the *logismoi* (repetitive obsessive thoughts) by ascetic rigour and continual penance.
- **Darkness without:** real demons were often seen as lurking behind the temptations, and the monks were engaged in a spiritual warfare.
- The search for **apatheia**, freedom from passions, which sounds negative – like our term 'apathy' – but is rather a kind of tranquillity, which a friend once likened to an air balloon, which is not buffeted by the winds, but rides them in stillness.
- **Solitude** and extensive periods of silence. The word 'monk' comes from the Greek *monas*, alone.
- **Community:** balancing this, a common life under the strict discipline of a spiritual father or *abba* (the origin of our 'abbot').
- **Poverty**: reducing worldly goods to the minimum and sharing them in common.

- **Virginity**: the patristic suspicion of the body intensified. Among the sins the sexual ones loomed large; even 'wet dreams' were tainted.
- However this also imparted a healthy sense of **solidarity in sin**, from which no one could claim to be free. There are many tales of junior monks wanting to condemn weaker brothers and sisters, but the wiser old monks intervened, identifying with the sinner (Williams, 2004).
- The beginnings of **spiritual direction**: people would come from the cities to seek advice, self-understanding and guidance in the spiritual life.
- Correspondingly the beginnings of an **analysis of the soul** and the inner life. The deadly sins were analysed: originally nine, of which two are particularly important in the spirituality of darkness: *akedia* or dryness, a listless indifference and loss of motivation, which was often seen as an inner desert; and *penthé*, grief, which we might now term depression. These were seen as negative demon-induced phenomena that had to be overcome; only later, with the likes of John of the Cross, would they be seen as sometimes the work of grace.

Anthony of Egypt (c.251–356)

It had long been common practice for Christians to live ascetic, celibate lives within or on the edge of their towns. But having explored these options in response to Jesus' words to the rich young man, 'Go, sell everything you have' (Luke 18.22), Anthony finally resolved to retire into complete solitude on a mountain in the desert near the Red Sea. The silence was interrupted only by the counsel he gave to those who came to him, words of wisdom such as 'He who knows that he is praying has not yet begun to pray.' Gradually others came to dwell in caves nearby, and begged Anthony to be their *abba*, and so the first monastic community was born.

In time *Pachomius* (d.346) organized such communities under the first monastic rule. Basil of Caesarea developed a more comprehensive rule that became widespread in the East, while *John Cassian* (c.360–433) founded a monastery in France and brought desert monasticism to the West.

Evagrius of Pontus (346–99)

A renowned preacher from Asia Minor, Evagrius became a monk to escape an adulterous affair. He found the practicalities of community life rather difficult, and retired to a deeper hermit-like seclusion. He connected desert spirituality and prayer with the theology of Origen, interpreting the desert way as an intellectual seeking of pure contemplation and *apatheia*. His analysis of the soul, the deadly sins and 'demons' is subtle, expressed in pithy aphorisms:

> Virtues do not stop demons attacking us, but keep us unscathed by them. (cited in Kadloubovsky, 1954, p. 102)

> If you are a theologian, you truly pray; if you truly pray, you are a theologian. (*Chapters on Prayer*, 1978, p. 65)

Makarios the Great (c.300–91)

Makarios, from Egypt, represents the contrasting, earthy side of the desert as a moral struggle to restore the will rather than the mind. He was full of wise advice: 'if an alien thought arises, never look at it but always look upwards'. Makarios was reputed to have achieved *theosis* and become a god on earth, on the grounds, significantly, not of his moral purity, but because just as God protects the earth, so Makarios covered the sins of the weaker brethren (Williams, 2004).

His spirituality (and that ascribed to him – so-called 'Pseudo-Macarius') readily assimilated both Jewish and Greek elements, as we find in this passage which beautifully unites the Jewish chariot throne of God with the soul which Plato likened to a charioteer:

> The soul . . . is privileged to be the dwelling place and the throne of God, all eye, all light, all face, all glory, all spirit, made so by Christ, who drives, guides, carries and supports the soul about and adorns and decorates the soul with his spiritual beauty. (1989, p. 38)

Lectio Divina

Origen had emphasized the need to read the Bible with prayerful attention to specific phrases, repeated and turned over in the mind. The medieval Carthusian, Guigo II (1978), describes four stages of this practice of 'divine reading':

- **reading** the passage slowly several times;
- **meditation**: reflecting on it in relation to oneself, focusing on phrases that stand out as important;
- **prayer**: responding with the heart, speaking back to God and so opening a conversation;
- **contemplation**: becoming free from one's thoughts in a total attention and listening to God.

The Jesus Prayer

The monks endeavoured to 'pray without ceasing' (1 Thess. 5.17) and used simple repeated phrases from the Psalms such as 'O God make speed to save us: O Lord make haste to help us.' From fifth-century Syria there rapidly spread throughout Eastern monasticism the practice of recalling the presence of Christ through a brief repeated prayer like 'Lord Jesus Christ, Son of God, have mercy on me a sinner,' or more simply, 'Jesus'. In Chapter 4 we shall see how this 'prayer of the heart' developed with the hesychasts.

Western Monasticism

The Augustinian Rule

Augustine wrote a simple rule for the monastic life, emphasizing friendship, social justice and evangelical equality under a prior (first among equals) rather than the discipline of the authoritative *abba* of Eastern and Benedictine monasticism.

Benedict of Nursia (c.480–547)

Benedict adapted from Cassian a monasticism centred on worship and the recital of the Psalms at regular hours of matins (in the night), the first, third, sixth and ninth hours of the day, vespers at sunset, and compline before sleep. The austerity of the Eastern traditions was relaxed in a balanced life in which the whole person, body, mind and spirit, was engaged in times for prayer, study, work and recreation. Humility, meekness and obedience were inculcated under the discipline of the *abba*.

Benedictine monasticism spread through Europe from the south, becoming, along with the more austere, Eastern-style monasticism of the Celts, the protector of Christian learning in a time of barbarian invasion and war. *Pope Gregory the Great (c.*540–604), a monk of great culture and tireless organizing abilities, pioneered this advance in England, and encouraged the use of music in worship. The chant used throughout Western monasticism still bears his name.

Celtic asceticism: the desert in the sea

The desert tradition soon spread to the Celtic fringes, where hermits sought out remote islands like the Skellig Rocks, Iona and Lindisfarne.

Celtic tradition speaks of the three martyrdoms:

- The **red** martyrdom of those who gave their life for Christ under persecution;
- the **white** martyrdom of virginity; and
- the **green** martyrdom of homeless travelling and pilgrimage. This was characteristic of Celtic saints who crossed remote seas to convert people to Christ: Patrick (*c.*390–460), David (*c.*520–600), Brendan, Bridget or Bride, Columba of Iona (*c.*521–97), Aidan of Lindisfarne (*c.*600–51) and the countless saints whose name lives on only in the names of Welsh and Cornish villages.

Whereas the Roman form of Christianity centred on the cathedrals in the great cities, the largely rural Celtic Church was focused on the monasteries. Though eventually weakened by Viking invasions and succumbing to the monarchical weight of Rome, Celtic spirituality bequeathed to the wider Church the practice of personal confession to a spiritual guide (latterly a priest), a lyrical asceticism and friendship with the earth that is increasingly valued today, and the unique art of its manuscripts. In the Book of Kells and the Lindisfarne Gospels, the work of austere monks, we see the words of scripture intertwined with humorous scenes and observations of nature as if forming the many lines of a visual polyphony – a 'Word made flesh' in a different way from before or since.

John the Scot Eriugena (c.800–77)

The greatest Celtic theologian, John (from Ireland) translated Denys the Areopagite and introduced his thought and that of Gregory of Nyssa and Maximus to the West. Following Gregory he identified God with the non-being out of which the world was created. God is 'nothing', radically unknowable, even to Godself. God does not know evil, which is non-being of a different kind; so sin need not stand in the way of our ultimate salvation and return to God.

John held that God comes into being and is created through the things God creates; creation is an adventure of self-discovery by God and theophany for creatures – everything that exists being a 'light' that leads the way back to God. All creation will ultimately return to the paradise of God, but only those who have learned to contemplate God in this life will enjoy to the full the paradise fruit, merging with God as lights blend into the one light, or voices in the one choir (1987, v.935c). 'Hell' will consist in remaining trapped in the fantasies of individual separateness and satisfaction vainly sought in this life, marring enjoyment of eternal life in God.

John's ideas sounded unfamiliar, especially his notion that in mystical union God becomes indistinguishable from our deepest self, being the one who experiences God in us, and that God is enriched and even 'created' by creation. But the ideas his translations had introduced in time fostered a distinctive apophatic tradition in the West.

Anselm of Canterbury (1033–1109)

An Italian Benedictine who became Archbishop of Canterbury and was later exiled, Anselm is renowned for being among the first to 'prove' the existence of God. As, by definition, the greatest being we can conceive of – he argued – God must exist, since a non-existent God would be less great! The 'proof' is a far cry from the thought of John the Scot, who would question whether God was either a being or conceivable! Nonetheless its context is not dry abstraction but prayer seeking an object worthy of adoration. *Credo ut intelligam*, he wrote: 'I believe in order that I may understand.'

Anselm wrote many devotions and meditations, and was one among many in the Middle Ages – including Julian of Norwich – to follow early Syrian tradition in addressing Christ as mother, as in this canticle composed of his words.

Jesus, as a mother you gather your people to you; you are gentle with us as a mother with her children. Often you weep over our sins and our pride, tenderly you draw us from hatred and judgement. You comfort us in sorrow and bind up our wounds, in sickness you nurse us, and with pure milk you feed us. Jesus, by your dying we are born to new life: by your anguish and labour we come forth in joy. (Preface to the *Proslogion*, 1973)

Monasticism Reformed

Though individually the Benedictines renounced possessions, the collective industry of the monasteries turned them into some of the richest landowners, employing many serfs for the physical labour while the monks attended to the increasingly demanding liturgy.

In the twelfth century a number of movements sought a return to the original simplicity of monasticism. The Carthusians adopted an extremely austere, silent rule based on the desert fathers. The Cistercians adopted more moderate but hugely significant and influential changes (McGinn, 1994, pp. 158–62):

- A co-ordinated structure of mother and daughter houses linked by convocations and visitations.
- Work was to be done by lay brothers who shared to a degree in the community life, not by serfs.
- Child oblates were not accepted, only adults by conscious decision.

Between them these changes made for a monasticism that was not merely a way of life for a spiritual elite, but a co-ordinated and committed movement for change in society at large.

Bernard of Clairvaux (c.1090–1153)

The greatest Cistercian mystic and theologian, passionate and combative by nature, Bernard was also a poet and an astute politician. He was merciless with those he disagreed with, like Abelard and the new scholastic theologians, and he gave strong support to the Crusades. Yet his was a mysticism of love: 'Life is only for loving. Time is only that we may find God.'[2]

Indeed, Bernard was among the first to emphasize the love of the fleshly humanity of Christ as well as the divinity, and he promoted devotion to the one who gave birth to and nurtured that human flesh, Mary. Where previously writers like Origen had seen the Song of Songs as allegorical of an intellectual and spiritual love of the Word, Bernard did not hesitate to apply its eroticism literally to the love of Christ, who became incarnate

> that he might return all the affections of carnal humans, who could only love carnally, first to the saving love of his flesh, and thus, little by little, lead them to spiritual love. (cited McGinn, 1994, p. 174)

We are led from the penitential kiss of Christ's feet, through the devotional kiss of his hand, to the contemplative kiss of the mouth, described in the Song. Elsewhere Bernard describes four stages:

1 Love of self for self's sake – pure selfishness.
2 Love of God for self's sake, for the benefits God can give.
3 Love of God for God's sake – the disinterested love of God, obedient and self-forgetting.
4 Love of self for God's sake. Of course, this entails love of other selves for God's sake equally; and we shall see below how Richard of St Victor developed this idea.

Courtly Love

The new emphasis on the spiritual role of carnal love, and the focus on the Virgin Mary, went hand in hand – part cause, part effect – with the new lyricism

---

2 This saying has also been ascribed to Augustine.

of courtly love. Troubadours were singing the delights of serving and adoring their beloved ladies just as 'troubadours of the spirit' like Bernard – and later Francis – were singing the joys of serving 'Our Lord' and 'Our Lady' (Lewis, 1977). Meanwhile in 1150 the Church officially recognized marriage as a sacrament, despite theologians' doubts about a sacrament whose outward sign was carnal love.

Ironically, one of the roots of our notions of romantic love may lie in celibate mysticism.

William of St Thierry (c.1077–1148)

Another Cistercian, William has only recently moved out of the shadow of his friend Bernard. His 'great contribution . . . is to have evolved a theology of the Trinity which is essentially mystical, and a mystical theology which is essentially Trinitarian' (Brooke, 1980, p. 8).

William combined a Western understanding of the Spirit, as the love that unites the Father and the Son, with an Eastern stress on the importance of the work of the Spirit fusing himself with the transformed soul, such that likewise 'our love toward God *is* the Holy Spirit' (cited by McGinn, 1994, p. 272). So through the Spirit the mystic comes to share in the life of the Trinity, God's love of God, the mutual love of Father and Son, which *is* the indwelling Spirit.

Richard of St Victor (d.1173)

Richard was an Augustinian canon and one of the early scholastics – theologians teaching in an academic rather than a strict monastic setting. He saw prayer as involving four stages rather than the three familiar from Origen onward.

1 **Meditation**: God enters into the soul and she turns inward into herself and begins to thirst for God.
2 **Contemplation:** The soul ascends above herself and is lifted up to God, thirsting to go to him.
3 **Jubilation**: the soul, uplifted, passes over altogether into God.
4 **Compassion**: the soul goes forth on God's behalf and descends below herself, impelled by God's own love of others.

So the journey culminates not in inward union, but in an outpouring of compassion. As for John the Scot and William, so for Richard, God is not only the goal of the mystical journey but the source. The journey begins with God's coming to the soul, and ends in the soul's moving out from God with God's own ecstatic love.

Hildegard of Bingen (1098–1179)

A Benedictine abbess, Hildegard was a visionary, mystic, artist, scientist, poet and musical composer. Her 'visions', which she transcribed accompanied with thoughts and verses set to music, seem to represent – as perhaps they do for Julian and other women mystics later – an artistic mode of theological reflection. The overall vision seems idiosyncratically to combine something remarkably akin to ancient chariot and apocalyptic mysticism with contemporary science and philosophy.

Conclusion

We have considered the period in which Christian spirituality and worship took their lasting form, and have witnessed the vital part played in this by monasticism, a contribution that emerges as all the greater when we consider that many of the mystics covered in other chapters were also monks and nuns. In the next chapter we shall see this monastic hegemony both confirmed and challenged.

For Reflection and Discussion

1 Is spirituality for you primarily something you experience, something you believe, or something you do?
2 Do you feel there are some spiritual truths that cannot be written down but only passed on by word of mouth? Or is it wrong to keep things 'secret' from the uninitiated?
3 Which of the ten listed monastic ideals (pp. 40–1) do you feel have enriched the Christian tradition, and which have impoverished or distorted it?

4 Which of the ideas of John Scotus Eriugena do you feel are worth further thought, and which do you find nonsensical or heretical?
5 Compare the 'classical' description of the spiritual journey in Table 2
   with those offered by Bernard and Richard. What are the strengths
   and weaknesses of each?

Further Reading

Elisabeth Behr-Sigel, 1993, *The Place of the Heart: Introduction to Orthodox Spiritual-
   ity*, New York: St Vladimir's Seminary Press.
Louis Bouyer, tr. Illtyd Trethowen, 1990, *The Christian Mystery: From Pagan Myth to
   Christian Mysticism*, Edinburgh: T & T Clark.
Marilyn Dunn, 2000, *The Emergence of Monasticism*, Oxford: Blackwell.
William Harmless, 2004, *Desert Christians: An Introduction to the Literature of Early
   Monasticism*, Oxford and New York: Oxford University Press.
Bernard McGinn, 1994, *The Growth of Mysticism*, New York: Crossroad.
Thomas O'Loughlin and Philip Sheldrake, 2000, *Journeys on the Edge: The Celtic
   Tradition*, Maryknoll, NY, Orbis.
Kenneth Stevenson, 1989, *The First Rites,* Collegeville: Liturgical Press.
Rowan Williams, 2004, *Silence and Honey Cakes*, Oxford: Lion Hudson.

4

Hierarchy and Heresy: Medieval Spirituality

In the previous chapters (see also Chapter 10) we touched on the patristic and monastic alienation from the physical body; this chapter charts the Church's tightening embrace of the sociopolitical body. In the medieval period, Christianity became perhaps the most all-embracing religious system the world has seen. Religion, law, politics, science and culture were all subjected to the theocratic rule of faith

In many ways this was the zenith of Christian spirituality, in which all life was sacramentally ordered around Christ, and 'mystics' were both more numerous and more highly regarded than before or since. But the period has also been seen as a nadir in which Christianity began to resort to the inquisition, torture, and burning at the stake, and to instil an all-pervasive terror of the eternal fires of hell; while theology, meanwhile, lost its spiritual roots and became a rationalistic, scholastic and legalistic pursuit, whose goal was not faith, but the production of an ideology for Christendom. In the process – on this view – the spirituality that had hitherto been inseparable from theology began to drift into an exile of emotional subjectivity.

Our historical exploration will raise the fundamental question to be considered in Chapter 9: is spirituality essentially linked to religious faith in a kind of 'mystical theology', or is it an independent force, seen at its best when liberated from theology?

The trends described were clearest in the Catholic West, but we will begin our discussion with the Orthodox East.

Developments in the East

The situation in the East was subtly different from that in the West. The Church favoured the use of the vernacular, and as Orthodoxy spread to Russia and other Slavic lands, indigenous variants easily developed. But urban development and church centralization were less in those lands. Lay theology developed, but without either the heretical or the feminine emphasis found in the West, and though there was a similar turn to the *experience* of God, it remained focused on the divine rather than the humanity and sufferings of Christ.

As in the West, tensions developed between corporate structure and individual simplicity (witness Joseph and Nilus) but without leading to any split like the Western Reformation. And while Enlightenment values began to be introduced in the time of Peter the Great, Orthodox spirituality as well as national feeling staunchly resisted them. For these reasons we will deal with Orthodox spirituality from medieval times *onward* in this one chapter, rather than artificially spreading it over the ensuing chapters in a manner that would confuse the discussion with historical movements that had no deep impact on Orthodox spirituality.

Symeon the New Theologian (949–1042)

Symeon's 'newness' lay not in theological innovation but a new emphasis – which was to continue in the East – on the Holy Spirit and on the need for doctrine to be experienced personally:

> Do not say that it is impossible to receive the Spirit of God . . . Do not say that one can possess Him without knowing it . . . Do not say that men cannot perceive the divine light, or that it is impossible in this age! (1975, Hymn 27, 125–32)

Hesychasm

An experiential technique of prayer developed out of the prayer of the heart (p. 43) in the Middle Ages among the numerous monasteries of Mount Athos in northern Greece. The 'hesychasts' sought the vision of God through

- **Silence** – *hesuchia*.
- The careful use of **breathing** co-ordinated with the praying of . . .
- . . . a set phrase, rather like a mantra, the most familiar being the **Jesus Prayer**, 'Lord Jesus Christ, Son of God, have mercy on me, a sinner.' The prayer was seen as summing up the whole mystery of salvation. The one praying would, as he inhaled, confess Jesus as Lord and Son of God, then exhaling, confess and expel his own sinfulness.
- **Bodily posture**. Unlike the erect spine and crossed legs recommended in several Oriental religions, hesychasts sat with head bowed between the knees, a womblike – albeit painful – posture designed to focus the mind on the heart.
- Taking the **mind into the heart**, the place of thought into the place of desire and integration, in which true prayer is formed.

Gregory Palamas (1296–1359)

For Palamas, the vision of God was attained, not by the mind or soul on its own, but by the whole person transformed by the grace of God. Obviously the spiritual eye of the mind is able to contemplate the glory of God in creation; this was quite acceptable Neoplatonism. But what interested Palamas was the opposite possibility of seeing with our embodied eyes the uncreated light that shone before the world began to be; the eschatological light, moreover, that all the redeemed will share at the end of time. Palamas based this possibility on a theme that has always loomed larger in the East than in the West: Jesus' transfiguration.

> The three disciples on Mount Tabor beheld the glory of the transfiguration through their bodily eyes. Yet what enables us to see the divine light is not the organs of sense perception by virtue of their own intrinsic power, but rather the grace of God that is active within them. (1983, I.3.16)

Using the now familiar Orthodox distinction, Palamas argued that the uncreated light seen by the saints is the *energy* of God, which continually streams from him like light from the sun, filling the created world for those with eyes to see. But the *essence* of God – the nature of God in himself – transcends vision and comprehension of any kind. So, following Gregory and Denys, God's light includes a darkness: 'There is an unknowing that is higher than all knowledge, a darkness that is supremely bright; and in this dazzling darkness divine things are given to the saints' (1983, 1.3.18).

Russian Spirituality

Monasticism spread with Christianity to Russia, developing some extremely rigorous and ascetic trends that were repeatedly counterbalanced by more moderate forms. In caves near Kiev, the first capital of Russia, *St Theodosius* (*c*.1002–74) pioneered a moderate asceticism.

Following the devastating Tartar invasions of the thirteenth century the capital shifted to Moscow. Monasticism was restored by *St Sergius of Radonezh* (1322–92), who was to become the patron saint of Moscow and all Russia. Like many Russian monastic leaders, Sergius began as a simple hermit with only wild beasts, including a bear, for company, until forced by his companions to become head of a great monastery which was the centre for social work and national renewal as well as contemplation.

Following the 'schism' of Rome (as the Orthodox saw it) in 1054, and the fall of Constantinople to the Turks in 1453, many Orthodox came to regard Moscow as the 'third Rome', the centre of the true Christian universe.

Rival Spiritualities

The tension between corporate and politically oriented monasticism and a more liberal and individual piety was epitomized in two great saints, *Joseph of Volokolamsk* (1439–1515) and *Nil Sorsky* (*c*.1433–1508). Nil learned from a visit to Mount Athos the value of small monastic groups of two or three living in simple huts with minimal possessions, dedicated to prayer, a surprisingly liberal and critical study of scripture and tradition, and deep friendship. Joseph on the other hand preferred strong well-endowed monasteries focused on the opulent beauty of the Byzantine liturgy. Discipline was severe, with confession and punishment an important feature. Joseph argued against Nil that possessions and property could help monasticism as an educative and charitable force. After bitter controversy his position prevailed and Nil's little groups were suppressed. These saints can be seen as the source of two strands of Russian spirituality: one authoritarian, disciplined, and rooted in *sobornost* (solidarity) and tradition, and the other idiosyncratic, soulful, radical and often defiant.

Fools, Guides and Novelists

In the latter tradition we find movements among lay people aiming to re-create the spirituality of the desert outside the cloisters. *Holy fools* wandered as vagabonds, acting in an absurd and self-humiliating but often prophetically challenging way, following St Paul's advice to be a 'fool for Christ'. They included *Blessed Basil of Moscow* (1468–1552), who publicly ridiculed Ivan the Terrible, before whom everyone else cowered in fear, and *Nicholas of Pskov* (d.1576), who after Ivan's massacre of the people of Novgorod, offered him meat in Lent. Ivan replied that as a fasting Christian he could not eat it, to which Nicholas retorted, 'Then why do you drink the blood of Christians?'

The *staretz* or spiritual guide, based on the desert *abba*, assumed a particular importance in Russian spirituality, immortalized in Fr Zosima in Dostoyevsky's *Brothers Karamazov*, and embodied in the humble yet penetrating wisdom of *Metropolitan Anthony of Sourozh* (1914–2003).

Meanwhile the prayer of the heart became a mainstay of lay as well as monastic spirituality, as immortalized in the nineteenth-century *Pilgrim's Tale*. And lay people would live for a time as hermits, following their own rule of life in a *poustinia* or shack in the forest (Doherty, 1977).

Among Russian writers, the intense, demon-laden spirituality of *Fyodor Dostoyevsky* (1821–81), the broad, radical vision of *Leo Tolstoy* (1828–1910), and the defiant, enduring integrity of *Alexander Solzhenitsyn* (b.1918) in their very different ways express these constant strands of Russian spirituality.

In the tradition of Joseph we can place that of the *Old Believers*, who rejected the Westernizing influences of Peter the Great in favour of the ancient Russian liturgy, plainchant, calendar and the minute details of everyday living. Small communities have survived persecution by both Orthodox and Communist governments. And it has been argued that Russian communism itself owes much to the *sobornost* and the authoritarian confessional disciplines of Joseph's strand of spirituality; Joseph Stalin, after all, began his career as a monk.

Seraphim of Sarov (1759–1833)

Another monk, Seraphim withdrew to the solitude of the Russian forests, where like Francis he lived in intimacy with the wild animals. He was spiritual director for many, and helped lay people to grow in Orthodoxy spirituality. Loved in the East as Francis is in the West, he came to embody the Orthodox ideals of asceticism, contemplation, divinization and the vision of the uncreated Light. The latter is explained to a disciple, who said to him

> 'I don't understand how one can be certain of being in the Spirit of God. How should I be able to recognize for certain this manifestation in myself?' ...
> 'My friend, [said Seraphim,] we are both at this moment in the Spirit of God ... Why won't you look at me?'
> 'I can't look at you, Father – I replied – your eyes shine like lightning; your face has become more dazzling than the sun, and it hurts my eyes to look at you.'
> 'Don't be afraid' said he, 'at this very moment you've become as bright as I have. You are also at present in the fullness of the Spirit of God; otherwise, you wouldn't be able to see me as you do see me.'
> (Conversation on the end of Christian Life, cited in Lossky, 1957, pp. 227–9)

Developments in the West

In the West, the twelfth and thirteenth centuries saw a cultural renaissance (McGinn, 1998, pp. 2–4). Towns and cities were developing on a huge scale. This moved the centre of learning way from the monasteries – where theology had always been pursued in the context of the contemplative life – towards the universities and cathedrals at the heart of the new cities. Power was becoming more centralized in the bureaucracies of the developing states, as well as in the

Church itself. But whereas in rural society people had definitively belonged to one kind of tight hierarchy or another – the military aristocracy, the feudal peasantry or the Church hierarchy – in the towns, with freer trade, freer association became possible. The economy began to be based on money and trade rather than feudal favour. Finally, literacy increased, especially in the vernacular, and this allowed lay people, and women in particular – not versed in Latin – to contribute theologically.

Reflecting all this was a momentous architectural change (García-Riviera in Holder, 2005, pp. 351–2) from *Romanesque* to *Gothic*, from churches that enclosed with geometric arches a finite, incarnational space for an earthly community, to architecture that emphasized space and height, soaring into the transcendent. The most significant art form ceased to be the icon or fresco, materially incarnating the presence of God in paint, and became the stained-glass window, lit by light from elsewhere, making the church a starting point for an infinite journey into the Beyond.

In the same manner, the old monastic spirituality, incarnating Christian values in a stable way of life, was giving way to two developments: the *university*, with its vision of the whole of knowledge and the whole of 'secular' society embraced, consecrated and ruled by a new, rationally agile, academic and speculative scholastic theology; and the *apostolica vita*, the desire of many, encouraged by the Church but extending way beyond its hierarchy, to return to an apostolic life of simplicity and mission.

The desire for simplicity was, of course, as old as monasticism, but the notion of a mission, not just to bring the gospel to the 'heathen', but to transform and convert to Christ an already nominally Christian society, was radical. The simplicity to which people felt called was not a withdrawal to the desert, but a movement *into* society, full of evangelical purpose. Christian faith was ceasing to be a way of life preserved in essentially closed communities, and was, like the architecture, opening out as a linear journey to which all were to be summoned.

In many ways the story of medieval mysticism is the story of the interaction between these two movements: a theology becoming more academic and 'professional', and a spirituality becoming more populist and 'lay'. Through the Middle Ages, the tension did not quite lead to breaking point, as later it did.

The Preaching Orders

The apostolic life bore two kinds of fruit: the development of lay and (especially) women's spirituality, to which we shall turn in due course; and the initiation of a new alternative to monasticism, the mendicant orders of friars, who made no vow of stability but (ideally) wandered from place to place as preachers, dependent on others for alms, rather like the early disciples. The two most significant orders were the Dominicans and the Franciscans.

Thomas Aquinas (1224–74)

The Dominicans were founded in 1215 with the primary aim of converting the Cathars or Albigensians, who had come to dominate the South of France. The Cathars saw themselves as living the purest form of the apostolic life, with their elite of 'perfect ones' having broken all ties with the material world, which like the Gnostics they believed to be the evil product of a false divinity.

The Dominicans' most celebrated theologian, Thomas Aquinas, developed a contrasting theology centred on the radical goodness of creation. Though seldom regarded as a 'mystic', the heart of his theology is a profound grasp of the intimacy of the transcendent God with all creation:

> God is present everywhere in everything; not indeed as part of their substance, but in the way agents are present to . . . what they act upon . . . During the whole period of a creature's existence, then, God must be present to it in the way its own existence is . . . more intimately and profoundly interior . . . than anything else. (1989, p. 22 (I.8.1))

> As Augustine says, 'if, at any time, the ruling power of God were to desert what he created, his creation would immediately lose its form, and all nature would collapse.' Whatever actually possesses form exists, given the influence of God; just as air that possesses transparency is lit up, given the influence of the sun. (1989, p. 154 (I.104.1))

Plato's eternal, geometrically based concepts could not do justice to such an intimate presence, and Thomas turned instead to Aristotle's organic, biologically based understanding of a world of matter always striving to grow and

realize itself in and through time. God was for Thomas 'pure act', the full reali-
zation of all potential for goodness, beauty and being.

Because God relates to the world as agent to act, God must wholly surpass all
the partially realized beings we know of, and yet they must all bear some analogy to the power that made them. As with Denys, everything (*kataphatically*)
speaks of God in some unknowable way, being his doing. All things are analogies, revealing something (*symbolically*) of God. But (*apophatically*) nothing is
literally true of God.

For Thomas, the Orthodox distinction between God's essence and energies
could not hold. God's being is fully realized in the act of creating, and leaves no
unexpressed potential. As Karl Barth later put it, unlike the moon, God has no
hidden side, but is wholly turned towards his creation, bathing it always in his
light. Nevertheless people cannot see God in the way the hesychasts suggested.
In visions, people do not directly see the uncreated light; God *creates* the vision
to convey some truth to them. This marked a fundamental divergence between
Orthodox and Western spirituality.

Francis of Assisi (1181–1226)

Francis was converted to the apostolic life by words he heard spoken from the
cross, bidding him rebuild his ruined Church, which he first misunderstood
as relating to a ruined church building, then realized as a call to simplicity.
Stripping naked, and telling his father that God was now his only father, he
renounced his inheritance and began to wander as a preacher and beggar. In
time a small group formed around him dedicated to the same way of life, while
his close friend Clare formed a community of nuns, the Poor Clares. After a
struggle he won the Pope's permission to found a new order.

Francis is perhaps the best loved of Western saints. Today he is associated
with a light, joyful, affirmative spirituality, close to every living creature. The
lightness and joy were certainly there in abundance, but intimately linked to a
desire to enter deeply into the poverty and passion of Christ, which bore fruit
in his receiving, through a vision, the stigmata, the wounds of Christ. His was a
spirituality of creation, crib and cross.

After his death there were terrible, and not entirely successful, struggles to
preserve his unique spirit of simplicity.

Bonaventure (1221–74)

Often Franciscan spirituality – emotional, visionary, simple, celebrating kinship with all creation, and seeing the love of God as the basis of knowledge of God – is contrasted with the Dominican spirituality of Aquinas and Eckhart – intellectual, speculative, convoluted, sceptical of direct experience of God, and seeing the knowledge of God as the basis of the love. However, Franciscans developed their own scholasticism with the likes of Duns Scotus and Bonaventure. The latter is perhaps the last theologian to be a mystic too, integrating a deep devotion to the life and example of Francis with an apophatic description of the spiritual journey.

The journey he described leads us from finding God in nature, through finding God in ourselves, to finding God beyond ourselves and all things. The journey moves from what Zaehner (see p. 117) would call 'nature' to 'soul' to 'theistic' spirituality. But each stage is further divided into two. At the first stage we move from sensing things in the world to the use of imagination to see through them, as symbols, to God. In the second stage we move towards God first through reason, and then by 'intellect', that is, through the virtues of faith, hope and love. In the third stage we contemplate the beauty of God's form, but then move beyond even that to embrace God in darkness and ecstasy, a move that is only possible through the passion and death of Christ. And there we note the cross-centred, Franciscan twist to a framework essentially based on Denys, not unlike the twist Maximus imparted in the East.

The Flesh of God: Women Mystics

As well as the new preaching orders, the *apostolica vita* found expression in the gathering together of lay people into communities run on semi-monastic lines. The towns, with the free association into guilds, made such free communities a natural development, though one which the Church viewed very ambivalently. One such movement, in Belgium, was the *Beguines*, whose members included the first three mystics discussed below.

The new lay – and particularly, it turned out, women's – spirituality had remarkable features. It was written in the vernacular, which was only then beginning to be used as a written means of reflection. Its startling use of down to earth, bodily images, contrasts with the stately abstractions of Latin scholasticism, and proved capable of generating new insights, whose orthodoxy proved remarkably difficult for the Church bureaucracy to assess.

The understanding of *heresy* was itself undergoing a shift. Where in patristic times heresy had meant *unorthodox* belief, mainly concerning the nature of the Trinity and the incarnation in Christ, now (according to the Council of Vierne, 1311) it was coming to be seen as *subversive* belief which undermined the Church's monopoly of the scriptures and the means of grace by viewing people as capable of independent spiritual growth and perfection (Jantzen, 1995, pp. 246–84).

The tension between this redefinition of heresy and the movement towards lay spirituality came to a head with the burning of Marguerite Porete in 1310. At the very time when *Dante* (1265–1321) was composing his *Divine Comedy*, in which cosmic, hierarchical, theological, moral and mystical visions are serenely integrated, a tragic rift appeared between theological hierarchy and mysticism.

Hadewijch of Brabant (thirteenth century)

Hadewijch is virtually unknown apart from her writings, which focus on *Minne*, a feminine, personified word for Love (sometimes translated 'Lady Love'). Hadewijch saw love expressed in the soul in a remarkable sequence of images: bond, light, live coal, fire, dew, living spring and finally – paradoxically the highest image of love – hell. For Hadewijch, love was an ecstasy of joy and pain, focused most clearly in the Eucharist, which she described as a mutual devouring of Christ and the soul:

> Each knows the other through and through
> In the anguish or the repose or the madness of Love,
> And eats his flesh and drinks his blood:
> The heart of each devours the other's heart. (1980, p. 358)

Hadewijch wrote of the Trinity as a whirlpool or spinning disc, and described the 'mutual abyss' of God and the soul in love, an abyss crossed through a paradoxical 'unfaith' or giving up of all faith and hope, leaving only the love itself. She also described the kiss of God and the soul as forming a single mouth, anticipating Eckhart's notion of an ultimate merging of God and the soul. Like Eckhart, Hadewijch believed Christ's incarnation only consummated an eternal existence of ourselves in God (Bouyer, 1990, p. 242).

Mechthild of Magdeburg (c.1210–85)

Mechthild was less sharply paradoxical than Hadewijch, more lyrical and dramatic with her beautiful, repeated metaphors of God's flowing, the love-play or courtship between God and the soul, and the metaphor of 'sinking' into God, which reverses the traditional imagery of ascent.

Marguerite Porete (d.1310)

Marguerite is known only from her book, *The Mirror of Simple Souls*, and her heresy trial at which she was condemned for teaching in it that the simple soul is entirely 'annihilated' in God, ceasing to have any will but his, and therefore becoming unable to sin.

The book takes the form of a dialogue between the Soul, Lady Love and Reason. The latter has to be given up, as conventional thought and morality are transcended by the perfected soul as it returns to its primordial nothingness in God. As noted, it was the suggestion that spirituality could transcend the need for the Church and its moral teachings that was now coming to be regarded as heresy.

Catherine of Siena (c.1340–80)

A Dominican tertiary, Catherine combined mysticism with a life of action, dedicating herself to the nursing of the sick, and later involving herself in Church politics, protesting its many abuses, and finally persuading Pope Gregory XI to return from Avignon – where he was beholden to French power – to Rome. Like Hadewijch and many contemporary female saints she had an intense desire for the Eucharist, which led her to extreme fasting (Bynum, 1988).

Julian of Norwich (1342–1417)

Mother Julian, lived as an anchoress, solitary apart from the spiritual direction she gave to many. She received a series of 'shewings', which were visions accompanied by interpretations given by God. In her humble way she combined the earthy (see p. 160) yet visionary language of the Beguines, something of the cross-centred simplicity of Francis, and a grasp of the metaphysics of Thomas Aquinas, manifest in her hazelnut vision, quoted on p. 134, where she goes on to express her desire to be 'substantially Oned' with God.

The Resurgence of Unknowing

The intense, creative and often sensuous imagination of the women saints was combined with a more intellectual, speculative and apophatic strand by the mystics who flourished in the Rhineland.

Meister Eckhart (c.1260–1328)

Eckhart can be portrayed as the antithesis of his fellow Dominican, Thomas Aquinas, but in a different way from Francis: Germanic rather than Italian, mystical rather than rational, heretical rather than orthodox. Yet Eckhart's 'heresies' can be read as radical, poetic expressions of what his fellow Dominican expressed logically, judiciously and prosaically. Alternatively they can be regarded as expressing in speculative and sometimes scholastic language what the Beguines had expressed poetically.

These are Eckhart's key concepts.

1 Beneath and prior to God the Trinity is undifferentiated God. God is forever 'boiling' or bubbling up into the Trinity.
2 All symbols or language about God can become idolatrous and an obstacle to spiritual growth – even Christ and God. So for the sake of God the soul needs in the end to 'let go of God'.
3 As there is a God beneath the Trinity, so there is an uncreated soul beneath the soul. Aquinas argued that when we act from our truest, freest selves,

God is acting in us. What Aquinas said about agency, Eckhart affirms about being. For him, God and the soul are ultimately one

4 The birth of Christ that matters is his birth now in the soul. Eckhart writes of the soul scintillating or sparkling with the light of the Godhead, mirroring Godhead so perfectly as to justify the idea that the soul like Godhead is uncreated. Godhead flowers in the soul as the blessed Trinity.

5 The most important virtue, surpassing even love, is indifference or detachment, an acceptance of whatever happens as belonging to a God-filled universe. Here Eckhart comes close to Porete's annihilation of the will in God.

Eckhart was condemned as a heretic, especially for point 3, but he died before the condemnation took effect, and remained influential among Rhineland Dominicans such as *Henry Suso* (c.1295–1366), *John Tauler* (c.1300–61) and Ruusbroec, as well as, later, John of the Cross.

John Ruusbroec (1293–1381)

What in Eckhart is expressed radically and abstractly is expressed more lyrically, and with a more orthodox balance, in Ruusbroec (or Ruysbroeck). He relates spiritual unity with God to the natural unity we have with God in creation, following Aquinas in speaking of God as a boundless dynamism that is closer to us than we are to ourselves.

Following Denys, Ruusbroec describes the unitive life as superessential, beyond being. In our heart is a fathomless ground capable of embracing the superessential unity of Godhead, which (as for Eckhart) is beyond the being of the three persons. To attain this we need to travel the 'wayless way' beyond the landmarks of being, to possess God in simplicity and nakedness of Spirit.

In this journey the mystic moves from being the 'faithful servant' of God, to being God's 'secret friend', and finally his 'hidden child'. And the journey involves a repeated inflowing of 'fruitive love' (love that is enjoyment of God for God's own sake) and outflowing of active love for the world.

More English Mystics

Mysticism flowered later in England than on the Continent, but richly, with the anonymous *Cloud of Unknowing* (fourteenth century) taking up Gregory of Nyssa's theme of Moses on the mountain. A 'cloud of forgetting' below the mystic shuts out earthly desires, while a 'cloud of unknowing' floats above, because God, following Denys, is beyond reason and knowledge. The mystic has to pierce that cloud with the darts of love, for 'by love may he be gotten and holden, by thought never'.

In the same broadly apophatic tradition was *Walter Hilton* (1343–96), whereas *Richard Rolle* (1300–49) and *Margery Kempe* (1373–1438) were far more centred on experiences and visions, closer in spirit to the women described above. Rolle felt full of the 'fire of love', declaring 'the name of Jesus is in my mind as a joyful song, in my ear a heavenly music, and in my mouth sweet honey'.

Nicholas of Cusa (1401–64)

Nicholas continued the tradition of seeing God and union with him as 'beyond being', but employs concepts that at times anticipate relativity and postmodernism. A Renaissance bishop, he was interested in mathematics and science as well as theology, and thought highly of Plato. He was fond of geometrical analogies, regarding God as a circle whose centre is everywhere and circumference nowhere. The cosmos, by contrast, has its centre nowhere, neither in the earth nor in the sun: here Nicholas as it were leapt beyond Copernicus to Einstein!

Both science and theology, he held, teach a 'learned ignorance'. Our goal is union with the Trinity who unites all opposites. God's unity is not unity as opposed to diversity or difference, but the transcendence of both. God is not the same as the universe, but God's ultimate quintessence or 'quiddity' is the ultimate quintessence of sun and moon and everything (1954, p. 71). Likewise God is not (as for Thomas) pure act, fully realized existence, but a union of actual and potential existence. Spiritually this might suggest that our goal is not to realize all our potential, but to allow God to reconcile our fulfilled and unfulfilled aspects.

Decline and Rebirth

The later fourteenth and fifteenth century witnessed a series of catastrophes – the Black Death from 1347 onward, the Hundred Years War (1337–1453), the papal schism (1378–1417) and widespread anarchy in which warlords competed for allegiance. Spirituality reflected this increasing atmosphere of fear, dwelling on the sufferings of Christ and mortifications of the flesh. We see 'religious thought crystallising into images' and a 'saturation of the religious atmosphere' (Huizinga, 1965, p. 147) with works of devotion and penance, whose intricacy and educative power have nonetheless been positively described by Duffey (2003). But there was also a reaction against this religious complexity, towards a humanistic and individualistic optimism based on classical Greek and Roman models, with the Renaissance in science and the arts spreading from fourteenth-century Florence.

Devotio Moderna

World-weary pessimism, devotionalism, humanism, individualism, anti-intellectualism and anti-clericalism were all paradoxically reflected in the *devotio moderna* ('new devotion') and the Brethren of the Common Life, a movement that included *Thomas à Kempi*s (1380–1471). Both abstract scholasticism and Church abuses were rejected in favour of personal devotion centred on Jesus' humanity.

All the above tendencies are found in the English poet *William Langland* (c.1330–87), whose *Vision of Piers Plowman* (2000) pilloried the representatives of the Church, and culminated in the ancient vision of Christ harrowing hell, entering it after his death to liberate its inmates with a mercy that extended wider than baptism and the Church, suggesting reformations to come:

> My kinship demands that I have mercy
> On man, for we all be brethren
> In blood, if not in baptism . . .
> My righteousness and right shall rule
> In hell, and mercy over all mankind before me

In heaven. I were an unkind king
If I did not help my kin. (*Passus* 18, lines 372–8, 397–9, modernized)

Theologians versus Mystics?

The fifteenth-century Church was in some ways the victim of its own success, divided between the achievements of a theology that was becoming ever more university based and scholastic, and a spirituality that – thanks to the Church's own preaching of Christian faith at grass-roots level – was passing into the hands of the laity. In the Reformation the social tension between ecclesiastical and lay piety and power would explode and divide Europe.

One aspect of this tension – that between an intellectual and 'objective' theology and an emotional and 'subjective' spirituality – had indeed already proven too great to sustain.

> Perhaps from the late fourteenth century, the canon of those now called 'mystics' ceases to include theologians of repute, and *e converse*, from that time to our own the canon of theologians includes no mystics. (Turner, 1998, p. 7)

Indeed most figures discussed in Chapters 1–3 and in this Chapter up to Bonaventure, were mystics *and* theologians; but few of the writers described from this point on rank as theologians, except those that, while influencing spirituality, cannot be termed mystics themselves.

For Reflection and Discussion

1 Which of the hesychast practices would you recommend as helpful to spirituality, and which not, and why?
2 List five aspects you consider distinctive in Orthodox spirituality as it has developed since Symeon. Then list them 1–5 in terms of what they have to offer the West, from the most positive to the most negative. Say what your reasons are.
3 Compare the quotations from Thomas with Mother Julian's 'hazelnut' saying on p. 134. What similarities and differences do you note in style and content?

4 Hopefully you do not condone the burning of Marguerite as a heretic, but which views of hers, if any, do you consider inimical to Christian spirituality?

5 List the similarities and the differences between the women mystics discussed in 'The flesh of God' and the men discussed in 'The resurgence of unknowing'. Do your sympathies fall more with the men or the women?

6 Consider Denys Turner's statement on p. 67 in the light of this book and whatever else you know about the subject. Is it true? Are there exceptions? And for what reasons, if any, do you think it matters?

Further Reading

Oliver Davies, 2006, *God Within: The Mystical Tradition of Northern Europe*, Hyde Park, NY: New City Press.

Monica Furlong, 1996, *Visions and Longings: Medieval Women Mystics*, London: Mowbray.

Hadewijch, ed. C. Hart, 1980, *Hadewijch: The Complete Works*, translation and Introduction by Mother Columba Hart, OSB, Mahwah, NJ: Paulist Press. The extract used on p. 61 is © 1980 by the Missionary Society of St Paul the Apostle in the State of New York. Reprinted by permission of Paulist Press, Inc., www.paulistpress.com.

Bernard McGinn, 1998, *The Flowering of Mysticism*, New York: Crossroad.

Bernard McGinn, 2005, *The Harvest of Mysticism in Medieval Germany*, New York: Crossroad.

Joan N. Nuth, 2001, *God's Lovers in an Age of Anxiety: The Medieval English Mystics*, Maryknoll, NY: Orbis.

Kenneth Wolf, 2003, *The Poverty of Riches: St Francis of Assisi Reconsidered*, Oxford and New York: Oxford University Press.

5

Foundations for Faith: Reformation Spirituality

The factors that led to the transformation from a broadly 'feudal' society dominated by a landed aristocracy to a 'modern' society dominated by the middle classes and capitalism need not detain us here, since they have been well explored. For spirituality perhaps the most important change was from *participation* in a divinely given hierarchy – metaphysical, cosmic, hierarchical, economic, social and personal – to *negotiation* in which the relationship with God, the Church and society was established by interaction between different individual powers – Godself, the sovereign, the pope, the believer, the merchant . . . And where before the nature of things, the world to which we all belong, had been obvious and given, in the modern period the individual quest for *certainty* became paramount. As the philosopher Descartes sought out the clear and distinct ideas on which certain knowledge could be founded, we find Luther, Ignatius, Calvin and Teresa in their different ways seeking in the Bible and the self for sure and certain foundations of the Christian life.

The year 1518 saw an individual refusing to recant his views before the representatives of the worldwide Church, Luther declaring 'here I stand, I can do no other'. The same year saw the Spanish 'discovery' or invasion of Mexico, and the beginnings of the slave trade, with 4,000 Africans imported to the new colonies. The old hierarchy was giving way to the rights of individuals, on the one hand, to pursue the truth as they saw it, and on the other, to trade and profit at the expense of the traditionally understood 'common good'.

The Continental Protestant Reformation

In this chapter we consider first the spirituality of the Reformation on the European Continent, where Luther's refusal precipitated it, before considering its different ethos in England, and finally the spiritual response it elicited from Roman Catholicism.

Martin Luther (1483–1546)

Luther was an Augustinian monk who was in earlier life obsessed with dutiful observance and a desperate desire to put himself right with a suspicious, angry God. What he later regarded as his conversion came when he read in St Paul that 'the just shall live by faith'. According to Taylor (2007) he 'reversed the field of fear' that had dominated the complex ritual of the late Middle Ages:

> Luther's message was that we are all sinners, and deserve punishment . . . Only in facing our full sinfulness, can we throw ourselves on the mercy of God, by which alone we are justified. 'Who fears hell runs towards it'. We have to face down our fears, and this transmutes them into confidence in the saving power of God. (p. 75)

The basic elements of Lutheran spirituality stem from this core experience of fear of judgement reversed into faith in grace:

1 The rejection of salvation by works in favour of **salvation by faith alone**. All the burgeoning late medieval panoply of methods, rituals and devotions, for Luther, reeked of salvation by works, a salvation that, he thought, starts from our end, and overestimates the natural human capacity for God, rather than starting from the work of God in Christ.

2 **A new understanding of faith**. For the Fathers and for medieval theologians like Aquinas, faith was primarily belief. For salvation it was essential to believe the right things, and great effort went into defining orthodoxy and heresy. But Luther focused on the more existential, personal dimension that is the other aspect of the Greek *pistis*: trust in God's saving action, which frees us to act in response. Who and what Christ is became less important

than what Christ had done on the cross – in Luther's characteristic phrase – 'for me'.

3 **A different understanding of grace and how we are justified**. For Catholicism, from Augustine onward, God's grace is 'closer to me than I am to myself', and for Aquinas and others, 'grace perfects nature'. Though we cannot achieve our salvation by our own efforts, or create our own virtues, we can 'merit' salvation, because the virtues God gives us are truly our own. In Luther, grace is seen as extrinsic. Christians are 'justified sinners' whom God decides to account as righteous.

4 **A rejection of vision and participation.** Luther criticized the *theologia gloriae* – theology of glory – that underpinned so much Orthodox and medieval Western liturgy and spirituality, whereby the material of this world participates in and mediates a wisdom and a vision of God, by way of analogy and symbolism. Luther replaced this with a *theologia crucis* (Williams, 1979, pp. 145–9), arguing that the believer sees God most clearly in the darkness and foolishness of the cross (1 Cor. 1.23–25). 'Unknowing' ceased to be part of the way to union with God, as it was for the apophatic mystics, and became the permanent state of the Christian. Like Moses, who saw the back but not the face of God (Ex. 34), the believer walks by blind trust rather than by sight.

5 **A new distance between God and humanity.** Though he rejected scholastic theology, Luther inherited the nominalism of the late scholastics, according to which words were convenient labels rather than indicators of the true essence of things. What was good was therefore so not because it participated in God's essential goodness, but because God labelled it good. Point 3 really follows from this: God does not share his goodness with us or transform our natures for good, but decrees us good in Christ. Point 4 likewise follows – we cannot contemplate God's goodness and make it our own, but only trust it as something over against our badness (Bouyer, 1968, p. 65).

6 **Intercession** – asking for things in faith – replaced contemplation as the highest form of prayer. Point 4 ruled out contemplative participation in God's being, but we could engage with God's will through our work of intercession.

7 **Monasticism** and asceticism were rejected as attempting salvation by works. Luther abandoned his own monastic status and married. In England and throughout the Protestant lands the monasteries were ruthlessly

suppressed, eliminating the institutions that had for centuries been the mainstay of Christian spirituality.

8 **A space for the secular** was correspondingly opened up. Because all people are fundamentally sinners, over against God, rather than participating in him to greater or lesser hierarchical degrees, we are all equal before him and all fundamentally share in the priesthood of Christ. Denys's 'fountain' model of grace, spilling over from the saints to the Church hierarchy to humanity in general to the 'lower' creatures, was replaced by the equal non-participation – if we may so put it – of everyone. Luther separated the kingdom of God decisively from the kingdoms of this world, enabling secular institutions to develop without respect for the divine rights of kings and popes. However, Luther and many other Reformers resisted the obvious political implications. Liturgically and politically conservative despite himself, Luther supported the ruthless moves undertaken against egalitarian movements like the Peasant's Revolt.

9 As well as giving space to the secular, Luther's spirituality gave space for the **body**. Luther took an unusually pragmatic approach to sexuality (Lawrence, 1989) and was remarkably down to earth in his use of language, full of scatological metaphors to describe his opponents. Some even regard his terms '*in cloaca*' to mean that he described his conversion as happening 'in the toilet', though this interpretation is disputed!

10 Though the sacraments of baptism, Eucharist and penance were retained, they and the Church lost their mediating role, and authority was vested **solely in scripture**. Moreover the focus shifted from the spiritual or mystical meanings of scripture to its plain literal meaning. Scripture ceased to be a broad land the learned elite could enter to explore an imaginative play of meanings, questions and aspirations. God's word moved from interrogative and optative to imperative voice, commanding obedience. At the same time it was torn from the hierarchy and democratized, being translated into people's everyday languages. Reading and reflecting on it became a core aspect of all Protestant spirituality.

The New Spiritual Journey

Origen's three stages of the spiritual ascent were invalidated:

1 Purgation, because according to (1), (2) and (3), we cannot cleanse ourselves, and asceticism is in vain.
2 Illumination, because according to (4) God does not shine through creation, and vision is in vain.
3 Union, because according to (5) we cannot truly participate in God, only trust and obey.

Instead of a continuously unfolding journey, Protestant spirituality came to focus on a discontinuous rupture of conversion, whereby (1) a deep conviction of sin led to (2) a grasp by faith of what Christ had done 'for me' and thence to (3) an ongoing life as a new creation in Christ in which we trust that we are counted righteous. It was still a three-part journey, but the emphasis was very different from the traditional ascent. Later, with the pietist stress on feeling, parts of Protestantism would adopt the characteristic modern evangelical stress on momentary conversion *experience*.

John Calvin (1509–64)

If Luther was a German monk emotionally and passionately struggling to free himself from medieval constraints, Calvin was a French layman of human-ist sympathies rationally working out the implications in terms of constraints appropriate to a modern theocracy. Though his theocratic vision has only fleet-ingly been achieved at certain rather unhappy moments in history, his theology has certainly been the biggest single influence on Protestant spirituality and social practice.

Calvin's endeavour was to work out the logical implications of the Refor-mation in a manner that harmonized with the early Church and the Fathers. Thus while for Luther God's grace acts externally to justify us while we remain sinners, for Calvin grace was a no less external but active and irresistible sanc-tifying power.

The corollary was that, if we were not being transformed into saints, we cannot have been justified, and this lack of justification – damnation – must equally be the work of God.

Since Augustine the Western Church had always believed in the predestination of the elect. God willed the salvation of all, but *allowed* those he had not chosen to save to fall into damnation, which was caused, not by God, but by their own sinful resistance. Calvin, as ever, grasped the logical nettle, and declared that God wills and causes the damnation of the damned, and this was good simply because deemed to be so by the sovereign God.

Calvin also grasped the political nettle Luther had left untouched. God in his sovereign grace had no mediators, so such authority as earthly sovereigns possessed must be grounded in their people, not in any divine right of kings. An ungodly monarch could justifiably be deposed. But Calvin's stress on God's sovereignty did not lead to democracy. His Geneva was, notoriously, an authoritarian, policed attempt at theocracy. The Puritan colonies formed in America – with the exception of Quaker Pennsylvania – were similar. Calvin's 'irresistible grace' could not rest until it had achieved its goal in a fully transformed human society of the elect, God's chosen. And achieving that goal meant, in practice, a great deal of human compulsion and punishments that anticipated those of God.

Calvin was not a 'Calvinist', or rather, not the grim 'killjoy' of the stereotype. He was in many ways a world-affirming pleasure-enjoying humanist with a keen eye for the glory of God reflected in creation (Mursell, 2001, pp. 174–6). The notion of the Bible as the *sole* revelation of God, rather than as that which makes the wider revelation of God accessible to the human heart, was not yet on the scene. Nevertheless his was essentially a theological system, with austere and exacting moral and political demands. For this static ethic to become a resource for a living spirituality, something needed to happen to Calvinism; and this is what we shall see in the Puritans.

Anabaptists

From around 1525 there arose in the Netherlands and Central Europe pockets of a more radical return to the scriptures, labelled 'Anabaptist' because of the belief that conversion that makes one a Christian, and that it was appropriate for adult converts to be 'baptized again' to express their new faith. The Anabaptists believed in a gospel-based pacifism, simplicity of life and abandonment to God. The rich shared their property with the poor. They met in homes rather than churches for worship, which included the washing of feet. They distrusted all secular authorities as corrupt, but despite severe persecution and martyrdom by Catholic and Protestant authorities alike, resisted non-violently. Arguably they recovered something in the spirituality of Jesus and the early Church that had been lost with the advent of imperialist Christendom.

Anabaptist understandings influenced radical groups like the Quakers in England and America, and shaped Baptist liturgical practice. Anabaptism itself survives today with the Hutterites, Amish and Mennonites, and finds challenging theological expression in the writings of Yoder (p. 105).

Jakob Boehme (1575–1624)

While Luther and Calvin were foundational to Protestantism, and the Anabaptists represented its radical edge, Boehme was eccentric and mystical, but a decisive influence on the growth of pietism, as well as on English writers like Law and Blake. A simple cobbler, he saw, while at work, sunlight reflected in a tin vessel, and at that moment came to understand the everlasting division between light and dark and the way from the darkness of sin to the light of God. Boehme's writings are dense and full of alchemical and astrological speculations, but are built around a simple apophatic core: 'When you can throw yourself into that, where no creature dwells, though it be for a moment, then you hear what God speaks' (cited by Mursell, 2001, p. 188).

If Luther gave the Reformation a feeling heart, Calvin a rational head, and Anabaptism a radical will, Boehme (with less success, perhaps) strove to give it a mystical imagination.

The English Reformation

The Reformation in England took a relatively milder course than on the continents of Europe or America. While there were many martyrs on both sides, there were no genocidal persecutions. The absolute claims of kings were tempered by a growing parliamentary democracy. Yet the radical wing represented by the Anabaptists, ruthlessly suppressed on the Continent, steadily grew in England, creating a politically and spiritually revolutionary Protestant fringe of Diggers, Levellers and Quakers, seeing the first execution of a European king, precipitating a bloody Civil War, and providing foundations for the Puritan colonies in America.

The English Prayer Books of 1449 and 1552 combined a moderate Calvinist theology with a retention of Catholic hierarchical structure and a curtailed sense of ceremony and sacrament. Despite its author, Thomas Cranmer's urging of a weekly communion, his compression of the Benedictine hours of prayer into Matins and Evensong gave the English what was to be their regular diet of Sunday worship. Some indeed have argued that a lay Benedictinism came to constitute the heart of an Anglican spirituality which avoided excesses of asceticism or devotion, and sought a balance of heart and mind, 'true piety and sound learning' (Thornton in Jones, 1986).

Meanwhile the great theologian of early Anglicanism, *Richard Hooker* (1553–1600) expressed the ideal of bringing the whole people under the one divine, natural and moral law of God through common worship. His vision was reminiscent of the efforts of the Church in the High Middle Ages, and owed much to Aquinas, but in this later context it could only feel – and in the end be – undermined by Catholic and later Puritan dissent.

Indeed the Anglican 'middle way' was constituted by a double fear: of Catholic dogmatic system and ritual devotion on the one hand, and Puritan enthusiasm and spontaneity on the other. Paths to passionate spirituality open to each extreme were therefore often closed to Anglicans. Nevertheless 'despite a seemingly artificial gravity, a restrictive tension, the whole becomes pervaded with a subdued optimism; a domestic gentleness' (Thornton in Jones, p. 434), and a restrained but intense devotion focused on the personal reception (rather than the corporate celebration) of Holy Communion. Characteristic too is a 'reserve' regarding the dogmatic formulation of the mysteries of faith, well described by an Orthodox commentator as a

> non-assertion, which both exposes the faithful to the suffering of personal conflict and decision, but also gives the freedom of integrating the theological teaching . . . and . . . at the same time, surpassing it, relying in the last count on the inexplicable Mystery of the love of God. (Sister Thekla, 1974, p. 12)

Caroline Divines

From late Elizabethan times, with the Catholic threat lifted somewhat with the defeat of the Armada, many Anglican divines shifted their polemical focus to the Puritan challenge. Theologians like Hooker began to look for authority, behind Calvin and the Reformation, to the Patristic age, seen as a golden 'antiquity' prior to Roman Catholic excesses and Puritan minimalist reaction. Some ceremonial was reintroduced, and the classical Anglican balance of scripture, reason and tradition began to operate, albeit never equally (scripture always came first, while the Anglican approach to tradition was pragmatic rather than either slavish or hostile). *Lancelot Andrewes* (1556–1626) wrote sermons, prayers and meditations that are sinuous concatenations of quotes from the Bible and the Fathers. A scholarly, resonant and memorable translation of the Bible – the *Authorized Version* of 1611 – became the bedrock of English people's spirituality well beyond Anglicanism. *Jeremy Taylor* (1613–67), imprisoned under Cromwell, wrote lyrically of the acquisition of the virtues and the importance of toleration.

Anglican Poets and Mystics

If Anglicanism ever achieves a distinctive spirituality, it is perhaps in its poets and dramatists (Countryman, 2000). Though some have claimed the author (not entirely convincingly) as a Catholic or even an atheist, the works of *William Shakespeare* (1564–1616) illustrate the breadth and universal sympathy of Anglicanism at its best. One repeated theme – echoing the contemporary struggles of Anglicanism itself, perhaps – is the conflict between a narrow 'puritan' morality and an earthy, anarchic human wisdom represented by the likes of Falstaff and Lear's fool, and the later, wiser Lear himself.

The seventeenth century saw a sequence of poets described as 'metaphysical' for their intricate metaphors drawn from philosophy and science. *John Donne* (1552–1631) – a convert from Catholicism – wrote intense, paradoxical poems in which his earlier earthly loves give way to the divine:

> . . . I
> except you'enthrall me, never shall be free,
> nor ever chast, except thou ravish me. (Holy Sonnets, 14 in 1929, p. 285)

George Herbert (1593–1633) renounced courtly life to become a simple parish priest. He combined Catholic sacramentality with a Reformed sense of dependence on Christ's imputed goodness (Sister Thekla, 1974, pp. 57–69). His dramatic dialogues between Christ and the soul are reminiscent of the protest-laden wrestling with God that features so much in Jewish spirituality from the Psalms onward.

The Welshman, *Henry Vaughan* (1621–1695) was perhaps the closest of these poets to apophatic mysticism, with his sense of God's 'deep and dazzling darkness' expressed in his poem 'Night', a meditation on the moment of Christ's resurrection.

If, as suggested, something of the Benedictine spirit lived on in lay form in Anglicanism, this was epitomized by the founding at *Little Gidding* in 1626 of a lay community dedicated to a religious order of life based on Anglican morning and evening prayer. Cromwell's army destroyed it in 1646, but the memory lived on to inspire the Anglo-Catholic revival of monastic life in the nineteenth century, and a poem by T. S. Eliot in the twentieth!

Mystical writings as such are few in Anglicanism, the closest being those of *Thomas Traherne* (1637–74), an Anglican priest forgotten till the twentieth century. They radiate a sacramental sense of God's glory in everyday life:

> You never enjoy the world aright . . . till the Sea itself floweth in your veins . . . till your spirit filleth the whole world, and the stars are your jewels; till you are as familiar with the ways of God in all Ages as with your walk and table: till you are intimately acquainted with that shady nothing out of which the world was made: till you love men so as to desire their happiness, with a thirst equal to the zeal of your own. (1960, p. 14)

Puritans

'Puritan' was the initially critical name given to those who desired to purify the Church of England – of which most of them were faithful members – of all Roman Catholic vestiges, and reform Church and society on strictly Calvinist lines. With Calvin they placed great emphasis on holiness of life as proving one's election, and emphasized the importance of personal holiness.

However, the Puritans took the Reformers' high view of scriptural authority further than either Calvin or the Anglican Articles of Faith, to the point where, in the Westminster Catechism of 1643, the Bible was seen as the *sole* place where God was revealed (Pacini, in Dupré and Saliers, 1989). The Puritans sought to govern the whole of life by reference to the Bible. All pictures and images were ruled out by the commandments, ceremonial and festivals that had no biblical warrant had to be abolished, and a strict Sunday observance was enforced on the basis of the Sabbath observance of the Old Testament. It could be argued that the Puritans were developing a legalism and an obsession with 'works' – at least, with the works one must *not* do – as great or greater than that of the Roman Catholics.

But the Puritans were not simply 'more Calvinist than Calvin'. They placed more emphasis on the heart's experience of salvation than on systematic clarity of doctrine. Some have argued (Bouyer, 1968, p. 134) that they were closer to late medieval *devotio moderna* than Calvin's Renaissance rationalism, in, for example:

- Their general **pessimism** regarding the world, which they regarded as under God's wrathful judgement and largely destined for hell.
- The consequent role of **fear and despair** in leading people to salvation. According to a leading Puritan, William Perkins (1558–1602):

  God smites the heart with legal fear, whereby when a man sees his sins, he makes him to fear punishment and hell, and to despair of salvation, in regard to anything in himself. (1970, 2.13)

- **Devotion to the humanity of Jesus,** especially his sufferings on the cross. Cromwell's chaplain, Thomas Goodwin (reminiscent of Bernard, and antici-pating the official ratification of Catholic devotion to the Sacred Heart) described how God's eternal heart of love became incarnate in the human heart of Jesus, enabling him to love us, and we to respond, in a human way. Tender friendship with Jesus remained central for pietist and modern evan-gelical spirituality.

Meanwhile other developments in Protestantism ameliorated the stark divide between God and humanity. *Peter Ramus* (1513–72) reintroduced a Platonic notion of real participation of creatures in God. He thereby turned the nomi-nalism of the later schoolmen and Luther on its head. For them, if God wills something, it must be good. Ramus emphasized the corollary: if something is good, God must will it. We can therefore know something of God and his will through our human intimations of what is good. For *William Ames* (1576–1633) this became the basis of a covenant theology, whereby grace and faith do not negate but restore nature and reason.

This enabled *Peter Sterry* (1613–72) to feel free – not without criticism from fellow Puritans – to make use of ancient Greek mythology as well as the Bible, and to speak, as few in the Christian spiritual tradition have, of the divine laughter:

> Abide in the Father's love by spiritual joy. Joy is love flaming. One saith, that laughter is the dance of the spirits, their freest motion in the harmony, and that the light of the heavens is the laughter of Angels. Spiritual joy is the laughter of divine love, of the eternal Spirit, which is love, in our spirits. (1683, p. 390)

Cambridge Platonists

In the Cambridge Platonists, we see these trends taken further. Pessimism gives way to the optimistic tolerance of the latitudinarians, a third, 'broad church' party – over against the Carolines and Puritans – within the Church of England. In *John Smith* (1618–52) we see restored the ancient notion of a hierarchy of participation in God: 'God made the universe and all the creatures contained therein as so many glasses wherein he might reflect his own glory. He hath copied forth himself in the creation' (2007, 8th *Discourse*, Chapter 8).

Sadly, the social and cosmic hierarchy on which such notions depended was by then being dissolved by political and scientific change, and the Platonists tended to write 'an inspiring muddle between learning, philosophy and personal piety' (Thornton in Jones, 1986, p. 437).

Late Medieval or Pioneer Modern?

Most people, if asked to cite a work that epitomizes Puritan spirituality, would quote not from Ramus, Ames or Sterry – in whose broad but biblical optimism we see the spirit that led to the great democracies of the ensuing centuries – but *Pilgrim's Progress,* written by the much persecuted Baptist *John Bunyan* (1628–88). In its allegorical portrayal of virtues and vices, and its overall shape of a spiritual ascent or quest, this is as medieval a work as one could wish for, though of course one of immense dramatic subtlety, which huge numbers have found spiritually inspiring. And if one wanted to see the Protestant exaltation of God's sovereignty over against humanity, and the modern struggles against earthly tyrannies, played out in mythical form, one need look no further than the *Paradise Lost* of *John Milton* (1608–74). For Milton, God was sovereign to a degree that demanded Arianism: not even the Son, let alone Satan, could share the Father's absolute sovereignty. However, Blake later argued that Milton (himself persecuted by the hierarchies of the state) was 'of the devil's party without knowing it'! It is Satan who wins the sympathies of radicals as he tries to establish his republic far away from the divine hierarchy, though conservatives might note that in doing so, Satan is the first of many revolutionaries to abandon heaven for the pit of hell.

George Fox (1624–91)

Fox – founder of the Quakers – took the Reformation rejection of all mediators between the individual and God to radical conclusions when he asserted that all people possess the inner light of Christ. He discovered this universal light at his conversion:

> I was taken up in the love of God, so that I could not but admire the greatness of his love. And while I was in that condition it was opened unto me by the eternal Light and power, and I therein saw clearly that all was done and to be done in and by Christ . . . And when at any time my condition was veiled, my secret belief was stayed firm, and hope underneath held me, as an anchor in the bottom of the sea, and anchored my immortal soul to its Bishop [Christ].
> (1997, section 14)

A Quaker meeting for worship has no priests, because all mediate the light of Christ to the others present. It has no liturgy, but – after early enthusiasm and spontaneity akin to the Pentecostals of today – developed under influence of the quietists to involve a unique kind of corporate spiritual direction, in which the movement of the Holy Spirit is discerned, both individually (by each member listening in the silence) and corporately (as the members listen to the Spirit 'speaking to their condition' through each other). And Quakerism has retained Fox's deep commitment to gospel-based simplicity and pacifism, and radical political engagement.

The Catholic Reformation

The attacks of Luther, Calvin and the other Reformers promoted a Catholic response that was partly violent reaction, but partly a considered attempt to rectify abuses and respond to criticisms. This 'Counter-Reformation' developed a distinctive spirituality, centred on a nation that, having recently overthrown its Muslim rulers, and begun to develop a vast world empire, was immensely confident of its role as champion of Catholic orthodoxy: Spain.

Ignatius Loyola (c.1491–1556)

'Inigo' (to use his Spanish name) lusted for the heroic life of a soldier, but was wounded in battle and forced to reassess his life. In the process he became a soldier for Christ, founding the Society of Jesus (Jesuits) as an army committed to mission at home and in Spain's expanding colonies.

He was close to his contemporary, Luther, in three respects:

- The centrality of **conversion**, which is the main goal of the spiritual exercises he wrote.
- His consequent stress on **evangelism**, the need to bring others to conversion.
- For Ignatius, as for Luther, the aim was not the vision of God, but **obedience** to God. The aim was not the union of our being with God's being, but (following the line that leads from Augustine through Luther) a choice to respond to God's choice of us.

> Ignatius builds his whole spirituality upon the concept of choice; that is, upon God's choice, accomplished in eternal freedom which is offered to

man to choose for himself. This new 'identity' or 'fusion' between the Creator's choice and that of his creature begins ever more surely to replace the classical ideal of identifying their essences, the ideal of 'deification'. (von Balthasar, 1954, pp. 225–6)

Spiritual exercises were familiar in Catholicism from de Sales onward, but Ignatius introduced a profound dimension of imagination and psychological insight into his version, and they have become very widely used. People are asked to imagine themselves present in biblical scenes, noting all they would hear and see and smell and feel, and to experience Christ relating to them personally through the story. Whereas the Orthodox icon seeks to focus on the eternal Christ, whom the worshipper sees in the eternal 'today' of the liturgy, the Ignatian directee tries to enter and imagine the biblical situation and become the 'contemporary' of the historical Jesus, so as to hear and obey his word.

Central to this process is the 'discernment of spirits'. 'Evil spirits' (like Ignatius's own thoughts about glory in his army career) are recognizable because they excite us superficially, but lead to desolation. 'Good spirits' (like his call to a change of life) disturb and challenge us, but eventually lead to the consolation that comes from harmony with the will of God.

John of the Cross (1542–91)

John and Teresa (see next) were close friends who collaborated in the attempt to reform the Spanish Carmelites, attempts for which John was imprisoned. His spirituality explores the heights of nuptial union, lyrically described in his poems, but is also familiar for his haunting, desiccating analysis of the 'dark night of the soul'.

John differentiated four kinds of dark night, and linked them with the traditional threefold ascent of Origen.

1 **The Active Night of Sense**, in which the soul makes deliberate ascetical effort to overcome her passions and desires and live in detachment from worldly pleasures: the traditional way of purgation.
2 **The Passive Night of Sense,** in which the light of God casts a shadow over the things of the world, and grace begins to detach the soul from them irrespective of our will. Paradoxically this is an aspect of the way of illumination.

John speaks of God's 'ray of darkness', for in the dazzling light of God, everything else looks dark.

3 **The Active Night of Spirit**. The ascent to God means the rejection of spiritual as well as material pleasures; indeed, anything that is not God. As for Denys and Eckhart, to persist on the way of illumination, the soul has to reject idols and consolations, and to begin to seek not just good experiences of God, but Godself, acquiring 'the condition in which nothing is happening in the mind but what God is doing' (Williams, 1979, p. 126).

4 **The Passive Night of the Spirit**: the most terrible night of all. The soul is plunged against her will into pain and desolation, This marks the upper bound of the illuminative way and the beginning of the way of union. God has at this stage to 'assault' and annihilate the ego – with all the pain that that entails – in order to love God through the soul; for only God can truly love God (Turner, 1998, Chapter 10).

Not all in John is negative. He allows, in the illuminative phase, the prayer of quiet which at times will pour forth effortlessly from the soul, suggesting the play of courtyard fountains and flow of conversation late into the Mediterranean night (Bouyer, 1990, p. 255).

Teresa of Avila (1515–82)

As a woman, as belonging to a family of Jewish converts, and as a radical struggling to reform the Carmelite order, Teresa was suspect in three ways (Williams, 1991). Yet she writes with a humble simplicity that belies the psychological depths she discovers in prayer.

She compares the four degrees of prayer to watering a garden.

1 Drawing water through hard work from a well, which sometimes runs dry.
2 Building a wind pump drawing water from deep down, allowing the gardener to rest in the 'prayer of quiet' drawing on the permanent 'water table' of the spirit.
3 Finding a spring that waters the garden. God becomes the gardener. The soul helps him, while enjoying the garden as it grows in a manner words cannot explain.

4 Rain falls directly from above. There is simply 'enjoyment, without any knowledge of what is being enjoyed'.

In *The Interior Castle*, Teresa describes seven mansions visited on the journey to God.

1 The mansion of **purgation and struggle** to 'break free of obsessive and defensive concern with the self' (Williams, 1991, p. 116).
2 A mansion of **suffering**: the beginning of illuminative glimpses of God, conveying the soul's painful distance from him.
3 The mansion of those who are **conventionally good**, having purged away and overcome a lot that is negative. People often rest content here in a rather smug and judgemental Christianity, experiencing many 'consolations' – pleasant satisfying experiences arising from achievements – but few God-given 'spiritual delights'.
4 The **beginnings of union**, where God's work in the soul begins to predominate and impart spiritual delights, rather as in the third stage of the garden.
5 A mansion of **death to self** in which the seeker is 'hid' in Christ like a chrysalis in a cocoon.
6 A disorienting mansion of **visions, and also sufferings**. Within an agonizing clamour of new experience the butterfly soul is struggling to emerge and flap its wings.
7 **Spiritual marriage**, in which the soul extends her nuptial wings and flies with God the Trinity.

And the basis of the mystical journey Teresa describes in all this richness is the search to which Teresa feels called by Jesus – simple to state, complex to achieve:

Seek yourself in me. Seek me in yourself.

French Spirituality

This was a creative period for French spirituality too, with the generous humanist *Francis de Sales* (1567–1622) who pioneered a method of meditative prayer, and also won back many Genevan Calvinists to the Catholic faith; his comrade *Jeanne de Chantal* (1572–1641) and the philanthropist *Vincent de Paul* (1581–1660) who founded the Sisters of Charity to work among the poor. However, French spirituality became mired in the conflict involving the anti-mystical Jansenists and the 'hyper-mystical' quietists, described in the next chapter.

For Reflection and Discussion

1 Write down the headings *salvation, faith, grace, vision of God, closeness of God, prayer, the secular world, monks, the body, scripture.* Brainstorm and jot down what comes into your mind in connection with these words – or leave blank if nothing does! Compare your response with points 1–10 regarding Luther vis à vis the Catholic tradition. Are you consistently closer to one or the other, or a mixture? Do you feel your views come from these traditions, or are they independent?
2 Evaluate the statement about Luther, Calvin, the Anabaptists and Boehme on p. 75.
3 List the features you think would have been lost to Christian spirituality if the Anglican tradition had never existed.
4 Which of the radical Protestants, Bunyan, Milton and Fox, do you find most spiritually inspiring? What do you value in them, and what if anything disturbs you?
5 Compare John and Teresa's descriptions of the spiritual journey in both style and content. Are they fundamentally similar or are there important differences? Which do you feel more drawn to, and why?

Further Reading

Louis Bouyer, 1968, *Orthodox Spirituality and Protestant and Anglican Spirituality,* London: Burns and Oates.

Louis Dupré and Don E. Saliers, eds, 1989, *Christian Spirituality III: Post-Reformation and Modern,* New York: Crossroad / Herder & Herder.

Alister McGrath, 1990, *Luther's Theology of the Cross: Martin Luther's Theological Breakthrough,* Oxford: Blackwell.

Gordon Mursell, 2001, *English Spirituality: From the Early Days to 1700*, London: SPCK.

Geoffrey Rowell, Kenneth Stephenson and Rowan Williams, eds, 2001, *Love's Redeeming Work: The Anglican Quest for Holiness*, Oxford: Oxford University Press.

Rowan Williams, 1991, *Teresa of Avila*, London: Chapman.

6

Revival or Retreat? Spirituality after the Enlightenment

The year 1789 saw in France the declaration of a republic based not on Christian faith but reason and human rights. It was the year when Blake wrote his *Songs of Innocence*, Bentham published his *Introduction to the Principles of Morals and Legislation*, and when the first steam-driven cotton factory opened in Manchester. The broad trend beginning in the later seventeenth century and continuing apace in the eighteenth, known as the Enlightenment, was bearing fruit in political revolution, a poetic celebration of original innocence, rationalist ethics and industrial technology. 'Man' was beginning to improve on God, creating for 'himself' a better world.

This process has been described in many ways, not least in Charles Taylor's monumental and subtle recent work (2007). But the following two aspects are probably among the most important in terms of impact on Christian spirituality.

- **'Detraditionalization'** (Heelas 1996) denotes a shift from traditional ways of *understanding* the world. Previously, a practice like prayer, an institution like bishops, or a teaching like the Trinity would have been justified by the authority of scripture and tradition handed down from the past. But in the Enlightenment the past began to be felt as a negative weight, responsible for war and social injustice. Thinkers began to appeal to reason, experience and common sense, which were believed to be universal.

- **Secularization**. The term 'secular' strictly means 'relating to this *saeculum*', this age, as opposed to sacred history or God's reign. Secularization means a change in relation to *time and hope*. Traditional Christian eschatology – belief in judgement, heaven and hell – was slowly but surely replaced by the hope of establishing a better, even a utopian society on earth, by means of the triumph of reason through steady progress or violent revolution. Previously society had been seen as part of a sacred order made by God, who delegated his power downward through royal and priestly hierarchies. Their efforts involved at best a 'damage limitation' of the effects of original sin. But with the Enlightenment, society and its institutions were increasingly seen as constructed by individuals coming together in a 'social contract', and so 'secularized'. Original sin gave way to a more optimistic belief in 'original innocence'. As Rousseau put it, we are 'born free, but everywhere in chains'. But people can unite to break their chains.

There are two ways in which Christian spirituality can respond to the Enlightenment understanding of the world, and two ways of responding to its ethical and political hopes, making the four broad possibilities for spirituality in Table 3. Though perhaps rather simplified, this structure will help us find our way through this complex period.

Table 3: Four Responses to the Enlightenment

Understanding ⇓ Hope ⇒	Christian eschatology	Secular utopia
based on tradition and story	1: fideism	3: romanticism
based on universal reason	4: liberationism	2: liberalism

1 The Christian understanding the world and hope of salvation are both retained by being aligned with a realm of 'faith' or 'experience' that lies beyond rationality: **fideism**.
2 The opposite: secular reason and its hope are both accepted, and spirituality submits to the disciplines they impose. Religion and spirituality welcome the secular, in a trend we can describe by the rather slippery term, **liberalism**.

3 The secular hope is embraced, often with revolutionary fervour, but rational understanding is challenged. Human traditions of life and their associated myths and stories – including the Christian – are seen as embodying their own truths. Nature, culture, art and imagination are trusted more than reason: **Romanticism**.

4 Christian hope and eschatology are retained, but harnessed to socialist and other secular understandings of the world and its history: the 'social gospel' and **liberationism.**

Fideism

Fideism denotes the position that faith alone is its own authority, needing no support from reason. When reason or science (a) conflict with traditional or biblical understandings, or (b) create their own utopian hopes, they are stoutly rejected.

Blaise Pascal (1623–62)

The great mathematician, Pascal, hails from an earlier period, but felt the terror of the vastness of the cosmos that science was unfolding, declaring 'the infinite spaces terrify me!' The God of reason seemed ever more remote from this cosmos, but Pascal experienced a conversion, which he recorded in notes: 'Fire. "God of Abraham, God of Isaac, God of Jacob," not of philosophers and scholars. Certainty, certainty, heartfelt, joy, peace' (1995, p. 285).

Pascal made a 'leap of faith'. Like Tertullian (p. 20) he now saw Christian faith as having nothing to do with reason.

Pascal followed *Jansenism*, an austere variant of Catholicism with a pessimistic view of human nature and destiny – embracing predestination – that was close to Calvinism and the Puritans. Along with dance, song and ceremony, mystical experience and intimacy with God were rejected in favour of the obedience of a disciplined moral life. Pascal even renounced his mathematics as a cause of sinful pride.

Quietism

The mystical was affirmed, on the other hand, by Quietists like *Madame Guyon* (1648–1717) and her supporter and friend, *François Fénelon* (1651–1715), who advocated annihilation of the individual will in disinterested love of God. Later, *Jean-Pierre de Caussade* (1675–1751) advocated a more reasoned 'abandonment to divine providence', enabling one to dwell in the present moment as a sacrament rather than filling the mind with memories and anticipations. *Thérese de Lisieux* (1873–97) and *Simone Weil* (pp. 103–4) can be described as moderate quietists.

Quietism however was condemned by the Catholic authorities, who associated it with so many varied views as to create what theologian Henri Bremond termed a 'rout of the mystics'. Strangely, whereas in the seventeenth and twentieth centuries, 'mysticism' was something many Protestants associated with Catholicism, through the eighteenth and nineteenth century it was seen by the Catholic hierarchy as a kind of Protestant heresy! Certainly it was to be the pietists and liberals who in their different ways gave pride of place to personal, inward spirituality. Mysticism was gaining ground in the hitherto less amenable soils of Protestantism (Bouyer, 1968, p. 260).

Pietism

Broadly speaking, 'pietism' denotes the notion that Christian faith is primarily a matter of feelings and morality, rather than, say, liturgy or doctrine, such that the latter serve the former, and are positively harmful if divorced from them.

There had certainly been a strong pietist strand in the Puritans, while the Lutheran *Johann Arndt* (1555–1621) had argued that Christian faith needs to be experienced at first hand rather than merely through dogma. But by the end of the seventeenth century, mainstream Protestantism had developed its own dry, scholastic orthodoxy. It was to combat this that *Philip Jakob Spener* (1633–1705) founded his *collegia pietatis*, small groups of Christians meeting together to reflect on scripture and share their personal experience of faith. Puritans had long supplemented what they saw as the dry diet of official church worship with groups of this kind, and the idea would continue with John Wesley's 'classes' and the housegroups widely familiar today. Nevertheless it provoked strong opposition and accusations of pharisaism and even crypto-Catholicism!

Herman Francke (1663–1727) and *Gottfried Arnold* (1666–1714) took Spener's ideas further. They affirmed the now familiar idea that a specific conversion *experience* (rather than conversion as such) is essential for true Christian faith. Christianity, for them, was a simple faith for simple people, flourishing better when uncluttered by theological ideas or sophisticated education, And women, because of their alleged link with the life of feeling rather than intellect, were closer to the gospel. Faith was becoming feminized, and the 'angel of the home' – the meek and pious wife – began to be thought of as the carrier of faith, while her husband engaged in the sordid, materialistic business of earning a living (Brown, 2001).

A 'feminine' quietism in this sense flourished in the Dutch mystic *Gerhard Tersteegen* (1697–1769) who urged that God must be all in our life, and the self must learn to be passive, desiring nothing but God. He criticized Luther for making faith into a good work, urging that 'salvation by faith' should mean that people put no faith in anything of their own, not even their faith, so that their whole life is liberated to be God's alone.

Two significant movements embraced aspects of pietism, the Moravian Brethren and the Methodists. The former was founded by *Nikolaus-Ludwig von Zinzendorf* (1700–60). For him, our personal 'Father' was not the austere Creator but the loving, intimate Jesus, while the Holy Spirit was a kind of mother. The piety that resulted was sincere, but the theology was a shade gnostic, and not surprisingly, Zinzendorf's grand schemes for reuniting the Church around his ideas met with failure.

John Wesley (1703–91)

Wesley was profoundly influenced by pietism, and the Moravians in particular. He experienced a conversion, in which his anxious heart was 'strangely warmed', and conversion became central to his gospel.

However, he and his brother, the hymn writer Charles Wesley, remained anchored in a robust sacramentalism, in which the Calvinist notion of sharing in the risen and ascended Christ through Holy Communion took on vivid form, combining with a notion of our own exaltation and perfection in Christ.

Against Calvin, Wesley believed the grace of God seeks a free response from us. In many ways Wesley reaffirmed – without the terminology – Eastern Orthodox understandings of *theosis* (participation in God) and *synergy* (the working together of God's Holy Spirit and ours). The Lutheran affirmation that saving righteousness is Christ's *not* mine gives way to the sense that it is Christ's *hence* mine, as in Charles Wesley's great hymn, 'And can it be':

> No condemnation now I dread;
> Jesus, and all in him, is mine!
> Alive in him, my living Head,
> And clothed in righteousness divine,
> bold I approach the eternal throne,
> And claim the crown, through Christ my own.

Like the pietists, but unlike the somewhat class-ridden Anglicanism of the time, Wesley had great empathy for the unlettered poor, who were beginning to crowd into the towns at the start of England's industrial revolution. Wesley preached in the open air to great masses, regardless of parish boundaries – to the alarm of the Anglicans – and developed a system of classes for the education of the new converts in faith.

When the Anglican bishops refused to support his mission in America, Wesley ordained his own priests. So it came about that, whereas the Anglican Church had combined a generally Reformed theology with a Catholic church order, Wesley had to reconcile the somewhat Catholic – even perhaps Orthodox – theology just described with a Reformed, non-episcopal church order.

Wesley had a non-fideist openness to the Enlightenment, and his emphasis on experience owed much to the philosopher John Locke (Brantley, 1984). However, his subtle synthesis of scripture, reason, tradition and experience gave way, in later Methodism, to the trend that was coming to be called evangelical.

Evangelicalism

Continental pietism combined with the English Puritan tradition and Methodism to form the evangelicalism that was a major force in the formation of Victorian Christianity and has grown to be of immense importance worldwide. Pioneers in this movement included the poet *William Cowper* (1731–

1800), the hymn-writer *John Newton* (1725–1807) – a slave-trader who became a forceful advocate of its abolition – and the saintly preacher *Charles Simeon* (1759–1836).

Gordon Wakefield (in Dupré and Saliers, 1989, p. 275) lists seven characteristics of English evangelicalism:

1 The centrality of the Bible as the word of God, in preaching, testimony and private conversation.
2 The need for conversion in response to the cross of Christ.
3 Moral responsibility as central to the new life in Christ.
4 The importance of private and family prayers to complement the corporate worship; and a respect for the Sabbath.
5 World mission using the British Empire as base.
6 Social concern and philanthropy, but not revolutionary activism, accepting the world order as God-given.
7 A deep suspicion of anything Roman Catholic.

American Evangelicalism and Revivalism

Evangelicalism took a different form in America, where Christianity represented the hopes – initially theocratic, but mellowing to the democratic – of refugees from the English establishment. Here the sober and loyal conservatism of English evangelicalism gave way to something more extravagant, pragmatic and sometimes anarchic, varying between extremes of reaction and radicalism.

Jonathan Edwards (1703–58) had prepared solid ground with a reasoned rather than fideist Puritan theology. He saw emotions as important in forming Christian virtue (see p. 196) rather than being themselves at the centre of faith.

From the late eighteenth century onward, a series of revivals known as the *Great Awakening* swept the country, led by great preachers like George Whitefield (1714–70) – the English founder of the Calvinistic strand of Methodism – Charles Finney (1792–1875) and Dwight Moody (1837–99).

Evangelicalism was dominant in the spirituality of black people, where it took on the often plaintive passion of gospel music, and imparted a sense of dignity that did not always rest content with the injustices of the social order.

Pentecostalism

The son of former slaves, *William Seymour* (1870–1922) initiated the Pentecostal movement among the urban black poor. The abolition of slavery may have failed to bring full liberty within the body politic, but the personal body was finding a new freedom in the Spirit. Worship became spontaneous, emotional and bodily involving, and marked by powerful signs of the Spirit such as speaking in tongues.

The early Pentecostals believed they were at the heart of God's plan to reawaken world Christianity to the gifts of the Spirit. Indeed Pentecostalism is now worldwide and among the fastest growing forms of Christian spirituality. It has triggered a more moderate *charismatic movement* in mainstream Protestant and Catholic Churches, emphasizing the need for baptism in the Spirit and other spiritual gifts, taking the not unjustifiable view that the Holy Spirit has long been the sidelined 'Cinderella of the Trinity' in Western theology (though the implications for the identity of the other two divine persons are seldom followed through!).

Søren Kierkegaard (1813–55)

The Danish writer Kierkegaard attacked theological system-builders like Hegel (p. 98) for the 'absent-mindedness' with which they allowed their intellectual edifices to distract them from addressing the fundamental despair and dread of human existence. Having broken off his engagement to his deeply loved Regina, Kierkegaard idealized Abraham, who was prepared to sacrifice his beloved son Isaac in his lonely faith in God, irrational and unethical though this seemed. (It has to be said, in Kierkegaard's thought the feelings of Regina and Isaac seem to be out of the frame!)

As Isaac was renounced but then 'given back' to Abraham, so the religious man, who surrenders all to God, finds the particular blessings of life given back. In this way the religious man succeeds in the primary task of life, which is to become a self. The aesthetic person, who lives only for particular momentary experiences, and the ethical person, who lives for abstract ideals, lose their selves in the particular and the universal respectively. But the religious man, believing against all reason in the paradox of the God-man, Jesus, finds the universal in the particular, and so finds his true self 'grounded transparently in God'.

This bald summary does scant justice to writings full of disconcerting irony and paradox, as well as a degree of neurosis. They are crafted to overthrow systematic thought and to bring the reader face to face with the dilemmas of her own existence. In them the Protestant tradition finds a new spiritual language of its own.

Karl Barth (1886–1968)

Early influenced by Kierkegaard, Barth saw all religious experience and aspiration as an impediment to Christian faith, since the latter relies not on the mystical ascent and return of humanity to divinity, but on the coming in Christ of a God who is 'wholly other' than the God of philosophical systems or human spirituality. For Barth, and the mainstream twentieth-century Protestant theologians who followed him, prayer meant not mystical union or pietist sentiment, but encountering in penitence the Word of God revealed in Christ and the Bible:

> My faith being small and my obedience slight, of what meaning are these words, 'I believe, I obey'? Deep is the abyss. The core of our being is put to question the moment we believe and obey as well as we can . . . Because of God we are in distress. God alone is able to heal us out of it . . . For the Reformers everything was reduced to the question, 'How is it possible for me to have an encounter with God? (1985, pp. 31–2)

Yet in the language of encounter, distress and abyss, familiar mystical notes seem to be sounded . . .

Liberalism

Contrary to fideism, but characteristic of the eighteenth century, were attempts to redefine Christian faith in a manner that was acceptable to reason. Miracles, the supernatural and the sacramental were downplayed in favour of a God who cohered well with the lawful universe that science was discovering. In the extreme case, the Trinity was rejected, and a 'deist' view prevailed for which God was the creator of the intricate design of the cosmos, but did not intervene in any special revelations through Christ or scripture.

Immanuel Kant (1724–1804)

Even as he completed the Enlightenment's rejection of traditional metaphysical understandings of God, Kant opened the way for Romantic alternatives. Though a philosopher rather than a spiritual writer, Kant cannot be ignored in any attempt to understand modern spirituality.

Kant argued that we structure the world around us according to the categories we understand. We can never conceptualize how things are in themselves, but can only know how they appear to us. Arguments for or against God, along with all metaphysical speculations, trespass beyond the bounds of reason. As in apophatic spirituality, God is beyond our understanding; but so is reality as such.

However, while speculative reason has to abandon God, and morality has likewise to reject the notion of a 'heteronomous' divine lawgiver (p. 188), Kant argued that practical reason requires the concepts of God, freedom and immortality in order to live an autonomous moral life. Meanwhile the way 'things in themselves' reach beyond our understanding leads to a baffling-yet-exhilarating sense of the 'sublime' (White, 1997) – feelings Otto later teased out in his idea of the holy (Chapter 7).

The limitation of reason, the sense of the sublime and the philosophical idealism – the 'world-creating' powers Kant gave to the human understanding – became key features of Romanticism.

Friedrich Schleiermacher (1768–1834)

Schleiermacher accepted the limits Kant placed on theological speculation, and sought to make Christian faith reasonable to its 'cultured despisers'. He distilled from the classical Christian doctrines a spiritual 'essence' of Christian faith, which could be translated into rational terms. For him – in the spiritual tradition of Luther and pietism – this essence was not dogmatic belief, but a sense of total dependence on and trust in God. The dogmas of faith served in one way or another to express this trust, which was both a sublime and awesome feeling, and a totally rational response to the greatness of God and the vulnerability we experience. Doctrine thus depended on a spirituality supported by reason.

Friedrich Hegel (1770–1831)

Schleiermacher's method was broadly followed by the liberal strand of nineteenth-century theology. Hegel effected a supreme – but as Kierkegaard pointed out, very abstract – reconciliation between Christianity and philosophical idealism. He understood all history as a rational evolution of ideas that are, in turn, the unfolding of the Trinity. History was at once entirely rational and entirely spiritual.

Liberalism remains a vital force in theology, but the phrase 'liberal spirituality' is seldom heard. Secular reason seems to find it hard to generate a spirituality, and liberalism seems to need to borrow either from pietism (like Schleiermacher) a spirituality of dependence; from Romanticism a spirituality of original innocence and 'natural piety' and their restoration through bold imagination; or from liberationism (as is perhaps the most vital option today) a spirituality of struggle and challenge to power.

Romanticism

It is possible to possess a revolutionary, subversive and utopian political hope, but to serve this not by rational abstraction but by means of Christian and other human traditions and cultures, as well as a venerated 'nature', appropriated by the liberating imagination. This, essentially is the move made by Romanticism.

William Blake (1757–1827)

Blake was steeped in the Bible, and his poems and pictures are full of its imagery. But the Bible lived in Blake in a new way that served his own radical vision. Blake's great enemy was precisely the God of rational and moral law that was so amenable to the deists of the Enlightenment. He ridiculed this 'God' in his famous picture of *The Ancient of Days* as a kind of scientist in the clouds, inspecting the deep and measuring it with his compasses. Blake believed, like Rousseau and many Romantics, in an original innocence. This is corrupted by the experience of society, and has to be recovered as 'innocence in experience'.

Blake's rejection of the rational 'creator' in favour of the God of Jesus has been criticized as gnostic, but Blake was by no means hostile to the created order. He was not 'against matter' but against the scientific materialism, industrial technology and productivity-driven morality that were epitomized in the 'dark, Satanic mills' of the Industrial Revolution.

Blake placed Christian scripture and tradition back in the service of liberation. He constructed elaborate and rather confusing mythologies, but is perhaps at his best with his simple illustrated poems in *Songs of Innocence and Experience,* and his parables from 'Auguries of Innocence':

> To see a World in a grain of sand
> And a Heaven in a Wild Flower.
> Hold Infinity in the palm of your Hand
> And eternity in an hour . . .
>
> A Robin Redbreast in a Cage
> Puts all Heaven in a Rage . . .
>
> Every tear from every eye
> Becomes a Babe in Eternity . . .
>
> The bleat, the bark, bellow and roar
> Are waves that beat on Heaven's shore . . .
> ('Auguries of Innocence', in 1971, pp. 431–2)
>
> Priests in black gowns are walking their rounds
> and binding with briars my joys and desires.
> ('The Garden of Love', in 1971, p. 215)

Later Romantics

The Romantics mined all traditions – classical mythology, local folk stories and ballads, as well as Christianity – for a language that would liberate the heart and the imagination. For some, such liberation entailed a rejection of the Christian tradition, but Christian spirituality thrived in many poets, including

- *William Wordsworth* (1770–1850), whose nature mysticism epitomizes much in Romantic spirituality, focusing not on the transcendent God in Godself so much as our own . . .

> sense sublime
> Of something far more deeply interfused,
> Whose dwelling is the lights of setting suns,
> And the round ocean, and the living air,
> And the blue sky, and in the mind of man,
> A motion and a spirit, that impels
> All thinking things, all objects of all thought,
> And rolls through all things. (1965, p. 116)

- *Samuel Taylor Coleridge* (1772–1834) advocated a fusion in theology between feeling, reason, imagination and doctrine, and wrote spiritually haunting verse, including his *Ancient Mariner,* an allegory of spiritual rebirth.
- *Emily Dickinson* (1830–86), whose deceptively simple verse conceals a passionate and intense questioning.
- *Gerard Manley Hopkins* (1844–89), a Jesuit who expressed a passion for God's presence in nature, as well as his own terrifying dark nights of the soul, in innovative, energetic verse.
- *T. S. Eliot* (1888–1965), whose expansive free verse, rich in Christian symbolism, expresses a philosophical, reflective spirituality steeped in reference to mystical writers.
- *W. H. Auden* (1907–73), whose tight-knit verse compresses, by contrast, a spirituality of political engagement and social concern.
- *R. S. Thomas* (1913–2000), whose short poems, in the tradition of Dickinson, reflect a restless questioning and a 'reaching out' to God in the darkness of modern unbelief.

This is to mention only a few of the English-writing poets whose work is often underestimated in its contribution to modern spirituality.

'High' Anglicanism

The 'high church' Anglican tradition represented by the Caroline divines had retreated in the eighteenth century before the advances of rationalism and pietism, but survived through the non-jurors, who refused to switch allegiance to the Protestant William of Orange. They included *William Law* (1668–1761) whose spiritual writings show a pietist emphasis on sin and the need for sincere inner change, plus the influence of Boehme, and a hint of Eckhart's divine birth in the soul:

> When, therefore, the first spark of a desire after God arises in thy soul, cherish it with all thy care, give all thy heart into it, it is nothing less than a touch of the divine loadstone that is to draw thee out of the vanity of time into the riches of eternity. Get up, therefore, and follow it as gladly as the Wise Men of the East followed the star from Heaven that appeared to them. It will do for thee as the star did for them: it will lead thee to the birth of Jesus . . . in the dark centre of thy own fallen soul. (2001, Chapter 2, 52)

In the 1830s the *Oxford Movement* – which included *John Henry Newman* (1801–90) – who later converted to Roman Catholicism – the poet *John Keble* (1792–1866), and the patristic scholar *Edward Pusey* (1800–82) – urged the Church of England to repent of its secularization and subservience to the state, and look rather to its identity with the universal Church in every age.

Towards a Catholic Socialism

With the next generation of Anglo-Catholics, the emphasis shifted to the recovery of medieval ceremonial splendour, partly in order to give a taste of God's glory to the poor, who were crowding into the rotten slums of the cities. At the same time monastic communities began to be re-established in the Anglican Church.

In this one respect remarkably like Karl Marx, many Anglo-Catholics saw the Middle Ages as a time when humanity expressed itself collectively in craft and culture, before these were alienated in mass production and the service of individual profit. They looked back to the Middle Ages in order to look forward to a sense of the common good that the individualist and middle-class values of the Reformation were believed to have obliterated. In this sense – using tradition to serve a radical goal – they tended towards a Romantic socialism.

Similar ideals developed in the Roman Catholic Church, leading in the twentieth century to the Catholic Socialism of *Dorothy Day* (1897–1980) and the worker priest movement. The Anglican Archbishops *William Temple* (1881–1944) and *Michael Ramsey* (1904–88) as well as *Pope John XXIII* (1881–1963) represented the same sacramental vision for the common good. The recent *Radical Orthodox* movement, which looks to a paradoxical mix of medieval theology and postmodernism for a radical critique of modern society, was pioneered by three Anglo-Catholics, and can be described as spiritually Romantic in the same sense.

Liberationism

There is a contrary way of being politically radical as a Christian. Those we have considered so far drew on Christianity as presenting a rich tradition of understanding, which could be used to effect those hopes which secular capitalist society possessed but could not achieve. But it is also possible to do more or less the opposite: adopt a secular, scientific understanding of the world and the soul, but harness this to the eschatological or 'end-time' imagination (Alison, 1996) expressed in the Bible and Christian tradition. It was this that nourished the strand of political spirituality that emerged, at first from the Protestant churches, in the late nineteenth and twentieth centuries.

America and the Social Gospel

While European evangelicalism had tended to be socially concerned but politically conservative, the United States was founded by Puritans and liberals in radical defiance of colonial power. The radicalism cooled but never died, continuing for example in the evangelicalism and later Pentecostalism of the black former slaves. *Sojourner Truth* (1797–1883) combined revivalist preaching with themes of black and women's liberation. *Walter Rauschenbusch* (1861–1918) likewise combined a sense of the urgency of conversion with what became known as the 'social gospel', as later did *Martin Luther King* (1929–68), and the pioneer of black theology, *James Cone* (b.1939).

Bonhoeffer's 'Religionless Christianity'

Dietrich Bonhoeffer (1906–45) defied the 'German Christians' who supported Hitler, by helping to form the Confessing Church and a secret seminary to train ministers for it. He rejected the 'cheap grace' implied by an easygoing nominal observance of worship and the sacraments, and advocated forming Christian communities on lay but quasi-monastic lines. He emphasized the 'cost of discipleship' not only in his writings (2001) but in his death at the hands of the Nazis following his part in an assassination attempt on Hitler. He urged (1981) a radical acceptance of secularism as a sign of humanity's 'coming of age'. Much outward religious practice needed to be abandoned, he argued, for Christians need to be subversives, working secretly for God's kingdom. Thus Bonhoeffer combined defiant politics with a pietist emphasis on the inward life rather than 'externals'.

Simone Weil (1909–43)

Weil could be argued, similarly, to have achieved a remarkable unity of political activism and quietism. An atheistic Jew who never quite converted to Christianity, she was drawn to the liturgy and spirituality of Catholicism, but could never accept its power structures. She believed that doctrines – especially the incarnational doctrine of God seeking out humanity in Christ – should not be imposed, but offered as beautiful intellectual objects for our attention with power to transform our lives. She advocated purifying the mind of all imaginary compensations and loving God in and through our and the universe's emptiness, which is paradoxically beautiful:

We must continually suspend the work of the imagination filling the void within ourselves.

If we accept no matter what void, what stroke of fate can prevent us from loving the universe?

We have the assurance that, come what may, *the universe is full.* (2002, p. 18)

Hospitalized, Weil refused to eat more than the food available to her colleagues in the resistance to Nazism, and died, joining the company of so many women mystics who fasted to extremes.

Thomas Merton: Activist Contemplation

Merton (1915–68) was a Trappist monk who came to see his earlier lofty impulse to withdraw from the world as a delusion, and thereafter saw contemplation only as a means to deeper love of humankind. This involved him in engagement with the spirituality of Zen Buddhism, Taoism and Hinduism, and alignment with contemporary protest against nuclear weapons and the Vietnam War. His was a spirituality characteristic of the 1960s, impatient with traditional boundaries in its search for justice, love and peace; something, perhaps, we have yet to catch up with?

Taizé

In 1940 a Calvinist minister founded an ecumenical 'Community of Reconciliation' to bring healing in time of war, and took the name *Brother Roger* (1915–2005). Its spirituality of simplicity and solidarity with the poor, as well as its liturgy of repeated mantra-like chants, candlelit icons and long reflective silences, has had a huge impact on contemporary worship and the activist spirituality of the young.

Liberation Theology

In Latin America from the 1960s a group of bishops and theologians began to see Marxist analysis as indicating the best way to overcome poverty and injustice. They made strong links between Marxism and the biblical themes of exodus and the coming of the kingdom, and developed the corporate spirituality of the 'base community' where oppressed people were encouraged to reflect on their own situation in the light of scripture and tradition with a view to identifying appropriate action. Their portrait of Jesus as a revolutionary, though partial, has left an indelible mark on Christian spirituality, as has the notion that theology, wherever it may travel, needs to begin and end with practice (see pp. 146–8).

Apocalyptic Politics

More clearly than any other writers, perhaps, the Mennonite *John Howard Yoder* (1926–96) and Methodist *Walter Wink* (b.1935) reconcile secular politics with that early language of biblical hope: apocalyptic. Both see Jesus as one who overcame oppressive structures of power by non-violent, pacifist means, and bids us do the same. They identify the demons, principalities and powers with which Jesus and his followers are described as doing battle (Eph. 6.12) with a 'domination system' which is primarily political, though it also has its 'bridgehead' in the human ego. The resulting spirituality involves identifying and naming the powers that imprison us, both psychologically and socially, and then doing non-violent battle with them.

Prayer in this context is the very opposite of quietist acquiescence in the will of God:

> Prayer infuses the air of a time yet to be into the suffocating atmosphere of the present . . . History belongs to the intercessors who believe the future into being . . . Praying is rattling God's cage and waking God up and setting God free and giving this famished God water and this starved God food and cutting the ropes off God's hands and the manacles off God's feet and washing the caked sweat from God's eyes and then watching God swell with life and vitality and energy and following God wherever God goes. (Wink, 1998, p. 186)

Conclusion

In this period we have seen Christian spirituality no longer as a formative influence on society, but responding to a society whose understanding and hopes were being shaped by independent economic and ideological forces. Spirituality responded in four characteristic ways, but which is to be preferred?

The historical part of this book can be left to close with this question, which is still with us today. However, Chapter 7 deals with a kind of interest in spirituality that surfaced in the late nineteenth and twentieth centuries, and so in a way represents a continuation of the history of spirituality itself. And since then, other 'postmodern' questions have been posed, which are explored in Chapter 13. Though a thematic rather than historical chapter, the theme it explores – human difference – is one that brings the history of spirituality up to the present day.

For Reflection and Discussion

1 What is your gut reaction to the four events described in the opening paragraph? And where do you stand in relation to detraditionalization and secularization? Do you feel the spiritual writers considered so far have always been (a) traditionalist in understanding and (b) other-worldly in hope? Can you think of exceptions?

2 What are the five main things spirituality more widely can glean from pietism, Methodism, evangelicalism and Pentecostalism? And what are the five main things these traditions can and should learn from the wider Christian tradition?

3 Do you agree that there is mysticism in Kierkegaard and Barth, or are they fundamentally anti-mystical? And do you agree with their rejection of philosophical and religious systems? State your reasons.

4 Does Romanticism seem to you an enrichment of Christian spirituality or its negation? What is the role of imagination, poetry and the arts in spirituality? What art and poetry, if any, has helped you especially, and in what way?

5 How do you respond to Wink's description of prayer? What can we learn from it, and what from the quietist notion of prayer as surrendering ourselves to the love and will of God? Are the quietist and activist understandings of prayer reconcilable?

Further Reading

Dietrich Bonhoeffer, 1981, *Letters and Papers from Prison*, London: SCM Press.

Widson Bridges, 2001, *Resurrection Song: African American Spirituality*, New York: Orbis.

Harvey Cox, 2001, *Fire From Heaven: The Rise of Pentecostal Spirituality and the Reshaping of Religion in the 21st Century*, Cambridge, MA: Da Capo.

James Gordon, 2000, *Evangelical Spirituality*, Eugene, OR: Wipf and Stock.

Carter Lindberg, 2004, *The Pietist Theologians: An Introduction to Theology in the Seventeenth and Eighteenth Centuries*, Oxford: Blackwell.

Gordon Mursell, 2001, *English Spirituality: From 1700 to the Present*, London: SPCK.

Jon Sobrino, 1987, *The Spirituality of Liberation: Toward Political Holiness*, Maryknoll, NY: Orbis.

Walter Wink, 1992, *Engaging the Powers: Discernment and Resistance in a World of Domination*, Minneapolis: Fortress Press.

Part 2

Themes and Connections

The lens through which Christian spirituality is viewed now changes from the historical to the thematic. From looking at causal developments through time we move to looking at conceptual relationships and connections with other aspects of human nature and enquiry. We ask in successive chapters questions like

- Is experience at the heart of spirituality?
- Is science inimical to, nourishing of, or even a form of spirituality?
- Is spirituality the 'mystical department' of theology?
- Why has spirituality been so ambiguous – to say the least – about the body?
- Is spirituality mainly concerned with the individual soul, and if so, does psychotherapy replace it?
- Does spirituality serve to make us morally better people?
- How does Christian spirituality relate to different spiritualities, and human difference in general?

The disciplines explored are not definitive. Limitations of space, for example, prevented a discussion of spirituality and the arts, or culture more generally.

In the first part of the book, the focus was very obviously on Christian spirituality and its antecedents. In this part the focus widens to questions about spirituality as such. And yet there is still a subtle focus on *Christian* spirituality because of the particular relations it has had with science, theology, psychology and secular ethics. Other religions did not encounter science and the secular in the same way as Christianity; indeed in some cases they did not encounter them at all until the expansion of the initially Christian empires dispersed science and, later, secularity worldwide. Meanwhile the religion of the incarnation had its own distinctive love-hate relationship with the body. So this part of the book will mainly be exploring the encounter – sometimes tense, sometimes mutually nourishing – of *Christian* spirituality with these other disciplines and concerns.

The reader or teacher using this book will probably be more focused either on themes or on history. Table 4 is offered so that the whole book will be of use in either case. This is a grid listing the historical Chapters 1–6 as columns and the thematic Chapters 7–13 as the rows. The table represents a kind of interchange where one can change 'trains' of thought from the historical to the thematic and vice versa.

Chapter 13 had to be placed in one part or the other. The issues it raises are primarily those confronted by recent spirituality, so it could have formed a historical chapter on 'postmodern spirituality', but it is hard to take a historical view of one's own times, and it seemed better to emphasize the thematic approach.

Table 4: How the History connects with the Themes

	1: Biblical	2: Patristic	3: 'Dark Age'	4: Medieval	5: Reformation	6: Modern
7: Experience	Theophany and absence: God encountered, yet often remote	Spirituality reaches beyond experience	Experience through liturgy and ways of prayer including prayer of heart and hesychasm	Experience becomes a rival authority among some mystics especially women	New stress on experience, including conversion	Pietism and Romanticism stress experience. Mystical experience begins to be studied
8: Science	Cosmos lawlike, logical, non-sacred and so science-friendly, but science begins among Greeks not Jews	Greek rationality inherited, but focus is on the eternal truths not material observations	Considerable monastic love of nature. The first stirrings of modern science	Shift to Aristotle increases empirical focus, but tradition retains greater authority than scientific enquiry	Reformation separates out a secular sphere for science, which provides technologies for growing capitalism	Spirituality becomes suspicious of the all pervading scientific vision, but for some science is the main spiritual resource
9: Theology	Bible and Christ form the subject of theology. Pauline and Johannine beginnings of theological thinking	Theological practice develops: formation of doctrines of Trinity and incarnation	Theology and spirituality remain united, but little theological development	Rise of academic theology. Redefinition of heresy. Tension between spirituality and theology	Mystics and theologians distinct and sometimes hostile	Pietist and Romantic suspicion of theological dogma. Many begin to claim spirituality without dogma or religion

10: Body	Embodied eroticism in Song of Songs, but beginnings of suspicion in New Testament times	Fathers generally hostile to body and sex	Monastic celibacy ideal dominates, but beginnings of courtly love and romance	Bodily and erotic imagery especially in women, combined with suspicion	Marriage rather than monasticism affirmed by Reformers. Feminization of piety	Reassertion of sex and the body, but resisted by Church
11: Psyche	Characters depicted very realistically, but no description of mental activity	With Augustine and others spirituality becomes an inner journey	Development of spiritual direction and analysis of the soul	Growing stress on feelings by some; the soul seen as a quasi-divine abyss by northern mystics	Turn to the subject as the foundation of knowledge. Outer expresses inner rather than vice versa	Development of psychology as a science, and secular psychotherapies
12: Ethics	Prophecy and wisdom different resources for ethics	Society and religious communities modelled as communities directed to a common good in God. Ethics of virtues and vices flows from this end-focused perspective			Protestant and Ignatian return to an ethic of obedience	A plurality of ethical approaches. Autonomy increasingly seen as central
13: Difference	Monotheism linked to imperialist demand for unity	Universal logos allows for assimilation of pagan diversity	Christianity becomes the civic religion of empire. Diversity increasingly mistrusted as heresy		Christendom fractures but uniformity required in each part	Collapse of patriarchies: postmodern affirmation of difference

7

Encounter or Escapism? Spirituality and Experience

> Many Christians are like deaf people at a concert. They study the programme carefully, believe every statement made in it, speak respectfully of the quality of the music, but only really hear a phrase now and again. So they have no notion at all of the mighty symphony which fills the universe, to which our lives are destined to make their tiny contribution, and which is the self revelation of the Eternal God.

Thus Evelyn Underhill (1937, pp. 18–19) contrasts a dogmatic assent to Christianity unfavourably with the Christian experience of God. She also likens creedal statements to signposts on the road pointing the way to Dover, which cannot substitute for the experience of Dover itself. The contrast between mere propositional belief and living experience is familiar in spiritual writers, and is surely behind many contemporary people's preference for such experience to 'religious dogma'. (To continue the analogies, however, one might ask whether the most 'real' driving experience is that which pays no attention to signposts or traffic signs at all? Or whether following a concert from a score can never enhance the listening experience?)

Ask people what they understand by 'spirituality', and a great many would probably respond in terms of experience. Spirituality is widely understood as the experiential side of a religion or belief system. When people say they dislike institutional religion but believe that having a spirituality is important, they are often referring to the importance of experiences gained through prayer, through meditation, or spontaneously. On the other hand, there is also a widespread feeling that this experience is not quite what it was, that the angels do not visit as they once did, and that spirituality has now to engage with the absence rather than the experience of God.

However, we have seen that these latter feelings are at least as old as the sense of the 'departure' of God in the Hebrew exile. People perhaps emphasize spiritual experience precisely when the societies that have embodied spirituality are threatened or breaking down, as Jewish society then was. The decline of Orthodox Byzantine culture in the wake of Muslim invasions was likewise accompanied by a growing focus on the direct experience of divine light (pp. 53–4). Perhaps the keen new interest in 'mystical experience' that arose in the twentieth century, as the empires and culture of Christendom crumbled, should be seen in this same perspective, as essentially an escape from the harsh facts of decline? Is 'spiritual experience' at the core of faith, or a denial of the vulnerability of faith's cultural embodiment?

Universal Spiritual Experience?

According to McGinn, in the West it was only the twelfth century that 'experience' began to be used in connection with the word 'mystical', and many continued to regard spiritual experiences as at best distracting from the spiritual journey, at worst suspect or even demonic. Only in the nineteenth century did people see fit to study spiritual or mystical experiences academically. However, from then on, until the mid-twentieth century, the study of spirituality consisted, more than anything else, in the study of spiritual experience. In this chapter we will consider what might be gained and lost in such a study, and why it has since come to seem, to many, a little quaint.

William James (1842–1910)

James was a psychologist from New England. His *The Variety of Religious Experience* (1983) is a great early example of such study, although some have criticized it for emphasizing, in the research, the experience of fellow American

Protestants. James distinguishes 'once-born' religion, based on an optimistic apprehension of God in creation, from the more anguished, 'twice born' according to which we need saving from our guilt through conversion. He concluded (p. 464) that the visible world is part of a more spiritual universe, union or harmonious relation with which is our true end, achieved in prayer, in which spiritual energy flows in and produces real effects, psychological or material.

Religion, he argued, contains universal psychological features – a 'zest' consisting of either 'enchantment' or 'earnestness'; and an 'assurance of safety and a temper of peace'. Religions have always added to this core 'over-beliefs' concerning the nature of the spiritual world; these, unlike the core, cannot be proved empirically, though 'the most interesting and valuable things about a man are usually his over-beliefs' (p. 490).

Friedrich von Hügel (1854–1928)

A modernizing Catholic, von Hügel argued against the division of experience into subjective emotions and objective perceptions. He argued that the world is so rich it can only be understood by a mixture of reason, mysticism and science. The three aspects he discerned in all religions – experiential/mystical, historical/institutional, and scientific/intellectual – were together necessary for a full grasp of reality.

Evelyn Underhill (1875–1941)

Von Hügel, himself a naturalized Englishman, was a major influence on Underhill. Her vast classic, *Mysticism* (1999) argued that an elite of mystics in all religions shares a similar experience of God, which takes them through stages of awakening, purification, illumination, the dark night and union with God. Von Hügel was a major influence on her becoming an Anglican; and her later work (e.g. 1937) was more dedicated to bringing spiritual experience to ordinary people within their tradition.

The Perennial Philosophy

The term was coined by the eighteenth-century German philosopher Gottlieb Leibnitz, but promoted by the novelist Aldous Huxley (1945), F. C. Happold (1963) and the Buddhist Ananda Coomaraswamy to denote the widespread view that mystical experience is universal and constitutes the common, valid core of all religions. Huxley also later argued (1954) that the experience could be attained by the use of psychedelic drugs such as mescaline, a view that led to much interest in the 1960s. This experience was identified by reference to a perennial philosophy, a kind of amalgam of Hindu Vedanta and Neoplatonism.

Martin Buber (1878–1965)

A philosopher steeped in the Jewish Hasidic mysticism of the eighteenth century, Buber placed the emphasis on personal encounter rather than mystical fusion. He believed experience could be divided into two fundamental kinds:

- *'I–It'*: as when we think and know about people and things as third person others, as objects to be used for our benefit or analysed by science.
- *'I–Thou'*: the experience of relating to another person or thing as a reality over against us, known through relationship, meeting, dialogue, challenge and love.

In his seminal work (1976), Buber argued that we cannot truly experience God as an 'it' or have factual knowledge about him at all; we can only experience God as an intimate 'thou', through prayer and spiritual encounter. Nevertheless we are always wanting to reduce God to an 'it', an idol of our imagination, and this gives rise to the dogmatic aspect of religion.

Rudolf Otto (1869–1937)

Otto focused likewise on the element of encounter with God as Other. In *The Idea of the Holy* (1958) he saw the core of all spiritual experience as an encounter with the 'numinous', a term derived from the Latin for 'presence' and defined as *mysterium tremendum et fascinans*, a mystery that makes us want to flee in dread and yet holds us with fascination. He saw this as operating throughout religion, from animist notions of *mana* or spiritual power, through the Greek tragic hero who appals us in his wickedness and yet draws us to compassion for his suffering, to the holy God of the monotheistic faiths, terrifying in his power yet infinitely attractive.

Otto believed numinous feelings gave us access to the noumenal realm of Kant (p. 97) – that is, to reality transcending the categories we use to understand things in the phenomenal world. His concept of the numinous has become widely used, but also criticized for not being as universal as he suggested, but seemingly absent from many non-theistic religions such as Buddhism and Taoism.

Walter Stace (1886–1967)

Stace, an English philosopher of religion, tried to produce a philosophically coherent account of spiritual experience as something that transcends subject and object and the laws of logic, and relates our 'pure self' to the World self in a fusion that is and is not identity.

Not all philosophers, of course, would agree that this makes for coherence! However, Stace believed in working from experience to appropriate concepts, rather than letting our concepts predetermine what kinds of experience there can be. His own concepts are partly drawn from the Hindu Vedanta philosophy.

Neo-Thomists

French theologians like *Jacques Maritain* (1882–1973) and *Étienne Gilson* (1884–1978) were anxious to understand spiritual experience in terms of the medieval categories they were reviving. For such thinkers, the direct experience of God was not compatible with God's transcendence. We cannot know God as an object corresponding to our image of him in our mind, since God transcends all images and concepts. These thinkers argued, however, that God through his Spirit creates a likeness of his own love in us, and the resemblance of this love in us to its source in God constitutes something like knowledge. Gilson went further than Maritain, arguing that in mystical union with God, it is actually the Holy Spirit in us who knows and loves God. The mystic participates in God's perfect knowledge and love of God (and by implication, the world). On this view – unlike those considered so far – rather than being our experience of the Spirit or of God, *spiritual experience is the Spirit's experience* in us.

R. C. Zaehner (1913–74)

A Roman Catholic writer with deep knowledge of Indian religions, Zaehner challenged perennialism by distinguishing (1969):

1 **Nature mysticism**: a 'panenhenic' ('all-in-one', p. 28) cosmic consciousness of the unity of everything, akin to what Stace had termed 'extrovertive' mysticism.
2 **Soul or monistic mysticism**: an inner state in which one senses, beyond all thought, an undifferentiated, 'limbo' state (p. 130) in which all distinctions of space, time and good and evil are transcended; akin to Stace's 'introvertive' mysticism.
3 **Theistic mysticism**, in which ego, space and time are also left behind, but in an embrace which goes beyond the universal One of (1) and (2) to reach out in love to a transcendent God. In distinguishing theistic mysticism, Zaehner went beyond Stace and the perennialists, but was arguably incorporating the encounter experience which Otto and Buber had described in different ways.

Author of some masterful surveys of religious experience (1976, 1998), *Ninian Smart* (1927–2001) criticized Zaehner's distinctions as simplistic, and urged that we consider social, narrative, dogmatic, ethical, ritual and material dimensions of spirituality as well as the experiential.

Two Challenges

The approaches to mysticism discussed so far have come to seem questionable owing to two kinds of development in the late twentieth century.

Constructivism

The status of *all* – and not just mystical – experience as an objective representation of reality has been challenged by philosophers such as Ludwig Wittgenstein and Michel Foucault, philosophers of science Thomas Kuhn and Michael Polanyi, and sociologist John Berger, among many others. From their very different angles they developed the view – described by some as constructivism, and an essential ingredient of postmodernism (Chapter 13) – that experience is socially constructed, being shaped by the language and concepts of one's culture.

Wittgenstein argued that there can be no private language, no way of describing experiences in an idiosyncratic way that only makes sense to ourselves. Language is essentially communicative, and we communicate through what he called 'language games' – logical and scientific systems, but also stories and rituals – that belong to a particular culture. Experience is 'story shaped' (Wicker, 1975) and so culture-shaped.

It is rare for Buddhists or Protestants (except a few who have previously been Catholics) to have visions of the Virgin Mary, or Roman Catholics (apart from converts from Buddhism) to encounter the Buddha. What we experience is determined by what we believe about reality – it is argued – because we cannot experience what we cannot interpret or share through language and culture, and language and culture are not everywhere the same.

The overall effect of such arguments was to render fruitless the preceding attempts to identify types of spiritual experience across cultural and religious boundaries. Spiritual experience had to be seen, on this view, as shaped and described, if not predetermined, by the religious culture of the experiencers.

Stephen Katz edited an influential anthology (1978) whose various authors argued strongly against both the 'perennialist' notion of a common core of spiritual experience, and attempts to classify together experiences of people from different religious cultures. All such attempts ignored the futility of trying to disentangle experience from culture. Indeed, as noted, the 'perennial' mystical experience was identified with a perennial philosophy.

On the same grounds, the American theologian *George Lindbeck* argued (1984) that we can only understand a religion, so to speak from the inside, by following it and embracing its practices, and so learning what its doctrines mean. He described this position as 'postliberal' because it defeated the liberal idea of trying to describe in 'neutral' secular terms the essence of Christian belief.

Constructivism has had an enormous impact on the study of spirituality, shifting it away from the classification of supposed spiritual experiences, towards the study of the religious practices and languages through which spirituality is conveyed.

Radical Negation

More recently, 'spiritual experience' has come under attack from another quarter. There have always been many, both outside and within the religious faiths, who have challenged the possibility or the meaningfulness of spiritual experience. But *Denys Turner* claims (1998) that this challenge to experience is actually the mainstream understanding of the Christian spiritual tradition itself.

Traditionally, he argues, mystics have not been advocates or describers of spiritual experience, but have argued consistently that such experience is at best irrelevant to the spiritual journey, and at worst an idolatrous distraction from it. Only in modern times, from about the sixteenth century onward, has the irrelevance or *absence of experience* in our relation with God been construed as an *experience of absence* or longing for God. Since then, mysticism has become removed from the exploration of God's mystery, which was the work of all theologians, to the description of the esoteric experiences of a not very theologically minded group of people called 'mystics'. As a result,

> Whereas our employment of the metaphors of 'inwardness' and 'ascent' appears to be tied in with the achievement and the cultivation of a certain kind of experience – such as those recommended within the practice of what is called, nowadays, 'centring' or 'contemplative' prayer – the Medieval employment of them was tied in with a 'critique' of such religious experiences and practices. (Turner, 1998, p. 4).

Here Turner is emphasizing the 'apophatic' or 'negating' tradition in mysticism, which emphasizes the way God transcends all thought, language or experience. The traditional writers he discusses – especially Dionysius, the unknown author of *The Cloud of Unknowing*, Eckhart and John of the Cross – all contain this emphasis, as we shall see. However, we have also noted strands of the Christian tradition – the hesychasts and Gregory Palamas in the Orthodox East, for example, the women mystics of the medieval West, and the pietist and Pentecostal movements – for whom spirituality is very experiential, and often bodily.

Are there Spiritual Experiences?

Turner's 'apophatic' turn was pitted against the trend of growing interest in spirituality of all kinds and a growing 'commodification' of it. Among the 'baby boomer' generation in the USA, W. Roof noted (1993) a widespread resurgence of interest in spiritual experiences in which 'mystics' (emphasizing feelings and values and an immanent God) were gradually displacing 'theists' (emphasizing cognitive descriptions, creedal statements and a transcendent God). Spirituality was looking more and more like E. Canda's definition: 'the human quest for personal meaning and mutually fulfilling relationships among people, the non-human environment and for some, God' (1988, p. 243).

Meanwhile, the argument for universal spiritual experience has by no means been lost. *John Hick* (1989, 2006) has argued that the experiences described in all religions are best explained by the hypothesis that their source is an ultimate reality, the cause of everything that exists. He believes Christians need to undergo a 'Copernican revolution' from a Christ-centred to a God-centred faith, analogous to Copernicus' shift from the earth-centred to the sun-centred universe. *William Wainwright* (1981) has argued strongly (against Stace) that spiritual experience does not transcend logic, but is similar enough to ordinary sense experience for us to believe it relates to spiritual reality. We should value spiritual experience, he argues, not because it makes us better people, but because it puts us in touch with divine reality. The Zen Buddhist philosopher, *Robert Forman*, has argued for a 'pure consciousness event' – 'a wakeful persistence going on for many hours, [in which] the subject recalls no content' (1999, p. 30) – which transcends language, and the categories of space and time. This can persist alongside, and deepen, normal consciousness in a 'dualistic mystical state'. And another Buddhist, the widely read *Ken Wilber* (2006) posits a 'unity-consciousness' in which self is united with its 'shadow', the ego with the unconscious, the mind with the body and the whole self with the not-self, in a rich and heady mix of psychology, politics, ecology and spirituality.

Concept and Experience: Cart and Horse?

Katz writes (1978, p. 25) 'there are NO pure (i.e. unmediated) experiences'. The Hindu does not have an experience which he *then* describes in Hindu terms; 'he has a Hindu experience'. But is this true? Do experiences always come ready-made in concept-shaped packages, so they can never challenge us to revise our concepts? Do we never have an experience which we find hard to interpret, until a new framework – perhaps years later, say after a conversion, or simply growing wiser – makes sense of it, or different sense to the sense we originally made? Do beings without language – animals, infants and the deaf-mute – have no experience? While it is certainly naïve to think we always first have an experience, and then find words to express it, the relation between experience and words is surely more mutually interactive than Katz suggests.

The interplay of experience and idea, such that sometimes experience demands new ideas, but also ideas shape experiences, is – as Turner points out – one of the things that moves us in writings like Augustine's *Confessions*. The book is both a biography of his own experience, and a theological exploration, *at one and the same time*. We see his conceptual framework changing from Manichaeism through Neoplatonism to Christianity, and this development is at once intellectual, emotional and experiential. Each factor grows through interaction with the other. Experience need not always be cart, in the way that Katz suggests, and never horse.

Without a framework of interpretation, spiritual experience is certainly impoverished. It is as it were left dangling as a kind of extraordinary curiosity, without impact on our lives as a whole. The descriptions of spiritual experience by Huxley, Stace, Wainwright and Forman are curiously empty, and remote from the richness of actual spiritual writings. The accounts get interesting only when some conceptual framework is applied to the experiences, whether that framework derives from the writer's own religion (Zaehner), from a philosophical framework (Otto, the perennialists), from a combination of the two (von Hügel, Buber, the Neo-Thomists, Turner, Forman), or including other sources like psychology and anthropology (Wilber). Frameworks like this are the conceptual machinery we need to make spiritual experience do real work in our lives.

So if some of the theophanies discussed in Chapter 1 proved formative for Christian spirituality, being retold time and again by the spiritual writers, it was through the frameworks generated by telling them – and also through the wisdom and apocalyptic frameworks thrown up by the later felt *absence* of specific theophanies – that they exerted this great influence. The experiences themselves, whatever they were, are lost in the mists of history.

So the critiques of Katz and Turner – in their different ways – have left their mark indelibly on the study of spirituality. If there is a return in some quarters to the emphasis on experience in spirituality, the focus is no longer on special 'experiences', but rather on the whole experience of people engaged – through the celebration of ritual and daily life, and the imaginative exploration of the 'faithscapes' their beliefs and imaginations map out – in some kind of spiritual journey of their life as a whole.

Experience or Experiences?

We use the term 'experiences' to denote specific events in our consciousness, but the singular term 'experience' is rather richer. Our 'experience' includes not just the experiences we have had but what we have made of them, and what they have made of us in our life as a whole. This includes the way we have felt them emotionally and the way we have interpreted them and been changed by them. So we 'put things down to experience'; and we speak of an 'experienced' person, meaning more than that they have had lots of individual experiences. In many languages, for example the Greek *pascho*, the word to experience, to suffer and to be changed is the same.

To conclude, *spirituality is and is not a matter of experience*. It is not mainly about experiences so much as experience. Experience is a matter of experiences *and* conceptual interpretation, which are always interacting. Experiences are not *caused* by our conceptual framework; for experience may take the lead and demand a change to the framework. But without a framework we will not be able to share what we have experienced, even with ourselves. We will not understand what we have experienced, though we may be able to remember it, and understand later. And it is not the experiences themselves, but the process of sharing and understanding those experiences and relating them to our and other life journeys, that is rightly termed 'spirituality'.

That is why the following chapters will look in turn at the possible frameworks of sharing, understanding and relating to life supplied by science, theological belief, embodied practice, psychology, ethics and human difference.

Spiritual Experience: God's Experience?

And in the process we will perhaps begin to grasp the difference a Christian stance might make to the role of experience. As Turner argues, Christians must never imagine they have experienced God if this means they have got God, as it were in their experiential or conceptual sights. But there is another way in which experience can function in a Christian spirituality. In line with Gilson, Rowan Williams argues: 'Knowledge of God is not a subject's conceptual grasp of an object, it is sharing what God is – more boldly, you might say, sharing God's "experience"' (1979, p. 13). For Christians – Gilson and Williams argue – God is the subject, not the object, of 'spiritual experience'. The goal of Christian spirituality, for them, is not to experience God, but to experience everything as God does.

If they are right, then the two matters considered at the end of Chapter 1 – the spirituality of Jesus, and the spiritual experience that he was and is for his believers – merge after all. If the spirituality of Jesus did not consist in ineffable experiences he had, but the experience of God and the world he conveyed, then that experience of God and the world might be what can still be glimpsed through encounter with his teaching and the people it has impacted. Christian spirituality – distinctively – might mean developing what St Paul termed 'the mind of Christ' (1 Cor. 2.16), or in more Trinitarian terms, being inspired by the Spirit with the love of Jesus for the Father, and the Father for him, and both for the world. But these are vulnerable claims you must test out as you read.

For Reflection and Discussion

1 Discuss your initial views of the following. Then see if your views have changed after reading the chapter.

- Are there such things as 'spiritual experiences' and can you give examples?
- Have you had any?
- Can spiritual experiences be artificially induced, and if so, how?
- Are such experiences 'cognitive' – that is, do they relate to any reality?
- Can they be scientifically explained, and if so, how?
- Are they all of one kind or several different kinds?
- Do they all relate to the same reality?

2 As you go through the accounts of spiritual experience in this chapter, note which accounts seem to tally with the Old Testament theophanies related in Chapter 1, and which seem to relate to a different kind of experience.

3 Which of the accounts of spiritual experience make most sense to you? And do you think it makes sense to try and classify it?

4 What do you find helpful in Canda's definition on p. 120, and what not?

5 Can you think of experiences you have had that you have only understood later? Or has understanding, in your life, always preceded experience?

6 Discuss the quotation from Williams on p. 123, and in what ways it rings true or not. Are the writers considered in Part 1 trying to communicate their own experience of God, or a divine experience of the world?

Further Reading

Martin Buber, 1976, *I and Thou*, Edinburgh: T&T Clark.

Aldous Huxley, 1945, *The Perennial Philosophy*, New York: Harper.

William James, 1983, *The Varieties of Religious Experience*, Harmondsworth: Penguin.

Steven Katz, ed., 1978, *Mysticism and Philosophical Analysis*, London: Sheldon.

Rudolf Otto, 1958, *The Idea of the Holy*, Oxford and New York: Oxford University Press.

Denys Turner, 1998, *The Darkness of God: Negativity in Christian Mysticism*, Cambridge, Cambridge University Press.

Evelyn Underhill, 1937, *The Spiritual Life*, London: Hodder and Stoughton.

R. C. Zaehner, 1969, *Mysticism, Sacred and Profane*, Oxford: Oxford University Press.

8

Contemplative Questioning? Spirituality and Science

People these days probably tend to place science and spirituality in very different categories. The scientific world of hard, clear objectivity and the precision of the machine and the calculator seem a long way from the subjective world of rather vague personal emotion which many associate with spirituality. Each 'world' has fierce advocates that insist that it alone has the answers to life's problems, while the other is a world of dangerous delusion.

And yet there may be aspects that unite both worlds. Both science and spirituality can be disciplined and rigorous (though the latter is not always so). Both can give rise to wonder and joy. Both – though some on either side would dispute this – can help give rise to wisdom. And God is found by many in both, and (witness Buddhist spirituality) necessitated by neither.

Both science and spirituality have connections with philosophy. In the English-speaking world, till recently, philosophers have often regarded science as the surest way to get at the truth, so that a lot of their effort went into understanding scientific method. But in its older sense of 'friendship with wisdom', philosophy is not far from spirituality in its aim.

In this chapter we shall explore the originally close relationships between philosophy, science and spirituality. We shall consider whether science and spirituality have more connections in their approach and method than either realizes, and then turn to look at the different 'worlds' these methods claim to access, and alternative ways of relating the natural and spiritual 'worlds'. Finally we shall consider whether spirituality can rightly claim, along (perhaps) with science and philosophy, to impart wisdom.

Science, Mathematics and Contemplation

The mystical quest seems to reach out beyond the scientific or the rationally knowable; but that does not mean it cannot include the scientific, or that it needs to be antithetical to it. While modern 'folklore' tells the story of classical science being driven underground by the mystical twaddle of the ages of faith, only to re-emerge at the Renaissance, another view (Jaki, 1986) notes that modern science (as distinct from the speculative intimations of science we find in the ancient world) developed mainly in lands dominated by Christianity, with its understanding of the universe as not itself too sacred to investigate, but rather, subject to divine laws we can discover. In medieval times several mystics were scientists, like Hildegard, or mathematicians, like Nicholas of Cusa, while the pioneer English scientist Roger Bacon was a Franciscan friar. Several great Renaissance scientists – including Johannes Kepler (below) – were inspired by Neoplatonic mysticism.

Moreover, though we read the likes of Dionysius, Maximus, Hildegard and Bonaventure as typically 'mystical' in intent, they can be argued to possess the embryo of scientific method. For them, the scientific contemplation of the forms taken by nature was the beginning of the contemplation of God.

> It is the work of the highest goodness not only to have created the divine and incorporeal natures of mental creatures as a reflection of the ineffable Divine glory ... but also to have imprinted clear traces of its greatness in sensory creatures ... for these traces can transport directly to God a human mind, which ponders deeply over them, making it soar above all visible things and leading it, as it were, into the realm of higher bliss. (Maximus in Kadloubovsky, 1954, p. 161)

The broad pattern of spiritual 'ascent' for these writers is:

1 observation of nature;
2 grasping of its underlying patterns or forms;

3 contemplating these forms as the names, outward expressions or energies of God;

4 reaching out in love to the unknowable being of God.

The first two stages are the familiar endeavour of science, while stage 3 is one that some contemporary cosmologists (Davies, 1992; Penrose, 1994) do not hesitate to make as they try to use their discoveries to probe 'the mind of God'. In an age dominated by science, however, many are remarkably ignorant of the contemplative beauty science and mathematics can evoke, so here we try to provide just a taster.

Mathematical Mysticism

Plato's philosophy of contemplative ascent was based on the discovery through geometry of the remarkably beautiful and 'eternal' order, shape and symmetry underlying the apparent chaos of the world. As an example, consider Plato's own discovery of the 'Platonic solids'.

At school we probably all learned about the regular polygons – ways of enclosing a two-dimensional space with a number of equal one-dimensional lines. Three lines form an equilateral triangle, four a square, five a pentagon and so on. We can form an infinite number of regular polygons in this way – see Figure 1. Plato was interested in the next step up: using a number of identical two-dimensional polygons to enclose a solid three-dimensional space, making a 'Platonic solid'. Plato discovered that there are only three ways of making such a solid with triangles, one with squares, one with pentagons, and none with hexagons or any higher polygon. These five possibilities are depicted in Figure 2.

Nowhere in any real or possible imaginary universe does any other Platonic solid exist. The laws constraining imaginative construction are so strict that not even God could invent a new Platonic solid! (He might change the laws of mathematics, but then Platonic solids, and geometry as we know it, would not exist.)

Now the mathematical imagination does not stop with a mere three dimensions! Space with four or more dimensions is another of those wonderful but barely imaginable ideas with which scientists work. So mathematicians inevitably asked what happens when we try to enclose 'four-dimensional space' with

Figure 1: Regular Polygons

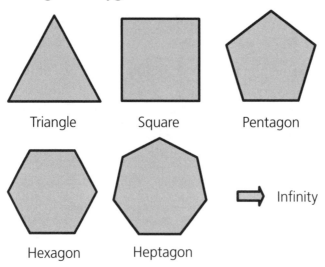

Triangle   Square   Pentagon

Hexagon   Heptagon   Infinity

Figure 2: The Platonic Solids

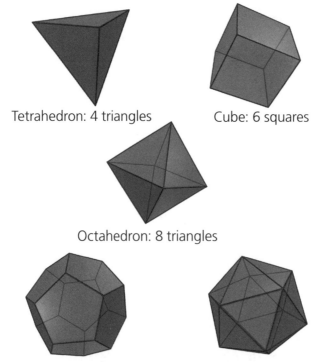

Tetrahedron: 4 triangles   Cube: 6 squares

Octahedron: 8 triangles

Dodecahedron: 12 pentagons   Icosahedron: 20 triangles

Figure 3: Four-dimensional Solids

Pentachoron: 5 tetrahedra   Hypercube: 8 cubes

Orthoplex: 16 tetrahedra   120-cell: 120 dodecahedra

600-cell: 600 tetrahedra   24-cell: 24 octahedra

a set of identical Platonic solids! One might have thought that four-dimensional space would be like Narnia, offering free scope for the imagination, but far from it. Mathematicians have worked out that there are no more and no less than six four-dimensional solids – they are depicted in Figure 3, and more information about them is to be found at http://math.ucr.edu/home/baez/platonic.html. (You must imagine all the lines are straight and of equal length, but distorted in

Figures 1 to 3 are constructed from figures in the Wikipedia site http://en.wikipedia. org/wiki/List_of_regular_polytopes (February 2008), which are licensed by the author, Fritz Obermeier, to the public domain.

the diagrams in order to flatten four-dimensional space onto a two-dimensional page.)

What about even higher dimensions than four? Do they offer more scope to the imagination? Apparently not. It turns out that in each higher kind of space – five dimensional, six dimensional and however high one wants to go – only three regular solids are possible.

Such speculation may seem pointless; but as well as being wonderful to contemplate, our speculations often turn out to be mirrored in reality. Indeed science can be described as the process of inventing (or constructing) mathematically coherent patterns (these days called 'models') and then finding out which pattern the actual world exemplifies. When we find that out we know Plato's eternal pattern or 'form' underlying the temporal. Plato himself tried to explain the basic elements of the world in terms of his five solids. He was wrong, but, in terms of scientific method, right to try.

Science, in this sense, involves a contemplative 'ascent', or some would prefer to say, a contemplative penetration beneath the surface, a search first to *imagine* or construct worlds that might be there, and then to *attend* to which of these 'worlds' is actually there.

Biophilia and the Infinite Regress

The beauty of the worlds of mathematics – including that particular mathematically described world we inhabit – is familiar to any who has explored it, and elicits what I have termed (1990) a 'spirituality of matter'. E. O. Wilson writes (1986) of his 'biophilia' or love of all the forms of life. To judge by the popularity of TV nature and science programmes, it seems that this is a love many people share.

In biology many who reject the notion of a designer or 'watchmaker' God (Wilson, 2006; Dawkins, 2006) do so not because they see the universe as lacking order, but because they believe it does not do justice to the kind of ordered beauty they encounter. It is arguable that such writers are rejecting a 'watchmaker' understanding of God because it suggests a mechanistic and rather prosaic and utilitarian Creator, and they feel this demeans the numinous mystery of the universe (Maitland, 1995), which has a remarkable habit of being amenable to rational analysis, but never completely. Each theory leaves something unsolved, forcing the scientist to reach out further, never reaching complete understanding but rather Nicholas of Cusa's 'learned ignorance' (p. 65). The scientist, probing ever deeper into this infinite regress of explanations, is perhaps not unlike Gregory's Moses on the Mountain, reaching out into the unknowable fastnesses of God.

Scientific and Spiritual Method

One might have expected the mathematical imagination to have spiralled away from the earth in its construction of fantasy worlds. But we have seen that its explorations 'discover' or 'invent' unexpected laws, and touch on what mathematicians like Roger Penrose and philosophers like Karl Popper believe to be a real world. Popper (1972) termed it 'World 3', believing it distinct from the worlds of matter and consciousness. Be that as it may, the mathematical laws prove profoundly productive of discoveries and inventions in those other two 'worlds'. Could the mystical imagination work in the same way? Many suspect that spirituality is fantasy, spiralling away from the earth. But the evidence of its history suggests that it too discovers (or invents?) unexpected patterns and regularities, which prove profoundly productive of wisdom and action in the world.

We can make this more specific. Denys's categories of kataphatic, apophatic and symbolic ways of knowing God (p. 28) suggest fertile comparisons and contrasts between mystical and scientific ways of knowing.

1 Science has a **kataphatic** interest in observing and correlating data, so that complex data are subsumed under simple laws. Spirituality likewise strives both to be sensitive to the complexity of experience and to seek simplicity and integrity within it. But of course, spiritual wisdom does not come about by way of experiments in which we manipulate experience and test out theories. If anything, the seeker is herself the 'experiment', who tests out her beliefs in her life, aiming for a grasp of the one reality unifying all her experience.

2 Science balances this with an **apophatic** dimension of critique. According to Karl Popper (2002) scientists actually try to ensure that their theories are falsifiable, and to be detached enough to dispense with them when falsified by

the facts. They are seeking the 'unprejudiced, unthinking blind sight we call scientific objectivity' (Daston and Galison, 2007, p. 16). Now while religious people have a reputation for dogmatism – refusing to countenance anything that would make them change their beliefs – the spiritual or mystical trend in religion combines such passionate commitment with provisionality and readiness to let go. Spirituality in the tradition that leads through Gregory of Nyssa, Eriugena and Eckhart, bids us let go of beliefs that no longer square with life, refusing to idolize concepts of God, but reaching out to the one who surpasses all expression.

3 Science operates, as we have seen, by constructing **models**, which give meaning to scientific laws and formulae in the process of subsuming a range of experience under them. Black holes, the atom, evolution, the ecosphere and superstrings are all models that make sense of a range of experiences by bringing them together under scientific laws. Models refer to no literal reality, but explain and predict real experience. In this they resemble the *symbols* of theology, which must not be taken literally, but must engage us with reality. However, scientific models are usually mathematically precise. Such precision is only claimed in poor, pretentious theology.

There is a tension in spirituality between the demands of 1 and 2. The experiment that proves a spirituality valid – if anything does – must be a whole life wholly committed to it. But if it is an experiment that is involved, a readiness to be found wrong, and to seek deeper, is also required. Can one be passionately committed to one's ideal and yet ready to let it go? Mystics like Eckhart suggest that is precisely the paradox Christian spirituality requires; and we are suggesting that only spirituality like that stands a chance of relating to reality in the way science does.

Theories of Everything and the Mind of God

It might be argued, then, that the big differences between spiritual and scientific method can be ascribed to the no less immense difference between God and creatures as far as understanding is concerned. Scientific method might be nothing other than spiritual method adapted to knowledge of creatures rather than the Creator.

However, Donald Mackinnon points out (in Katz, 1978) that the mystical vision is not the same as a kind of synoptic all-embracing vision that some scientific 'theory of everything' might one day provide. 'The transition from such experience to the mystical involves a *metabasis eis allos genos*' (transformation into other categories – p. 134). For mysticism is not a matter of subsuming everything that is under a single formula; rather it is 'to see ourselves as God sees us . . . to grasp . . . what we are in God's love' (p. 135). Contrary to the hopes of cosmologists (e.g. Davies, 1992) not even a 'theory of everything' will reveal 'the mind of God' in that sense.

Spirituality and the Universe of Science

So much for parallels and contrasts between the way science and spirituality approach reality. But probably more people are aware of contrasts between 'reality' as conceived by science and the 'reality' – if such it is – experienced on the spiritual journey. Does the spiritual journey take place in the world we know from science, does it construct the world in a different way, or does it access another, 'supernatural' world? These are the questions we turn to now.

Here are some possible answers, each of which gives rise to a different kind of spirituality in relation to the scientific universe.

- **Dualism.** Spirituality and science belong to different worlds. For classical Western Catholicism, there is a hard distinction between the 'natural' and the 'supernatural' realms, though of course the latter is the ultimate foundation of the former, and spills over into it as 'grace'. For Pascal (p. 90) the God of faith had nothing whatever in common with 'the God of the philosophers'. Dualism has taken many forms throughout the history of spirituality, and despite being out of favour as a concept, is very much alive today in practice.
- **Deism.** The scientific world is a vast machine perfectly following God-given laws. God makes the cosmic 'watch' and winds it up, but thereafter it follows its own devices. Spirituality may include wonder at the marvellous devices of nature, but the remoteness of the watchmaker makes personal relationship difficult to establish.
- **Existential awe.** This is our term for something that requires a name: the

spirituality that abandons the deists' concern with pattern and design to the scientists, on the grounds that 'it is not *how* things are in the world that is the mystical, but *that* it exists' (Wittgenstein, 1961, p. 149). Spirituality focuses on the fundamental miracle of the world's contingency: that there is something rather than nothing at all. Such wonder is beautifully expressed in Mother Julian's fifth 'shewing' (1952, p. 9):

> He shewed me a little thing, the quantity of an hazel-nut, in the palm of my hand; and it was as round as a ball. I looked thereupon with eye of my understanding, and thought: What may this be? And it was answered generally thus: It is all that is made. I marvelled how it might last, for methought it might suddenly have fallen to naught for littleness. And I was answered in my understanding: It lasteth, and ever shall, for that God loveth it. And so All-thing hath the Being by the love of God.

- **Observer participation.** The 'that' and the 'how' of things, however, may not be so distinct. Many current cosmological theories explain the fact *that* the universe exists by reference to its 'anthropic' structure, that is, by *how* it is structured to give rise to beings like us, capable of knowing it and wondering about its origin. We would not be here to wonder *that* the universe exists, if *how* it exists were not such as to make us exist. Some cosmologists, like John Wheeler, go further, arguing that quantum theory is best explained by the notion that the observer 'collapses' the field of possible worlds into the actual world observed. This means that human consciousness, which has evolved from the universe, actually also generates the universe, in a strange loop. Figure 4 depicts how this might work in the case of Mother Julian as she ponders the universe; the numbers and arrows correspond to the following stages.

1 Mother Julian and her consciousness have evolved from the universe. She is depicted as herself emerging from the 'universe' she marvels at in the palm of her hands.
2 From her and other minds, in turn, emerges a world of thought and imagination, including science, mathematics, theology and her own spiritual writings. As we have begun to see, this 'world' has its own laws, constraints and surprises.

Figure 4: Mother Julian's mystical loop

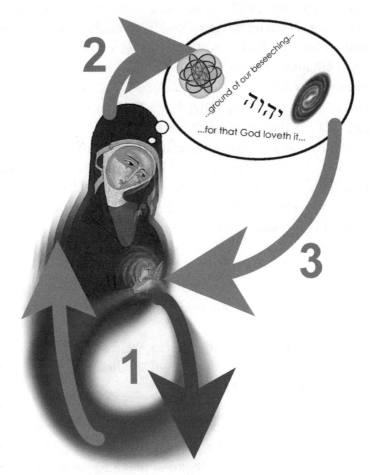

3 But out of this infinite array of imaginary and conceptual 'universes', Mother Julian's wonder and awareness 'select' the one that makes wonder and awareness possible. In a sense, her and our understanding and wonder are what sustains this universe and makes it, among the many possible universes, exist, rather than collapse into unknowable nothingness.

Penrose describes a more philosophical version of this loop (1994, pp. 413–4 developed in Thompson, 2002), while Hofstadter (1980, 1982) contains enchanting variations on the same theme. It suggests a 'mystical' quandary even greater, perhaps, than that which Wittgenstein pondered. However the loop gives to human consciousness a Godlike role in the creation of the

world, suggesting that when we feel we see a consciousness that has benevo-
lently chosen to create this world, it is our own world-creating human mind
we are in fact seeing. Though Mahayana Buddhists might see here the workings of Buddha-Mind, probably few Christians would be happy with this
notion, except perhaps the likes of Eriugena, Eckhart and Cupitt.

- **Gaian or pantheist spirituality.** God is ultimately identical with the universe, or relates to the universe as soul to body. This has not been a popular
alternative in the Christian tradition. It has too many links with the pagan
cultures with which Christianity contended in its early days, and is felt to
compromise God's transcendence and render the incarnation redundant.
However it is certainly recovering popularity in feminist and 'New Age' spirituality. Ursula King notes the resurgence, against the widespread dualism of
the older Christian tradition, of 'a more integrated, naturalistic and panen-
theistic spirituality' (2002, p. 6), while Grace Jantzen has argued strongly
for seeing the world as God's body (1984). However, if we see the self or soul
as 'emerging' from the body and constituting a distinct 'level', this account
develops into the next, which may answer some of the criticisms regarding
transcendence.
- **Spirituality of Emergence.** The idea of emergence emerges from two con-
siderations (see Thompson, 1990, pp. 205–10; Kaufman, 1995, pp. 23–4;
Goldstein, 1999; Johnson, 2001; Morowitz, 2002).

1 Different discourses are appropriate to different levels of reality. A physi-
   cist may investigate the molecules my blood is made of, a biologist my
   arm and how it has evolved, a psychologist the causes of my behaviour,
   an ethicist its effects in wider society, and a theologian the relation of my
   whole life to God.
2 In time, however, one 'level' gives rise seamlessly to 'another'. Atoms give
   rise to life; my mind or brain gives rise to moral (or immoral) actions, and
   so on.

Emergence is essentially that seamless causality which operates from a
lower level to a higher one. Life emerges from matter, consciousness from
life, and so on . . . The seamless unity of causality (1) negates dualism, while
the discreteness of the levels (2) defies mechanistic, reductionist or pantheist
accounts.

Emergence can be explained in a number of ways. Aristotle provided a better account than Plato, believing as he did that the forms were not eternal, but always linked with matter as it strives to realise itself in ever new ways, in a process he termed *entelechy* (inward purpose). *Pierre Teilhard de Chardin* (1881–1955) with his optimistic notion of a sequence of spheres of reality giving rise to ever higher forms – the biosphere or sphere of life giving rise to the noosphere or sphere of thought, and all converging on Christ as the Omega point at the end – may be seen as an early proponent of a spirituality of emergence. More recently, Murphy and Ellis (1996) have boldly presented ethics and theology as higher levels resting on a rather over-tidy hierarchy of natural levels.

Spirituality is and is not Wisdom

In Chapter 2 we saw how, as Christianity spread into a world of alien Greek concepts, it was able to ally the wisdom inherent in its own tradition, not least in the teaching of Christ, with the Greek 'love of wisdom'. By marrying the traditions represented by Moses' mountain and Plato's cave, arguably, the Christian mystical tradition came into its own. Though this process was not without loss (p. 32) it made Christian faith intelligible while safeguarding the unintelligible, the mystery. At least until the Middle Ages developed a rationalistic, academic theology, and late medieval and Reformation spirituality responded by becoming more subjective and psychological, spirituality was primarily engagement with the mystery of participation in God, Father, Son and Spirit.

Christian spirituality emerges as both being and not being identifiable with philosophy, science or wisdom. There is deep spirituality involved in scientific method and enquiry, but spirituality cannot be reduced to any theory, not even a 'theory of everything'. A category leap – or perhaps, a leap of levels – is necessary if we are to pass from a synoptic vision of the universe to the knowledge and love of God.

Overpowered by our own Omnipotence?

We also know today – with the H-bomb, the technological rape of the environment, and growing possibilities of 'eugenic' gene manipulation – that scientific knowledge does not of itself impart the wisdom to use its knowledge well. Just as spirituality that spirals away from scientific understanding can be escapist and arrogant, so science without spirituality can be terribly vulnerable to fascination with its own technological inventions.

> Mysticism provides us with a reason above rationalism; it forbids us to live contentedly in that world of half-lights which the lower reason is so ready to systematise, and in so doing, to distort fatally. (Inge, 1959, p. 61)

A spiritual wisdom, purified by the asceticism of scientific objectivity, is necessary if humans are to temper and master the very omnipotence science seems to open up for them. If people are not to be paradoxically overpowered by their fast growing omnipotence, they need to grow patiently in humble understanding of the human and ecological ends it should be serving.

For Reflection and Discussion

1 Write the ten words that first come to mind in connection with the word 'scientific'. (Try not to think to hard, just use free association, bearing in mind there are no 'right' answers.) Now write the ten words that first come to mind in relation to the word 'spiritual'. Now place the following words under the headings 'scientific' and 'spiritual' or both or neither, as seems appropriate to you:

hard	clear	objective
subjective	machine	calculation
precise	power	personal
dangerous	rigour	discipline
wisdom	feeling	wonder
delusion	mind	heart
joy	suffering	God.

Compare your answers – are there similar words or are they very different?

2 Write the first ten words that come to mind in connection with 'philosophy', and again, compare this with the lists you have made for 'spirituality' and 'science'. Can you summarize the similarities and differences between these concepts?

3 If God cannot invent another Platonic solid, what does this say to you about God, the world and the imagination?

4 Discuss the notion that spirituality differs from science only because God is other than the universe. In particular, what do you make of the notion that our lives are the experiment in which our beliefs are put to the test?

5 Which of the views on pp. 133–7 makes most sense to you, and why?

Further Reading

John Davies, 1992, *The Mind of God: Science and the Search for Ultimate Meaning*, Harmondsworth: Penguin.

Bede Griffiths, 1990, *A New Vision of Reality: Western Science, Eastern Mysticism and Christian Faith*, Springfield: Templegate.

Stanley Jaki, 1986, *Creation and Science*, Edinburgh: Scottish Academic Press.

Steven Johnson, 2001, *Emergence: The Connected Lives of Ants, Brains, Cities, and Software*, New York: Scribners.

Sara Maitland, 1995, *A Big Enough God: Artful Theology*, London and New York: Mowbray.

Ross Thompson, 1990, *Holy Ground: The Spirituality of Matter*, London: SPCK.

9

A Kind of Knowing?
Spirituality and Theology

Anthony de Mello (1983, pp. 46–7) relates a probably apocryphal story of a walk the devil once took with a close friend. Ahead of them, they saw a man pick up something from the road. On being asked what it might be, the devil declared that it was a piece of truth. The man voiced his worry that such a discovery might disturb the devil, but the devil made light of it, saying that the man would probably make a religion out of his piece of truth, so there was nothing for them to worry about!

For some, spiritual truth and religious belief are integrally related; for others, spiritual truth emerges from religious systems; for others, it is the grit around which the theological pearl is formed; while for yet others, like de Mello, the systematization of truth into religion is the devil's work, always distorting the truth and cramping the spirit.

The history of Christianity can be told as climaxing in the Church's attempts – at first full of apostolic zeal and comprehensive vision, but later, perhaps because of the very spiritual hungers and ideals it unleashed among the laity, increasingly desperate and oppressive – to bring the whole of society under the reign of religious faith. After that it is possible to discern the gradual emergence of personal spirituality from the theological framework that arguably gave it birth – an emergence that some argue is still proceeding apace in our time (Heelas, 2004). In other chapters we relate spirituality to wider aspects of human concern, but here we ask whether this emergence of spirituality from the reign of theology is liberating or disastrous; whether spirituality really 'belongs' to theology or not.

Mystical Theology

In Chapter 2 we saw how Christian theologians bent concepts derived from Neoplatonism in increasingly radical ways to make sense of their apprehension of Christ, generating in the process the classic doctrines of creation, Trinity and incarnation. Louth describes the interaction involved (1981, xi):

> Mystical theology provides the context for direct apprehensions of the God who has revealed himself in Christ and dwells within us through the Holy Spirit; while dogmatic theology attempts to incarnate those apprehensions in objectively precise terms which then, in their turn, inspire a mystical understanding of the God who has thus revealed himself.

On this view dogmatic theology tries to conceptualize the direct experience of mystical theology, in a manner that can lead in turn to further spiritual encounters. Meanwhile from a Russian Orthodox perspective, Vladimir Lossky (1957, p. 8) writes:

> We must live the dogma expressing a revealed truth, which appears to us as an unfathomable mystery, in such a fashion that instead of assimilating the mystery to our mode of understanding, we should, on the contrary, look for a profound change, an inner transformation of spirit, enabling us to experience it mystically.

Louth and Lossky, taken together, suggest that doctrines are rather like seeds, which grow to produce mystical fruit, which contain in themselves the seeds of further doctrine, which produce further mystical fruit, in an ongoing cycle.

Seed or Fruit?

If horticulture were our concern, it would be 'fruitless' to ask whether the 'core' of what we were growing lay in seed or fruit. But for theology there is an important question about where the knowledge lies, or where the process engages with God or reality, which different theologies answer differently. Is God primarily communicated in the 'word' of conceptual thought – in the words of scripture or creed, for example, or in dogmatic and systematic theology – which spirituality then clothes as it were in the 'flesh' of human experience and transformation? Or is God primarily revealed in the 'flesh' of transformed human experience – in Christian spirituality – which doctrine encapsulates and passes on for future generations in logical and systematic terms? Is theological truth – if such there is – clarified primarily through logical reflection on the mysteries once revealed to it, or through the ongoing human experience of the Church where the Holy Spirit dwells? We need a little more reflection to clarify these contentious issues.

In this chapter we will try to achieve a little of this clarification by examining three models of the possible relation between mysticism or spirituality and conceptual or systematic theology. Then we will move on, in the light of a positive critique of those models, to suggest a theory of theological knowledge that places spirituality at its heart. But we will have to be brief, and can only offer a preliminary sketch-map of the issues, to help you in your own reflections and investigations.

Climbing the Mountain: The Traditional Place of Mystical Theology

The monks and scholastics were agreed on a point that would now be contentious: that contemplation lies at the summit of both monastery and university. We are already familiar with the model, current (with subtle variations) from Denys through to Bonaventure, illustrated in Figure 5, where we move through three stages:

- **Kataphatic** affirmation of God's presence in the things he has made. The natural and human sciences can clearly have a role here, as well as the natural or philosophical theology which begins to move by the power of reason up the slopes to the next stage.
- **Symbolic** theologies, using the things of this world as analogies or pointers to the unseen and unimaginable God. Aquinas argued that the act of creation itself means that all things are analogies of God. But the incarnation, God's own choice to express his life in material and human form, realizes

Figure 5: The Original Mystical Mountain

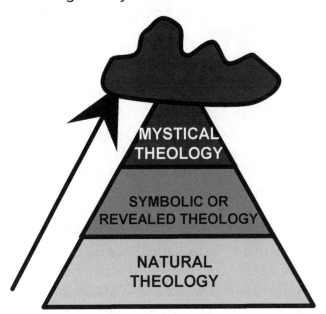

the potential of matter and humanity to symbolize God, forming the basis of
systematic and doctrinal theology, which takes us further up the mountain.

- **Mystical or apophatic** theology, at the summit, contemplating God in his
naked, inexpressible transcendence. Some writers emphasize that the view
from the mountain-top encompasses the lower slopes. Others stress the
dark cloud of radical unknowing that is entered at this stage, shutting out
things below and God above, the latter being reached not through reason but
through a love that means an eternal 'reaching out'.

Despite the immense authority this model has in the Christian tradition, it
would be hard indeed to adopt it in the universities and academies of today.

1 It is a linear march, without the circles of feedback we now expect in any
   genuine knowledge. Though she may have been inspired by the scientific
   stage, the mystic at the highest stage has nothing to learn from doing any
   more science.
2 It is unclear in the tradition itself whether mystical theology completes or
   subverts all knowledge.

3 It is inherently confessional, binding spirituality to a Christian understanding of revelation, and giving theology an imperial role that few in the academy could now accept.

So while spirituality and religion can be studied in the university, claims to theological truth are greeted with the embarrassment and sarcasm described by Brummett (in Buley-Meissner, 2000, p. 125). However, Brummett notes that it is not so much the case that theology has surrendered its reign in the academy to a democracy of equal disciplines, as that the physical sciences have taken over the reign, and now constitute the paradigm for all academic method in the way that theology once did. The anti-theological rhetoric of Dawkins and Wilson is reminiscent of the heresy-hunting theologians of old, yet many find it academically acceptable. And the main contender for academic hegemony is a deconstructive 'cultural studies' no less hostile, in general, to theology.

Nevertheless, contemplative attention in some sense can still be seen as lying at the heart of scientific enquiry (Chapter 8) and academic enquiry in general (Weil, 2001; Thompson, 2004). And it may be integral to the understanding of ideas and the listening to students that academic learning requires (Lindholm in Buley-Meissner, 2000, pp. 55–67). The challenge remains – to develop a model for the place of theology, with spirituality and contemplation within it, based on a sound theory of knowledge, without making imperialistic claims for theology or for any limited confessional understanding.

Up and Down the Mountain: Lonergan's Theological Method

A big step in this direction, arguing a precise – perhaps over-precise – place for spiritual love at the heart of the academic enterprise of theology, has been taken by Bernard Lonergan, a Canadian theologian in the tradition of Thomas Aquinas.

Figure 6 is our depiction of Lonergan's method as the ascent *and descent* of a four-level mountain. The levels are those Lonergan discerns in the process of knowing (1973, p. 9):

Figure 6: Lonergan's Mountain

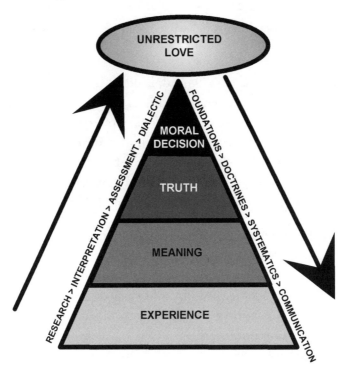

- **Empirical**: assimilating data – experiencing and perceiving things, and imagining possibilities.
- **Intellectual:** grasping meaning – understanding what we have experienced, and rightly expressing what we have understood in statements.
- **Rational**: judging truth – evaluating the truth, falsity, certainty or probability of the meaningful statements we have formulated.
- **Responsible:** discerning the best course of action on the basis of these truths, making moral decisions and carrying them out.

In theology (Lonergan, 1973, pp. 127–33) the process of knowing requires the same ordered process of empirical *research*, *interpretation*, historical *assessment* and '*dialectic*' to grapple with moral issues raised. This is the progress up the mountain towards integrated theological understanding. But theology also concerns the expression of faith, and in this process we descend the mountain from *foundations* (the moral expression of religious faith) through *doctrine* (general expression of Christian truth), *systematics* (making those truths meaningful to people today) and *communications* (creating things that convey those meanings).

At the apex of the whole process lies what Lonergan describes as unrestricted love:

> Being in love with God, as experienced, is being in love in an unrestricted fashion. All love is self-surrender, but being in love with God is being in love without limits or qualifications or conditions or reservations . . . [This] is not the product of our knowledge and choice. On the contrary, it dismantles and abolishes the horizon in which our knowing and choosing went on, and sets up a new horizon in which the love of God will transvalue our values and the eyes of that love will transform our knowing. (pp. 105–6)

In other words, after we have pieced together our experience into meaningful wholes, and used those to put together an objective world, and further, used our judgement about this world as a basis for sound ethical decisions, a further integration is required: surrender to the infinite horizon of unrestricted love, which for Lonergan is God. This 'conversion' then forms the basis of a new Christian life and the struggle to communicate it.

That unrestricted love is reminiscent of the mystics. But Lonergan sets his mysticism within a very ordered, linear rational process. What is missing is the way the 'descent' can feed back into the 'ascent': the fact that at any level of the mountain that we can, instead of going on up or down, as it were creep round the ledge to the other side. Thus our decisions and actions can feed back into our experiences. Differences in doctrine often feed back round into differences in historical judgement And perhaps the unrestricted mystical love should not just dwell at the apex of the process, but inform the whole of it?

Once we bend the process round in this way we arrive at a major alternative to the systematic and linear process that Lonergan describes, the 'pastoral cycle'.

Round and Round the Mountain: The Pastoral Cycle

The pastoral cycle combines theories of experiential learning (Kolb, 1984; Moon, 2004) with liberation theology and its prioritization of praxis. It has become

Figure 7: The Pastoral Cycle

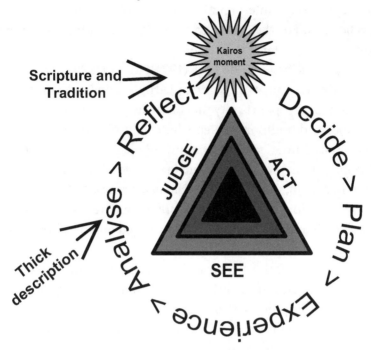

central to what is variously called pastoral or practical theology. Figure 7 is one illustration of it, developed from versions by Andrew Todd (unpublished) and liberation theologians. It describes an ongoing process of 'theological reflection' which is becoming recommended practice for all engaged in ministerial or pastoral practice (Graham, 2005; Thompson, 2008).

The central 'mountain' describes the core threefold process of seeing, judging and acting that is arguably involved in all practical knowledge. The rest of the diagram elaborates the systematic process of theological reflection, which has a varying number of stages and aspects for the different authors, from which this summary is distilled.

1 As with Lonergan's mountain, we begin with the raw data of **experience**.
2 The effort is made to **analyse** this experience. As with Lonergan, we try to interpret it and give it meaning. Very often a 'thick description' is composed where the experience is described from as many points of view as possible, including sociological and psychological insights.

3 Again, as with Lonergan (though often by a less defined gradation) we then move on to assess these interpretations and make judgements about truth through **reflection**. For the Christian believer, insights from scripture and faith tradition will be vital at this stage

4 Some writers, like Killen and de Beer (1994), Todd (1999) and Thompson (2008) emphasize a moment of insight, called by Todd a ***kairos* moment** from the Greek word for an opportunity that has to be grasped when it arrives. In this, experience and tradition suddenly 'inter-illuminate' and shed light on each other. It has a mystical quality akin to Lonergan's 'conversion' at the peak of the mountain, though it is by no means identical to that.

5 And as with Lonergan, this leads to a *metanoia*, a renewed understanding or change of heart leading to new goals to work for and new **decisions**.

6 Finally these goals and decisions have to be worked out in a **plan for action**.

This action, however, creates an objective difference in the world. Partly because of these objective changes, and partly because our understanding will have been changed in the reflective process, there will be a new experiences available and new ways of reflecting on them, thus setting the pastoral cycle turning once again. This is the process Lonergan does not describe, and which leads to a circle (or even a spiral – see Green, 2002) rather than a linear ascent and descent.

Essentially Lonergan is describing a one-off linear process whereby Christians reflect on the revelation they believe to have been given to them, and translate it into proclamation appropriate to today's world. The pastoral cycle, on the other hand, describes an ongoing process of reflecting on experience in the light of scriptural, traditional and contemporary resources. Lonergan and the pastoral theologians differ fundamentally over the 'seed or fruit' issue raised above. For Lonergan, revelation is the raw material, processed in the light of a spiritual conversion; for the pastoral cycle, ordinary experience is the raw material, processed in the light of revealed and other resources.

The Role of Spirituality

For both, however – though neither seems to say so explicitly – spirituality seems central. Lonergan's 'unrestricted love' is certainly reminiscent of many Christian mystics. Meanwhile the pastoral cycle concerns the inter-illumination of life and belief. It is most often presented as a way of enabling pastoral practitioners to process their experience in the light of their tradition, so as to achieve better practice: the focus is on 'life'. But if we shift the focus to achieving truer 'belief' about God, or a truer world vision in the light of belief, it comes closer to a mystical theology.

Indeed, theological reflection develops and enhances many of the practices – such as *lectio divina* and Ignatian meditation – that have long been familiar in the Christian spiritual tradition (Thompson, 2008, Chapter 4). But it tends – though there is no reason why this need be the case – to be situation-based and fragmentary. Spirituality might be said to name *the integrated discipline of relating one's whole experience to the whole of the tradition as one understands it, leading to a whole transformation of life that in turn regenerates all one experiences.* And mystical theology may then be nothing other than the *whole* of theology conceived on the model of the pastoral cycle, as an inter-illumination between experience and revelation leading to ethical practice that generates further experience and further inter-illumination . . .

The Cycle of Interactive Knowing

But can such cycles and spiralling ascents be seen as a basis of knowledge? Should spirituality be studied as an interesting human phenomenon, or should its truth claims be taken seriously alongside the truth claims of the many other disciplines studied in the academy?

Arguably, all knowledge involves interactive cycles of experience, reflection (applying belief and imagination) and often emotion, leading to decision and action and so to further experience. Consider the knowledge of the one who knows how to sail:

> As I pull on the sheet and feel the sail pull against me as it fills with the wind, as I move the rudder to give the maximum speed for the course I select . . . I live and I know the sea and the wind . . . There is . . . an area of control: my body, my limbs, and the boat . . . At the other end of the continuum there is an area of possible accident – unseen rocks, sudden gusts, unknown currents – which may just happen to me, outside my control . . . I know of the me and the not-me, through coming to know my powers and limits . . . The good

sailor, the one who has knowledge [of sailing], is the one who neither lets wind and wave take him where it will, nor sticks to a rigid preconception of where tiller and sail should be, but who adjusts what he controls sensitively to the changes he cannot control [in order to reach his goal]. (Thompson 1990, p. 125)

Knowing how to sail means being receptive to the experience of the wind and sea, processing this experience according to the sailing skills I have learned, and using these skills to effect changes to the rudder and sail that in turn change my relation to the environment and my experience of it. Could spirituality involve an analogous kind of know-how?

Spirituality as a Theological Cycle of Knowing

The pastoral cycle is arguably just this same cycle of interactive knowing, in which the belief brought to bear is not derived from the lore and expertise of sailors but the lore and expertise handed down in a religious tradition.

- In Chapter 7 we investigated the first part of what we now recognize as the pastoral cycle, **experience**. We suggested that spirituality was not a matter of special experiences conveying special knowledge to special mystics, but ordinary experience seen in the light of one's spirituality and faith tradition. This is experience as the pastoral cycle engages with it.
- We have considered the **philosophical and theological traditions** whereby spirituality processes experiences. In Chapter 2 we witnessed the way Greek philosophical categories were transformed in the light of the experience Christians were struggling to express. In Chapter 8 we suggested that the contemplative path of mystical theology was not alien from the methodology of science.
- In Chapter 3 we considered the **bodily practices** – sacramental, liturgical and communal – engendered by spirituality. Despite its historical hesitations about the body, spirituality can be thought to consist in the meanings that arise when we do religious things together with our bodies. But these meanings do not arise automatically, as it were, from our bodies, but from practice

that is informed by religious ideas and leads to new experience of the world; that is, from bodily practice that is part of the cycle that includes also experience and reflection.

But we can also now suggest that experience, tradition and practice hold together in a cycle that merely extends our ordinary practical ways of knowing the world. Just as the skill of sailing can give the sailor deeper knowledge of the world of sea and wind, enabling him to adapt his course if need be to reach his goals, so a religious tradition and the skills it embodies can, possibly, impart a deeper knowledge of God and the world, enabling us to change our course in the light of this knowledge to achieve the goals that matter. If that is so, then spirituality can be affirmed as the place where theology becomes knowledge through its impact on, and its impacting by, our everyday experience of the world. It is through spirituality that theology becomes a *kind* of science, imparting insights that, like those of science, lead us ever deeper into unknowing.

To develop our analogy, systematic theology strives to ensure that manuals of sailing are consistent with previous manuals and themselves, and written in up-to-date language that those without sailing expertise can understand. But it is spirituality that invites us to use them to learn to sail, and tests the manuals by the practice of sailing!

This means that *spirituality is and is not theology*. It is not simply the 'experiential' or 'moral' or 'practical' application of theology. It is no longer a linear theology at all, whether of ascent or application. For the cycle that enables knowledge disables any assurance of linear progress because it has to be open to the surprise of the not yet known. Spirituality is theology precisely in so far as theology can allow experience and practice to feed back into its systematic, theoretical formulations in something like the pastoral cycle.

Those are bold claims, which you must judge for yourself in the light of this book as a whole. Of course there is no claim here that any particular statement made by a spiritual or theological writer conveys knowledge. The claim is rather that there is a possibility that spiritual writings may embody the interactive engagement we call knowledge, so that those writings need to be taken seriously, and properly evaluated vis à vis contrary claims, by the academy, as well as – of course – by those engaged in the Christian spiritual search.

For Reflection and Discussion

1 What is your response to the de Mello story, and which of the suggested views about the relation between spiritual truth and religious belief do you take?
2 Do you find yourself embarrassed by, or embarrassing others by, religious truth claims made in academic or other settings? What do you think might lie at the root of this embarrassment?
3 What are the strengths and weaknesses, in your view, of Lonergan's notion of unrestricted love, and the role he gives it in theology?
4 Describe your experiences of 'theological reflection', whether structured or informal. In what way do you think one's spirituality can affect the outcome of theological reflection, or vice versa?
5 Is spirituality concerned with a knowledge of how to relate our potential to that of the world around us, similar to that required of the sailor? How does spirituality mediate between a passive 'go with the flow' and a rigid dogmatism about the course of our life? Can you think of spiritualities that fail to keep this balance?
6 Evaluate the suggestion that in spirituality, theology becomes a kind of science.

Further Reading

Joseph Flanagan, 1997, *Quest for Self-knowledge: An Essay in Lonergan's Philosophy*, Toronto: University of Toronto Press.

Elaine Graham, Heather Walton and Frances Ward, 2005, *Theological Reflection: Methods*, London: SCM Press.

G. D. Kaufman, 1995, *An Essay on Theological Method*, Cambridge: Harvard University Press.

Andrew Louth 1999, *Discerning the Mystery: An Essay on the Nature of Theology*, Oxford: Clarendon Press.

Judith Thompson with Stephen Pattison and Ross Thompson, 2008 (anticipated): *Studyguide to Theological Reflection*, London: SCM Press.

Andrew Todd, Michael West and Graham Noble, 1999, *Living Theology*, London: DLT.

10

Temple or Temptation?
Spirituality and the Body

In James Morrow's black comedy, *Towing Jehovah*, God has unexpectedly died of unknown causes, and his vast body has fallen out of the heavens into the Atlantic Ocean below. God's death is decidedly bad PR for the Church and prompts the obvious need for a good old Vatican conspiracy. So rather than leave God's two-mile-long corpse floating face up in the Atlantic, a grieving archangel recruits a former disgraced sea captain, Anthony Van Horne, to haul the Corpus Dei to a secret ice-hewn tomb prepared for a discreet burial at the North Pole. Bury God where he cannot be found and nobody need be any the wiser and the Church can go on functioning as if nothing of any real significance had happened. God might be dead but the Curia decide that the faithful need know nothing about it. Van Horne readily agrees, eager to redeem himself for indirectly causing the century's worst oil spill. And so he resumes command of his newly repaired supertanker, and speeds north, with God in tow.

En route Van Horne is faced by marauding predators who attack from air and sea. He meets a series of setbacks as absurd as the notion of the divine cargo he is towing. Perhaps the most amusing setback is an attempt at bombing and sinking the tanker made by a feminist castaway whom Van Horne had rescued. Eyeing up the cargo, the feminist notices that God has male genitalia and so she sets out to castrate the patriarchal corpse and then destroy it for the sake of oppressed womankind. For she opines that if the world were to discover that God really was male, then, as a corollary, males would indeed be God. So it is that on board the tanker sailors, theologians, atheists and feminists hammer out the stark implications of God's demise with questions like: Could God ever have a body?

God was male? God is dead? The Church is embarrassed by divine corporeality? Insight is laid upon insight as the whole sacrilegious comedy unfolds; the
journey is a slow one but one laden with amusing episodes, as through the icy
waters the divine corpse is hauled, by its ears, to the North Pole.

Now the point of our beginning with Morrow's story of fiction is that we
want to suggest that his tale raises issues pertinent to this chapter. We have
already noted a deep ambiguity at the heart of the Christian spiritual tradition.
On the one hand Christian ideas centred on the incarnation expressed themselves in ongoing bodily and corporate ways of life, but on the other hand, and
especially in monasticism, a prevailing suspicion of the body began to dominate
and thus tilt the Christian spiritual tradition in the direction of an asexual form
of spiritual life.

However, as the twentieth century closed and the twenty-first century began,
this ambiguity in the Christian spiritual tradition came under siege, and
remains so. Witness the current Anglican split on the issue of human sexuality
and you will appreciate that the body and its passions have become increasingly problematic for the Church. Witness too a whole host of voices with which
the Christian spiritual tradition must dialogue on issues of corporeality: the
critique of the dualist model of 'the ghost in the machine' by philosophers
like Gilbert Ryle (1970); the feminist critique of patriarchy; and the prevailing
notion of a 'permissive society' in which sex is liberated from procreation and
repression. It is not just feminists who are now on board the mythical supertanker. Many seek answers as to how the Christian spiritual tradition became
so emasculated and why the body was viewed as a thing to be tugged through
life and its passions put on ice. This chapter seeks to provide some.

The Bible and the Body

It is one of the great mysteries of the history of Christian spirituality, never
adequately explained, that a religion so grounded in the belief that God created
a 'good' world – a world in which God is best conceived through God's self-
expression of Godself in human flesh – could become so suspicious of the
body and so terrified of sexual pleasure. 'The Word made flesh, is here made
word again' (Muir, 1960, p. 228). Despite Christianity's central beliefs that God
created all matter, that the divine is revealed in and through human history and

that, most important of all, God has become incarnate in a human body, much of Christian tradition has been troubled by the whole concept of embodiment, both God's and our own.

The blame for this corporeal concern is often laid at the feet of Neoplatonic philosophy (Chapter 3) but, in reality, the roots of this discomfort can be found closer to home in aspects of the Judaism into which Christianity was first conceived. At its most extreme, Judaism could manifest its suspicion of both passion and the body (especially in its female form).

> The culture of patriarchy into which both Judaism and Christianity were born affirmed the normativity and superiority of men. Women and their bodies were regarded as dangerous sources of uncleanness. When this mentality met with Greek dualism which associated the rational with the male and the non-material and women with nature, corruptibility and matter, the stage was set for the emergence of a body-denying theology. (Stuart and Thatcher, 1996, pp. ix–x)

Despite the Gospels' focus on bodily healings, or Jesus' power of touch, or their mention of several anointings, washing of feet and the raising of the odd body, Matthew's Jesus declares, 'Do not fear those who kill the body but cannot kill the soul; rather fear him who can destroy both soul and body in hell' (Matt. 10.28). While not especially derogatory towards the body, what is implied here is the beginnings (in the Christian tradition at least) of the body's subordination to the soul in terms of its spiritual significance; an inference that would be made more explicit in the centuries to follow.

In the New Testament, however, the body is not yet viewed as something inherently evil. St Paul writes to the Corinthians: 'Do you not know that your body is a temple of the Holy Spirit within you . . . and that you are not your own? For you have been bought with a price. Therefore glorify God in your body' (1 Cor. 6.19–20). As elsewhere in the New Testament, and in later Syrian spirituality, the language of the Temple is projected onto language about the body. Similarly, Jesus attacks the Temple and describes his own body as the temple that will be raised up (John 2.19). This 'relocation' of the Temple at once secularizes the Temple and spiritualizes the human body, and is one deep root of Christian spirituality.

Yet alongside this high appreciation, Paul also expresses a regret that bodily existence gets in the way of our homecoming to God. So he could also write: 'while we are at home in the body we are away from the Lord – for we walk by faith, not by sight . . . we should rather be away from the body and at home with the Lord' (2 Cor. 5.7ff).

Back to Patristics

The same ambiguous spirituality, which locates goodness in the body as exceedingly precious, yet nevertheless considers the body to be a deadweight that acts as a drag on human salvation, or an animal needing to be tamed, became accentuated in the second century AD as Christianity began (Chapter 2) to dialogue with the Greco-Roman world into which it began to expand. We call four very different witnesses to this same development, all previously mentioned: a Neoplatonic Jew, a Neoplatonic Christian, an Eastern monk, and a bishop and theologian formative for the West.

Philo

In the language that St Paul echoes, Philo uses the imagery of the athlete but casts it in a destructive direction towards the body. Philo contrasts the athlete as the 'body-lover' who would easily abandon the soul for the sake of the flesh with the philosopher, 'the soul carer' who 'disregards that which is in reality a corpse, the body, with the soul aim that the best part of him, his soul, may not be wronged by an evil thing, the cadaver to which it is bound' (*Allegories of Laws*, 3.72, in 1993).

Clement of Alexandria

Clement adds theological credence to the view that the body is no more than a cadaver which the soul tows through life at the expense of the soul's purity and freedom (Ryan, 2004). Under the influence of Hellenic thought in general and of Philo in particular, Clement is driven to conclude that if the body is so antithetical to salvation, then for Christ to be considered humanity's Saviour he must not have shared in the kind of human embodiment humans experience. Instead Clement conjectures that Christ had a heavenly body sustained by a kind of holy energy that gave the illusion of human cravings but in reality left him devoid of the material passions of hunger, thirst and the like. Though Christ appeared to exhibit human traits of the body, Clement maintains that he knew no 'movement of feeling – either pleasure or pain'. Thus in terms of spirituality, if people are to be Christ-like, Clement argued that they too must aim to be without passion (*apatheia*, p. 40) and endlessly tame the body through the exactions of the censorious soul.

Anthony of Egypt

Athanasius described Anthony as a man 'radiant with joy' who, despite the extreme austerities of his life, lived to the advanced age of 105 still with all his own teeth. Though Anthony did not wear his asceticism on his sleeve or parade it in the form of an emaciated spectre, what Athanasius writes about him nevertheless reveals his dark ambivalence towards his own body. Athanasius observed:

> When [Anthony] was about to eat and sleep and provide for the other needs of the body, shame overcame him as he thought of the spiritual nature of the soul. Often when about to partake of food with many other monks, the thought of spiritual food came upon him and he would beg to be excused and went a long way from them, thinking that he should be ashamed to be seen eating with others. (1980, Chapter 45)

Moreover, Anthony may well have died with all of his teeth but Athanasius reveals that he never washed them nor did he bathe his body or allow anyone to see him naked (Ryan, 2004).

Augustine

Augustine's main struggle was fought not against food but against a strong libido. In his *Confessions*, Augustine does not so much confess but rather hints that he had a real problem with erections. Far from impotent, what exercised Augustine was that his spontaneous erections were a clear indicator that bodily lust could distort an individual person's otherwise good will and literally take control over the entire human person. So it was that Augustine was endearingly and boyishly impressed by people who seemed to have a measure of control over their bodies and could, at will, wiggle their ears or distort their faces. For Augustine, the spiritual life was above all a controlled life.

In a theological system that was to become the bedrock of Western Christendom, Augustine reasoned that the fall had left humanity with a weakened will, leaving us abandoned and enslaved by our desires like brutish beasts. Prior to the fall, humanity had enjoyed a unity of body and soul, and sexuality had been under the control of human will. When humanity usurped God's superiority, desire and will ceased to be friends and conflict became ingrained within the human condition; thus the body becomes, quite literally, a battleground in which spiritual advancement is hard won and nowhere is this more felt than in the genitals:

> When it comes to children being generated, the members created for this purpose do not obey the will, but lust has to be waited for to set these members in motion ... and sometimes it will not act when the mind is willing, while sometimes it will act even against the mind's will! Does the freedom of the human will not blush at this? (quoted in Singer, 1996, p. 317)

Augustine calls this spontaneous desire for material satisfaction 'concupiscence', of which sexual desire is the most obnoxious form: here lust overpowers the human mind and brings it down into the sensuous desire of the body, making rational thought impossible.

In this analysis, Manichean gloom regarding the subversive power of evil is laced with Neoplatonic distrust of the body. Richard Price (1996) sums up Augustine's influence succinctly when he writes:

> In the age of ... Augustine, we find already what was to remain the medieval compromise – government of the Church by a celibate elite, unique respect accorded to monks and nuns safely shut away in monasteries, whilst the traditional family under its male head remained the basic social unit in the outside world. (p. 25)

The Body Politic in Late Antiquity

Peter Brown (1988) helps us understand and place these anti-sexual trends, arguing that the culture of late antiquity tended to regard the body and its orifices as needing to be policed and ruled by the soul. Brown sees this as the spiritualizing of the actual threat of invasion of the body politic by barbarians. In time of threat, passion and vulnerability were to be despised, and Christianity followed suit.

But Brown also notes that in early Christianity procreation was as much an issue as sex itself. Whereas Judaism and pagan antiquity alike restrained sex in order to channel it to procreation, for early Christians (and later the monks) procreation itself was to be avoided. Christians should dedicate themselves to the kingdom to come not the propagation of a world that was passing away.

The Body: Alternative Scriptings

The connection between sexuality and spirituality in Christian theology has been almost completely severed by this nascent and pervasive dualism, in which the body is reduced to vile matter.

> If people could see what is underneath the skin . . . they would find the sight of women sickening. Her charm consists of slime and blood, of wetness and gall . . . And if we cannot bring ourselves to touch vomit and faeces, not even with our fingertips, how can we bring ourselves to embrace the dirt bag itself. (Attributed to Odo of Cluny, cited in Taylor, p. 65)

Significantly, this is written from a male perspective; as the onlooker who is 'spiritual' enough to recognize, with his X-ray eyes, the vileness of women, the man somehow rises above the perception that 'underneath' he is no different. Yet among the fault-lines in the medieval period we noted threads of a feminine counter-tradition that make possible, in our own day, the weaving of an integrated Christian spirituality that dares to embrace our embodied sensuality and celebrate the sacramental embodiment of God. An example may be taken from Mother Julian's *Showings* (a passage significantly omitted from one of the two extant manuscripts):

A man walks upright, and the food of his body is shut in as if in a well-made purse. When the time of his necessity comes, the purse is opened and then shut again, in most seemly fashion. And it is God who does this . . . for he does not despise what he has made, nor does he disdain to serve us in the simplest natural functions of our bodies . . . For as the body is clad in the cloth, and the flesh in the skin, and the bones in the flesh, and the heart in the trunk, so are we, soul and body, clad and enclosed in the goodness of God. (2004, Chapter 6)

Here Julian affirms even the down-to-earth activity of the bathroom – which later Benedictines renamed 'the shame-house' – as a sign of our divinely ordained embodiment. Our ensoulment within the body is not entrapment but rather an enclosure in the unitive goodness of God. For Julian, then, 'our sensuality is grounded in nature, in compassion, and in grace. In our sensuality, God is' (quoted in Nelson, 1988, p. 24).

Reuniting Body and Spirit: Ricoeur

Mother Julian's work of unitive integration between body, earth, soul, spirituality, sensuality and sexuality anticipates what Paul Ricoeur (1979, pp. 13ff.) referred to as the age of reunification. Ricoeur proposes that there have been three stages in the Western understanding of the relationship of the body (and sexuality) to religion (and spirituality).

1 The earliest stage was unitive in that sexuality and spirituality were interwoven through religious myth and ritual. Sex, procreation and the fertility of the earth were celebrated as numinous, spiritual powers.
2 With the rise of the major world religions we see a segregation of the two spheres: the sacred becomes other-worldly and transcendent while sexuality becomes demythologized and confined to procreation within institutionalized marriage.
3 We are now emerging into a third period characterized by a desire to reunite sexuality and spirituality prompted by a more psychophysical understanding of the person, in which sexual expression is not seen as needing restraint and discipline but rather exploration and celebration.

A Paradigmatic Shift: Nelson

The theologian and ethicist James Nelson, meanwhile, distinguishes seven significant signs of a paradigmatic shift in the understanding of the relation of sexuality and spirituality.

1 A shift from theologies of sexuality to **sexual theologies**. Theology can no longer 'presume to look down upon human sexuality from some unaffected Olympian advantage' (in Stuart and Thatcher, 1996, p. 214). Now the question before theologians is not a unidirectional enquiry into what God has to say about sexuality, but rather a dialogical reflection on what our sexuality reveals to us about God, and vice versa.

2 An unprecedented attack on dualism represented in a second shift away from understanding sexuality as incidental to, or detrimental, to experience of God toward understanding the **erotic as intrinsic to the divine–human experience**. Of course, the erotic had been intrinsic to Christian spirituality at least since Origen's commentary on the Song of Songs (Chapter 2) or Bernard of Clairvaux's analogy of the kiss (Chapter 3). Yet both these writers still feel the need to spiritualize the erotic, and thus tend to the prevailing view that inter-human eroticism is a distraction and a gross, inferior version of the real thing, the embrace of the soul and God. But as Friedrich Oetiner contended, 'The end of all God's work is embodiment' (cited in Nelson, p. 216). If it is the case that God's ongoing work is the work of embodiment, then sexuality and spirituality can be grounded together in what Weber termed 'incarnational consciousness'.

3 A shift from understanding sexual sin as a matter of intrinsically wrong sexual acts to understanding **sexual sin as alienation from our intended sexuality**. Whereas traditional Church teaching has tended to define sexual sin in terms of neatly defined and heavily categorized physical acts, Christian theology at its best now views sin as a condition of alienation from which harmful acts may arise. Nelson explains that sexual sin lies in 'a dualistic alienation by which the body becomes an object, either to be constrained out of fear (the Victorian approach) or to be treated as a pleasure machine (the Playboy philosophy)' (p. 216). It lies in the dualistic alienation by which females are kept from claiming their assertiveness and males kept from acknowledging their vulnerability.

4 A shift from understanding salvation as antisexual to knowing that there is **'sexual salvation'**. In Riceour's second phase Christians promoted a dis-embodied notion of salvation where deliverance denotes release from the flesh into freedom in the spiritual realm. Thus the typical saint was asexual, rarely washed, emasculated and – especially in the case of females (Bynum, 1988) – starving and emaciated. Now, however, a doctrine of salvation that stresses human becoming is beginning to explore what it means for God to embrace humanity in its entirety and fleshly particularity. Nelson refers to this as a form of 'sexual sanctification' understood as a 'growth in self-acceptance, in the capacity for sensuousness, in the capacity for play, in the diffusion of the erotic throughout the body (rather than in its genitalization) and in the embrace of androgynous possibility' (Nelson, p. 216).

5 A shift from act-centred sexual ethics to a **relational sexual ethics**. For Nelson, our sexuality is the physiological and psychological grounding for our capacities to love and thus ethics is about finding the life that best appro-priates the sexual meanings of the Word become flesh among us; to put it another way, ethics becomes inherently relational.

6 A consequent shift from understanding the Church as asexual (or perhaps the chaste feminine bride and mother) to understanding it as a **sexual com-munity** in which sexuality is no longer incidental or inimical to its life.

> [The] sexual revolution resulted in a growing self-consciousness and empowerment on the part of the sexually oppressed. Religious feminism articulated the ways in which the Church has always been a sexual com-munity – the ways it incorporated patriarchy into its language, worship, theological imagery, leadership patterns and ethics. A rising gay/lesbian consciousness performed a similar function in regard to the Church's heterosexism. Gradually, other groups – singles (including the widowed and divorced), the aging, those with handicapping conditions, the ill – have begun to recognise how churchly assumptions and practices have sexually disenfranchised them. (p. 217)

The rise of the disenfranchised – feminist, womanist, disablist, les-bi-gayist – has questioned, once and for all, the dichotomy of spirituality and the body in the Christian spiritual tradition. Radical theology has reclaimed the body from the jaws of patriarchy as the two divergent paths between a 'theology of (or about) sexuality' and Nelson's 'sexual theology' wrestle with each other.

Those whom patriarchy previously disenfranchised from theological discourse have discovered their voice through the reclamation of the holiness of their bodies. They have learned to trust what their embodiment and their sexuality teaches them about God.

7 A shift from understanding sexuality as a private issue to understanding it as a **personal and public issue**. The evidence of this last sign is writ large on the agenda of mainline denominations today as issues of gender and sexual orientation are hotly debated amid endeavours to dichotomize reality, armour emotions and deny our bodily concreteness.

Conclusion: From Dualism to Welcome Ambiguity

It would be naïve to suggest that if only free sexual expression replaced the old constraints, all would be well. But our sexuality is often where men (especially) wear their deepest wounds. Some kinds of wounded sexuality – like that of the paedophile or the compulsive rapist – may only find redemption, and avoid wounding others, through a celibacy supported by the Christian community, with a combination of care and rigour that society at large seems now quite incapable of offering. However, the Christian fear of sexuality can too easily collude with society's ongoing need for scapegoats, leading to an impulse to cast out, rather than to restrain and if possible transform.

Certainly the best test of whether a sexuality should be freely expressed is whether that expression heals wounds ('sexual salvation') or perpetuates and propagates them in self and others. But we have seen how the Church from Augustine onward has blurred this vital distinction by viewing all sexuality as, in effect, the propagation of a primordial wound. At best the Church has viewed only 'orthodox' sexualities as escaping this dismal curse, as if the distinction between saving and wounding did not cut across so called 'normal' and 'deviant' sexualities alike.

Recognizing this plunges us into a transformation in our spiritual understanding of sexuality that is quite unfinished. Spirituality is itself about human transformation or, at its simplest, the way people change in the light of their beliefs. Nelson's work reminds us that though such change is underway it does not, indeed it cannot, happen through a didacticism that merely rehearses ancient dualistic certitudes. Change only happens through what Brueggemann (1997, p. 29) has termed 'the playful entertainment of another scripting of reality that may subvert the old given text and its interpretation and lead to the embrace of an alternative reality'.

If Ricoeur is correct, then at present we live in what Victor Turner termed the 'in-between' phase of liminality. In terms of embodiment, the old dualistic configurations of the second age are noticeably dissonant with our fleshed-out experience, but the new alternative scripts are not yet finished. So perhaps in what all too often can appear as the Church's timid call for 'tolerance' over issues of sexuality and gender we might more graciously hear a bold and more insightful recognition of the need for a safe place to host the kind of ambiguity that enables change and transformation to happen. This is the very ambiguity that the patriarchal dualism we have inherited anathematized and yet which we, in our present age, know our liminality pre-defines. Reaching a more creative, unitive, non-dualist relationship between the body and the soul, and between spirituality and sexuality, will not be reached by threat or coercion, nor will it drop onto us from somewhere 'on high'. Salvation is written on the flesh and we are quite literally in this ambiguous struggle together as we await the truth of what is yet to be written.

For Reflection and Discussion

1 Imagine you are on board Van Horne's tanker, looking out onto the divine cargo he is towing. Describe what you see. Then consider what you might want to do, or say to the others.

2 Think of a time when you felt most 'at home in your body'. Try and recapture the thoughts, feelings and emotions you experienced at this time. Reflecting on this experience, do you agree with Paul when he says 'while we are at home in the body we are away from the Lord'?

3 While Clement accorded Christ merely a 'heavenly body' Christian orthodoxy eventually gave God the Son a continuing full-bodied humanity, not abandoned after the ascension. What implications might this have for Christian spirituality?

4 'Manichean gloom laced with a neo-platonic distrust of the body.' Is this a fair summary of Augustine's position?

5 Julian locates God in our sensuality. What would that mean for (a) a heterosexual couple in a committed relationship, (b) a homosexual couple in a committed relationship, (c) a paedophile, (d) a heterosexual couple having an affair?

6 Re-read the remark on and quotation from Nygren on pp. 130–1. If possible in a pair, take the roles of Nygren and Nelson and imagine how a conversation would flow between them on the role of the erotic in spirituality.

Further Reading

Peter Brown, 1988, *The Body and Society: Men, Women, and Sexual Renunciation in Early Christianity*, New York: Columbia University Press.

Sara Coakley, ed., 1997, *Religion and the Body*, Cambridge: Cambridge University Press.

Paul Ricoeur, 1979, 'Wonder, Eroticism and Enigma', in Hendrick Ruitenbeek, ed., *Sexuality and Identity*, New York: Dell.

Thomas Ryan, ed., 2004, *Reclaiming the Body in Christian Spirituality*, New York: Paulist.

Elizabeth Stuart and Adrian Thatcher, eds, 1996, *Christian Perspectives on Sexuality and Gender*, Leominster: Gracewing.

Mike Yaconelli, 2001, *Messy Spirituality: Christianity for the Rest of Us*, London: Hodder and Stoughton.

11

Serious about Soul? Spirituality and the Psyche

Religion . . . does not mean doctrine, or piety, or purity, or 'faith', or 'belief', or my life given to God. It means a willingness to be a fish in the holy water . . . to bow the head and take hints from our own dreams, to live a secret life, praying in a closet, to be lowly, to eat grief as a fish gulps and lives. It means being both fisherman and fish, not to be the wound but to take hold of the wound. Being a fish is to be active; not with cars or footballs, but with soul.

So Robert Bly (1990, p. 38) offers his own interpretation of religion, which is perhaps closer to what we understand by 'spirituality' – or at least, spirituality since the modern turn inward to the human subject. Spirituality in modern times has arguably come to mean being active and responsible about something called the psyche or soul. So now we turn from the body to consider the soul.

Spirituality in Tension with Morality

Of course, spirituality has always involved the mind or soul, but in the period covered by Chapter 5 especially, the balance had shifted in the relation between 'outer' objective and 'inner' psychic worlds. While theology still strove to pin its claims to the former, the spiritual had come to align itself with the latter. For Origen, Augustine, Ephrem and Denys through to Bonaventure, the soul's journey was defined and mapped by hierarchies believed to be objective, defined by Temple and mountain, by the Church's liturgy and the celestial spheres. In John and Teresa we find the same inter-illumination between inner and outer, but now the mountain or garden or series of mansions is an imaginary device defined in terms of the inner journey, which is mapped out with increasing subtlety. Spirituality – in Luther, Ignatius and Teresa alike – begins to focus on the subjective qualities of experiences themselves, and the assurance or otherwise they can provide for the individual's faith, rather than the spiritual truths they relate us to (Bouyer, 1968, pp. 250 and 279).

Meanwhile ideas were coming to be seen no longer as Plato's eternal entities in the divine mind, in which we participate, but as Occam's human constructs, existing inside our head (Louth, 1981, p. xv). Chapter 5 described how the Catholic faith – an objective system appropriated by the believer – moved with Luther to personal faith – something the individual confesses from the heart. The creed remained the same, but the focus became the act of trust made in it by the believer.

Again, in the metaphysical poets, scholastic metaphysics survives, but as a source of metaphors and paradoxes for the soul and human relationships. And a comparison of Michelangelo's – or Blake's – *Last Judgement* with their medieval predecessors, or of Bunyan's *Pilgrim's Progress* or Milton's *Paradise Lost* with Dante's *Divine Comedy*, shows how the fixed, objective orders have dissolved into a world whose defining features and focus are intrapersonal emotion and interpersonal drama.

Through the Looking Glass?

Objective and subjective structures remained, mirroring each other, but what was once the reflection – the soul – was now the reality; and what was once the reality was now the outward reflection, supplying metaphors for the soul. Spirituality, which had sought to acquaint itself with the spiritual and divine worlds in order to map a path for the soul, now traced the soul's path in order to learn about the divine and the spiritual. From inside the looking glass the 'outer' world now looked dull and 'disenchanted' (see Taylor, 2007, pp. 425–42) by contrast with the soul's rich inner meanings.

So spirituality was becoming an early form of psychology. With the

Enlightenment the traditional 'objective' structures themselves would begin to be questioned, so that Romanticism would feel free to trawl classical mythology and folklore as well as scripture in its search for metaphors for the soul. And as we shall see, the psychotherapists followed suit.

Marginalized Mystics, and Psychoanalysts?

According to de Certeau (1995) early modern mystics were to be found mainly among the parts of the aristocracy that were being undermined and marginalized by the advance of the new bourgeoisie and the printing press. As theology, both Protestant and Catholic, tried to align itself with written systems rather than living speech and experience, the mystics

> took up the challenge of the spoken word . . . They formed a solidarity with all the tongues that continued speaking, marked in their discourse by the assimilation to the child, the woman, the illiterate, madness, angels, or the body. Everywhere they insinuate an 'extraordinary': they are voices grown more and more separate from the field of meaning that writing had conquered, ever closer to the song or the cry . . . So it is that the passing figure of mystics continues to ask us what remains of the spoken word. That question, moreover, is not unrelated to what, in its own area, psychoanalysis restores. (p. 13)

De Certeau's final question introduces the subject of this chapter: whether the language of psychology and psychoanalysis, as it developed in the nineteenth and twentieth centuries, represents a continuation of the mystical focus on the soul and its guidance, that developed especially in the sixteenth and seventeenth centuries What does spirituality have to learn from psychology, and vice versa?

We shall examine intrapersonal, personal and transpersonal approaches to psychology (broadly following Hurding's classification (1986)) – not for their own sake, but to see what connections might be made with spirituality. After this we shall consider two models in which Christian spirituality has utilized psychological understandings, before evaluating the overall relationship between psychology and spirituality.

Intrapersonal Psychology: Freud and his Successors

We consider first the psychoanalytic approaches, which claim to explain the human psyche 'scientifically' by reducing it to component elements. In practice these approaches employ a range of hypotheses and narratives, often drawn from mythology, in a manner that is more reminiscent of spirituality than science. From this rich and influential tradition we will sample just two thinkers with which Christian spirituality must wrestle: Freud and Lacan.

Sigmund Freud (1856–1939)

Freud saw people as composed of various drives seeking pleasure, especially sexual pleasure. However, the search for pleasure is modified in childhood through relationships with mother and father in successive phases: 'oral' (suckling mother's breast), 'anal' (gaining control of excretion) and 'genital' (identifying with the appropriate gender). In the process the psyche divides into the conscious, rational 'ego', the unconscious 'id' and the internalized father who becomes the nagging conscience or 'super ego'. The aim of Freudian therapy is to unmask the secret workings of the unconscious so as to achieve a greater degree of rational control over our behaviour: 'where id was, there ego shall be'.

The scientific basis of Freud's theories has been much challenged, while feminists have criticized its 'patriarchal' focus on the father–son dynamic. Freud rejected religion and spirituality entirely as a kind of neurosis, with God as a projection of the persecuting father. It is unsurprising that Christian spirituality has seldom drawn directly on Freud.

However the concept of the unconscious – the idea that we are, like icebergs, 90 per cent hidden even from our own and others' view – is something Christian spirituality needs always to bear in mind. And Freud's typology of the early phases of childhood is not without its relevance to spirituality. Thus the language of drinking at the breast of Christ, and eucharistic feeding generally, can be seen as typically oral. Spirituality can be 'anally retentive' if it is tightly and legalistically controlled and lacking in generosity. Many people find such bodily analogies demeaning to spirituality, but then one has to consider the questions raised in Chapter 10.

A series of post-Freudians – including Melanie Klein (1882–1960), Donald Winnicott (1896–1971) and Arthur Janov (b.1924) – have taken the formative stage for the personality ever earlier, to the traumas of birth in Janov, and since Janov, even into experience in the womb. It is as if a spiritual ultimate is being sought by way of primacy in psychic time.

An Anglican priest, *Frank Lake* (1914–82) developed clinical theology, a heady but inspiring mix of evangelical, biblical and spiritual concepts with those drawn from post-Freudian psychology, focused especially on birth and the first nine months of life.

Mind made of Language: Lacan

Jacques Lacan (1901–81) saw himself as giving Freudianism a surer scientific basis than Freud, through the new theories of structuralism. However, most would argue that he went well beyond Freud into territory that many find bewildering and hard to evaluate. His thought developed through many phases, but towards the end he had come to see the human being as needing to tie a knot between three domains:

- The **imaginary**, in which the child understands his body, and hence himself, through seeing it, as it were, imaged in the mother's body and those of others.
- The **symbolic,** in which the child sets this imaginative life at the mercy of language, accepting the equivalent of Freud's castration complex as he submits to the 'law of the fathers'. So children palpably lose their infant fancy and become sober little adults. In return the child acquires intelligibility, but never a final meaning, because the meaning of words is always defined in terms of other words. By resorting to language to define ourselves, we inevitably defer any definitive significance for our life.
- The **real** – which for Lacan is not the hard world of scientific fact (which is part of the symbolic order) but something that eludes the imaginary and the symbolic, and cannot be captured in words. The real is known in 'jouissance', a kind of overwhelming physical trepidation and excitement, experienced by

the unconscious as joy but by the conscious mind, immersed in symbols, as a shattering dread. The forbidden excitement of jouissance often generates compulsive behaviour, but Lacan came to believe jouissance could spill over into the symbolic domain of language with more positive effect.

Though Lacan's speculations may seem remote from therapy, let alone spirituality, there is more to be said. The notion that the real exceeds language, but nevertheless can trickle over into it, makes sense of much mystical writing. This can involve a 'language of unsaying' (Sells, see Chapter 13) that ruptures systematic thought and enables reality as it were to spill through in our delight in language and its paradoxes. Jouissance itself suggests at one and the same time the pain that in the 'dark night' destroys the rational ego, and the erotic joy and bliss of the nuptial union.

One of Lacan's most interesting commentators, the Marxist Slavoj Žižek, perhaps fancifully, links Lacan's triad to the Christian Trinity:

> God the Father is the 'real Real' of the violent primordial Thing; God the Son is the 'imaginary Real' of the pure shining, the 'almost nothing' which the sublime shines through his miserable body; the Holy Ghost is the 'symbolic Real' of the community of believers. (2001, pp. 82–3)

Though he does not use the term himself, 'spirituality' might well denote the tying of the Lacanian knot between the *symbolic* rational and the ethical demands of society; the intimate play of the *imaginary*, and the unutterable ecstasy, at once painful and joyous, that constitutes the *real*. The good and rational life, harmonized with society; the aesthetic life, self-absorbed in its passionate desires, striving to create beauty; the silent, monastic, God-intoxicated life, reaching out towards the inexpressible: to tie a knot between these three, from which they will never again unravel and go their separate ways, is, perhaps, the task of Trinitarian Christian spirituality.

Personal Approaches

For Lacan, the ego is the rationalizing part of us, always too ready to supply a meaning to what we do. It is something therapy must mistrust and overcome.

Another tradition in therapy takes the opposite line, addressing not inner dynamics within the self, but the person as a whole, seeing the ego as central to the therapeutic process.

Person-centred Therapy

Carl Rogers (1902–87) pioneered person-centred therapy, which has become central in a great deal of counselling. Here the therapist discards all prior theories and offers the client empathy or 'unconditional positive regard'. The ideas, experiences, values and aims of the client are to be regarded as paramount, and the therapist serves only to help the client find out what they are. This will, it is argued, lead naturally to a process of catharsis, or purification, as buried feelings are allowed to surface and be discharged, leading successively to insight into problems, greater closeness to and reliance on experience, and growth towards self-realization.

In terms of Christian spirituality, Rogers' empathy is close to Christian *agapé*, unconditional love, which must be a *sine qua non* of Christian spiritual direction. His catharsis and insight are reminiscent of mystical purgation and illumination respectively. However, Rogers' exaltation of the self and its experience is unlike the Christian goal of self-abandonment in union with God. Christian spirituality has much to learn from Rogers, but Christian spiritual direction clearly cannot be identified with person-centred counselling.

Transpersonal Approaches

We turn now to two approaches that are explicit about the transpersonal, spiritual and relational aspects of psychic healing.

Carl Gustav Jung (1875–1961)

Jung broke with Freud primarily over this use of the spiritual and transpersonal in psychoanalysis. Where Freud saw in religion a neurosis to be cured, Jung saw a powerful source of healing symbols. More even than Freud, he mined ancient mythologies and fairytales as well as the Bible and detected universal 'arche-types' which led him to believe the unconscious to be 'collective', extending beyond the individual mind.

His therapy was addressed less to childhood trauma and more to the crises that beset people in mid-life. He believed people then often had to renegotiate with their 'shadow', that is, the qualities and drives they had early on split off from the conscious self and buried in the unconscious. The male has to come to terms with his shadow female or *anima*, and the female likewise with her masculine *animus*. He criticized the all-male imagery of the Christian Trinity, but regarded the Catholic dogma of the Assumption of Mary as supplying a welcome feminine fourth person!

Despite (or because of) his affirmation of religious symbols, Jung rejected his father's dogmatic Protestantism. He believed that in following the lofty ideal of Christ, Christians were often led to split off their regressive and sexual instincts; only to find these re-emerging in the violent 'shadow-side' of Christianity, in the burning of heretics and witches, and the imagined torments of hell. Rather than try to imitate Christ's life, Jung suggested, Christians should try 'to live their own proper lives as truly as he lived his' (1961, p. 273).

In enabling Christians to reappraise their tradition and open up to the resources and stories from other traditions, as well as relating their own traditions to the soul in new ways, Jung's impact on Christian spirituality has proved very fruitful.

In particular, the *Myers-Briggs indicator*, developed from Jung's theories of personality, is as much used in spiritual direction as it is in business. Bruce Duncan (1993) has related Jung's four basic dimensions of personality – intuitive, sensing, thinking and feeling – to four kinds of prayer and to the four Gospels. We will leave it to you to decide which Gospel is which!

Psychosynthesis

Roberto Assagioli (1888–1974) developed Jung's notion that there is a difference between the conscious ego and the higher self, the true being that seeks to realize itself in us. He also believed the unconscious contained positive levels inspiring art, science and works of love. Therapy involved these stages:

1 **Personal synthesis**. Exploration and harmonization of the various areas of the personality including the unconscious and the complexes which function within it as sub-personalities.

2 **Spiritual synthesis**, in which these synthesized elements are brought under the control of the ego. This involves 'disidentification' with negative psychic forces. Instead of saying, 'I hate x', for example, one is encouraged to think 'a wave of hatred regarding x is trying to engulf me'. Thereby the ego finds freedom to control elements that previously controlled it.

3 **Transpersonal synthesis**, in which the higher self is discovered or created and the psyche rebuilt around it. The higher self may appear first as a sense of something unresolved even after autonomy and integration have been achieved; or as another person, like the therapist or a loved one, in the absence of whom an inner dialogue persists. This process may be assisted by techniques like music therapy, and imaginary journeys in which the ego talks with an ideal guide.

Assagioli's approach arguably sits well with Christian spirituality. 'Dissociation' is surely involved in the desert tradition of ascribing sins to demons and doing battle with them. And many Christian traditions encourage dialogue with a guardian angel, a saint, an actual spiritual director or soul-guide, or Jesus in the Ignatian exercises.

Two Psychological Models used in Spirituality

Having considered psychotherapies that envisage progressively greater kinship with spirituality, we turn to spiritual models that have made extensive use of psychology. We have already mentioned one of the most widely used, the Myers-Briggs indicator; space will allow us to consider a further two.

Fowler's stages of faith

It has often been noted that spirituality develops (and sometimes declines) with our age. James Fowler (1981) produced an often-used classification of 'stages of faith'. He regarded faith as 'an orientation of the total person, giving purpose and goal to one's hopes and strivings, thoughts and actions' (p. 14), which is what now might be described as spirituality. Fowler related his stages to Piaget's theories of the development of cognition, and to Erikson's 'psycho-social stages' whereby at different times of life a person needs to resolve crucial issues before passing on to the next. Table 5 lists his stages, with the symbols he gave them and Erikson's corresponding stages.

Fowler's scheme can be criticized for imposing his own ideal of spiritual maturity on the evidence, and for seeing the journey of faith in terms of triumphing over a linear set of obstacles, rather than the non-linear spirals and tangles most of us experience. It has nevertheless proven useful and is frequently cited. As with all such models, it can be either a pseudo-scientific, life-inhibiting straitjacket, or a helpful stimulus to self-awareness and imagination.

The Enneagram

The Enneagram has emerged not from psychology but from ancient spiritual traditions. The origins are obscure; it seems to have been taken up in Islamic Sufi spirituality, before being promoted by the Russian writer Leonid Ouspensky; and recently being popularized for use by Jesuits and others in Christian spirituality.

Enneagram means 'nine points', and essentially that is what it is: a circle of nine points joined by a series of arrowed lines in a crown shape (Figure 8). Each point denotes a basic compulsion lying in one of the three centres of personality: head or cognition, heart or emotional relationship, and guts or basic drive. If the compulsions are overcome, the energies behind them can hold the key to spiritual transformation. Table 6 puts together suggestions from a wide range of writings relating the points of the Enneagram to biblical examples of the relevant personality, what God primarily is for that type, the associated virtue and compulsion, a relevant text, and what is sought in spirituality.

The Enneagram is a map for the spiritual journey rather than a static definition

Table 5: Authors' Summary of Fowler's Stages of Faith

Symbol	Age	Fowler's Stages	Erikson's Stages (and my questions)
	Baby	**Undifferentiated Faith:** baby and mother, as shown, form a unity. But mother is not always there – can she be trusted to return? Faith in its most primitive, pre-linguistic form resides in a trust in the nurturing goodness of the world around, as opposed to fear of relationship and the other.	**Trust vs mistrust:** will mother continue to feed me?
	Infant	**1: Intuitive Projective Faith:** Child learns to use language but relates to reality through vivid, non-linear imagination in which she intuitively projects herself into world as in the figure. God is another very real fantasy. Negatively, there can be fantasies of evil, primeval shame and guilt.	**Autonomy vs shame and doubt:** do parents accept me or am I disgusting? **Initiative vs guilt:** when am I bad, and how can I make up?
	Junior	**2: Mythic-Literal Faith:** reality is distinguished from fantasy as the child learns what it can make and do in the world in the context of society's and family's expectations. Beginnings of a moral sense, sometimes perfectionist. An ability to co-ordinate fantasies into linear stories, and to distinguish these from literal matters of fact and order an objective world, as shown.	**Industry vs inferiority:** can I do as well as my peers and earn teacher's approval?
	Adolescent	**3: Synthetic-Conventional Faith:** friendships begin to loom larger than family, as the adolescent becomes hyper sensitive to how she looks to others. A major time for conversion as faith within a faith-sharing peer group may be decisive for the forging of a new, personal identity in the context of others, as shown. To that end an extreme, distinct and idealistic faith may be preferred.	**Identity vs role confusion:** how do I look to my friends?
	Young Adult	**4: Individuative-Reflective Faith:** faith is put at the service of moral issues and conflicts and hence has to become more rational and critical, as the individual works out a form of faith that really works for life's complexity, balancing the demands of different worlds (see figure) like work and family.	**Intimacy vs isolation:** do my spouse and children love me, and I them?

		5: Conjunctive Faith: as children leave home and career perhaps reaches its limit and perhaps encounters 'the sacrament of defeat'. Deeper forces (Jung's 'shadow'?) need to be listened to alongside the conscious and rational. A 'second naïveté' (Ricoeur) in which childhood's symbolic power is reunited with adult conceptual meanings (triangles and circles in the figure?)	Generativity vs stagnation: what are my real goals in life and will I achieve them?
	Mid Life		
	Senior (if ever)	6: Universalizing Faith: a stage only reached by 'saints', whose faith becomes no longer a statement of the goal but a means to the end of abandoning oneself wholly and sacrificially to the needs and destiny of the world and humankind and what Christians term the kingdom of God. In the diagram we see the self vanish and a wider all-embracing circle appear.	Integrity vs despair: what have been my goals, and was it all worthwhile?

Figure 8: The Enneagram

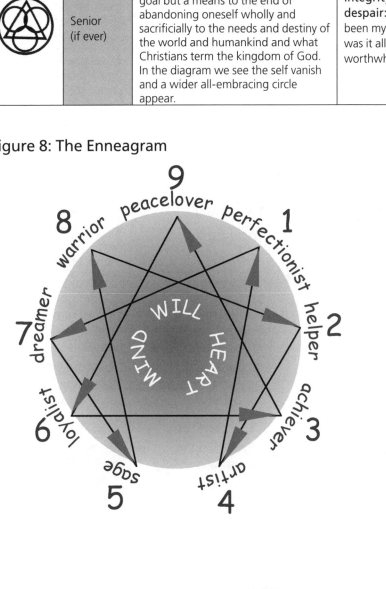

Table 6: The Enneagram and Spirituality: Authors' Summary

Point	IDEAL and Bible examples	God as ...	Spiritual Gift or Virtue
1	PERFECTIONIST: Jeremiah, Paul	THE MOST HIGH the challenging ideal	**Goodness** zeal for God, earnest desire to do the best
2	HEPLER: Rahab the prostitute, Martha of Bethany	LOVE unconditional generosity	**Love** deep concern and care for others
3	ACHIEVER: David, Peter	PURE ACT (Aquinas), achievement and fulfilment	**Excellence, usefulness** ability to organize and get things done
4	ARTIST: John the Divine, Mary of Bethany	GLORY majesty, awe, beauty	**Gentleness** sense of beauty, imagination
5	SAGE: Solomon, Thomas	WISDOM omniscience	**Faith, faithfulness** hunger for truth, objectivity, reason, ability to accept hard reality
6	SERVANT: Moses, James	LAW-GIVER faithfulness, order	**Endurance, long-suffering** desire to safeguard the truth even at cost to oneself, martyr spirit
7	DREAMER: Joseph, Mary Magdalen	JOY subtlety and wit, hopefulness	**Joy, delight** sense of fun and play, ability to dream dreams
8	WARRIOR: Elijah, John Baptist	ALMIGHTY anger empowering the oppressed	**Mastery, self-control** righteous anger on behalf of others
9	PEACE-LOVER Mary mother of Jesus: Barnabas	PEACE reconciliation, 'Let it be'	**Peace, well-being** reconciling others, creating calm and reassurance

Compulsion or Sin	Relevant Text	What Spirituality Asks of God
Judgementalism criticizing self and others for not measuring up to own ideals	Be perfect, as your Father . . . (Matt. 5.46–48)	**Uplift** me – focusing on the holiness of God, inspiring a desire to 'be perfect, as God is perfect'
Needing to be needed overwhelming and mothering others	Come to me, all who labour (Matt. 11.28–30)	**Affirm** me – times of fellowship or the stirring of love of neighbour
Obsession with success inability to accept failure and weakness	Go, and make disciples (Matt. 28.18–20)	**Involve** me – a sense of active participation in which I get something done
Narcissism being in love with own image, having to do it all 'my way'	Holy, holy, holy is the Lord (Isaiah 6.1–4)	**Inspire** me – firing the imagination with beautiful artistic images, ceremony and symbolism
Ivory tower attitude, hoarding knowledge, coldness towards others	With you is wisdom (Wisdom 9.9–10)	**Teach** me – or rather, give me something to question and reflect on. Give room for my doubts, to test and deepen my faith.
Intolerance of difference and change, conformist approach, stuck in outmoded tradition	If you obey . . . the Lord will bless (Deut. 30.15–16)	**Challenge** me with moral teaching: especially the weight of tradition versus my own and other modern views
Superficiality inability to take anything seriously; addiction to pleasure and fun	Arise, my love (Song 2.10–12)	**Delight** and entertain me – a sense of fun and laughter
Ruthless seeking of **power** for own sake, uncontrolled anger with those who oppose it	The Lord is my strength (Exodus 15.1–3)	**Empower** me with a feeling of God's invincible justice and majesty
Laziness manyana attitude, wanting everything to be comfortable, hating to see suffering	Peace I leave with you (John 14.27)	**Refresh** me – times of rest and quiet

of the soul. It can prove a remarkably rich and subtle tool to use in practice, even if the obscure origins and lack of scientific grounding trouble some. In particular, the notion that what we think of as our finest defining points may be compulsions limiting our growth and needing to be overcome, and yet also the key, once overcome, to transformation, resonates with the repeated biblical theme whereby the rejected stone becomes the keystone of the building (e.g. Matt. 21.42; Mark 12.10; Acts 4.11; 1 Pet. 2.7).

Psychotherapy: Secularized Spirituality?

Although it has often presented itself as a science, perhaps the most useful way to see psychology is as secularized and privatized spirituality. Our modern understanding of the 'soul' or psyche – as an inner life of intellect, feeling and will – owes a great deal both to Augustine's exacting self-analysis, and to the modern turn to the subject described at the start of this chapter. The disciplines of confession represent an early way of laying bare in confidentiality the depths of the soul, to bring it to healing and reconciliation. Analysis and counselling can be viewed as developments of such practices.

Freud, Jung, Lacan, Assagioli and the other great psychologists all speak in an idiosyncratic, metaphorical and myth-laden way. Often psychological language seems more obscure and counter-intuitive than any theology, perhaps because theology mines one tradition for the stories that bring salvation and healing, whereas psychology mines many old mythologies as well as inventing new ones. If we accept that we can only speak of the 'inner' by analogies taken from the 'outer' or the imaginary worlds, this obscurity may be forgivable.

Thus where traditional spirituality speaks of temptation and sin, psychology speaks of complexes and neuroses; where spirituality speaks of demons and angels, psychology speaks of the unconscious and its forces; where spirituality speaks of salvation, psychology speaks of therapy and integration. The concepts are of course parallel, not identical. In particular, psychological language loses many of the cosmic, social and Christocentric resonances of Christian theology, privatizing it into the individual mind. But we have seen that these tendencies were already at work, for better or worse, in post-Reformation spirituality. All the same, there seems to be a continuum here, such that a transpersonal psychotherapy and a Christian spirituality that is open to psychological insight shade into one another. Of course, a strict behaviourist and a fundamentalist theologian (not unalike, perhaps, in approach?) might equally see this shading as losing the clear contours of their respective sciences!

Psychological Insights for Spirituality

There are indeed certain psychological insights that a Christian spirituality can hardly now afford to ignore.

- **The unconscious**. Ruth Burrows (2007) distinguishes between 'lights on' and 'lights off' spirituality. In the former case the person experiences the work of God in her, in the latter case the work of God in the soul goes on unseen, beneath the veil of consciousness, manifest only if brought to light by a spiritual director, or in the fruit it bears in life as a whole. Acknowledging the unconscious dimension of spirituality in this way can release it from too much focus on experiences. Moreover, Paul was the first to recognize that 'the good I would do, that I do not' (Rom. 7.19). An understanding that the self we present to ourselves and others may not be our true self, and a struggle towards congruence between flesh and spirit (or unconscious and conscious?) must be an essential aspect of spiritual development.
- **Dreams**. Freud was not the first to recognize their importance; the Bible is full of dreams (witness those of Jacob, his son Joseph, and Joseph the husband of Mary) as well as visions. Dreams are not straightforward allegories, and their interpretation is often best done with the help of another. But spirituality has to be open to the possibility that God may speak through them, or (to put it in the psychological mode) that in dreams one's true self may be crying out.
- **The possibility of neurotic religiosity**. To regard all religion as neurotic, as Freud did, is hardly compatible with a Christian spirituality. But the latter was busy identifying the neurotic malformations and abuses of the Christian religion long before Freud. The desert fathers were quick to unmask a proud, self-deceiving piety based on works, as was Luther. And latterly Ronald Bullis (1996) has drawn on traditional and psychological insights to distinguish spiritual detachment from schizophrenia, and the dark night of the soul from depression. The difference, he argues, lies not in the

symptoms, which may be similar, but in the fruit. In neurosis and psychosis the individual withdraws from others and collapses into himself. He finds himself unable to sustain his own existence, let alone that of others. In the case of spirituality the same withdrawal or ego-loss releases the person into creative self-giving and the deep love of God and neighbour. It is certainly possible to use spirituality to evade rather than confront complexes, fears and guilt, and there will be times when psychotherapy is needed to help a person move forward spiritually. However, if spirituality were always an evasion, we would expect spiritually oriented people always to be sad, cramped and maladjusted, whereas manifestly they are often free, integrated, witty, healthy and long-lived.

- **Prayer and personality**. The personality classifications we have noted must never become boxes to imprison prayer in. But a healthy awareness that not all people will pray or relate to God or grow spiritually in the same way is vital. Such classifications can liberate people from thinking they have to be like others, or others like them, and offer a sketch-map, rather than a simplistic linear path, for spiritual growth.

Differences

So was Bly right to identify 'religion' or spirituality with being 'active with soul'? To be sure, spirituality involves being responsible for the soul, and caring about how one develops, and acting in ways that will help one to do so. But is spirituality therefore to be identified with psychotherapy or soul-care? There are at least three reasons why not.

- **Length**. Spirituality is more than psychotherapy as life is more than medicine. Medicine and psychotherapy are what we use when the body or soul go wrong in some way. Psychotherapy is a very expensive process many cannot afford, designed to deal with specific problems. Spirituality is for anyone who wants it, and is a lifelong.
- **Depth**. Psychotherapy plumbs the depths of the individual soul, and aims at self-discovery and healing. It does not (or should not) impose its own values, but tries to work with those of the client. There is – or should be – no such thing as 'Christian' or 'Islamic' psychotherapy. But spirituality incorporates

a value system taken from a religion or other source. Hence there is such a thing as Christian spirituality, the subject of this book, which includes a particular understanding of humanity and a vision of God. This vision reaches beyond the depths of the soul towards the uncreated depths of God.

- **Breadth**. With a few exceptions, psychotherapy mainly aims to adjust the individual to the world she lives in, making it easier for her to cope with life in it. Spirituality may have the opposite effect, creating a 'divine discontent' with a society that is seen more and more to be at odds with God. Life may become more confused and jarring, because spirituality has a prophetic edge. For those committed to it, spirituality can be like the birth-pangs of a new age (Rom. 8.22–23), being God's way of motivating the Christian to create a new and better world. So a full picture of spirituality requires that this chapter, relating spirituality to the *psyche*, be broadened by the next, which will relate it to the *cosmos* and the *polis*, to moral life in the political world and the city or state.

For Reflection and Discussion

1 What is your initial reaction to Bly's remark? Will it serve as a definition of spirituality, or can you describe important features it leaves out?

2 Which of the approaches to psychotherapy discussed do you feel is most useful for developing spirituality, and why? And which are the three most important challenges these thinkers have brought to spirituality?

3 Reflecting on your own life and those of people you know, can you identify in it Fowler's stages of faith? In what ways has your experience departed from this model, and what insights have you gained from it?

4 In what ways do you think your spiritual journey may be constrained or enabled by your personality? Do you find the Enneagram helpful in illuminating this influence, and if so, how? Where would you place spiritual writers such as Origen, Augustine, Benedict, Bernard, Francis, Julian, Luther, Calvin or Blake in this scheme?

5 On balance do you think psychology is a secularized spirituality? Do you think psychology can ever be scientific, or can we only understand the soul through myths and parables, as spirituality has tended to?

Further Reading

Naria Beesing, Robert Nogosek and Patrick O'Leary, 1984, *The Enneagram: A Journey of Self-Discovery*, Denville, New Jersey: Dimension Books.

Bruno Bettelheim, 2001, *Freud and Man's Soul*, London: Pimlico.

Bruce Duncan, 1993, *Pray your Way: Your Personality and God*, London: DLT.

James Fowler, 1981, *Stages of Faith: The Psychology of Human Development and the Quest for Meaning.* San Francisco: Harper and Row.

Roger Hurding, 1986, *Roots and Shoots: A Guide to Counselling and Psychotherapy*, London, Sydney and Auckland: Hodder and Stoughton.

F. LeRon Shults and Steven Sandage, 2006, *Transforming Spirituality: Integrating Theology and Psychology*, Grand Rapids: Baker Academic Press.

William West, 2000, *Psychotherapy and Spirituality: Crossing the Line between Therapy and Religion*, London, Thousand Oaks and New Delhi: Sage.

12

Training in Transformation? Spirituality and Ethics

What is the relation between spirituality on the one hand, and ethics, politics, and morality on the other? How does the spiritual quest relate to the various ways in which humans organize their lives together?

Spirituality Beyond Morality?

At one extreme, there are those who consider that spirituality transcends ethics. Quietists like Marguerite Porete and Madame Guyon were persecuted by the Church – we noted – for their belief in a total union with God's will that rendered moral restraints superfluous.

A degree of immorality may even be viewed as necessary to spirituality. The ancient Catholic *Exultet*, sung near the Easter candle on the night before Easter, proclaims 'O happy fault, O necessary sin of Adam, to have brought the world so great a redeemer!' The sin is seen as justified because without it Christ would not have come, to die and to rise again; as if the spiritual positive of salvation far outweighed, and even 'necessitated', the negative of sin. In the same vein Luther bids us 'sin boldly, and rejoice in Christ even more boldly, for he is victorious over sin, death and the world'. We noted how Kierkegaard saw Abraham as suspending morality in his readiness to sacrifice Isaac. And the twentieth-century Lutheran, Emil Brunner, took to radical conclusions the Lutheran teaching on the contrast between the moral law and divine grace when he wrote 'in the last resort it is precisely morality which *is* evil' (1937, p. 71).

Morality Without Spirituality?

Such ideas can promote a reaction, however. Humanists and Christians alike have felt that we can actually live better moral lives without spirituality, or even without religion altogether. For example, W. G. McLagan argued (1961) that the Christian notions of sin and grace can undermine moral autonomy by detracting from human freedom and responsibility, encouraging people to wait on God's energizing power rather than pursuing the good by their own energy. He was attacking especially the Calvinist notion of God's irresistible grace, which overrides the recipient's moral choice or merit.

McLagan argued that religion can be thought to support morality in two ways: by inculcating a belief that the universe is favourable to morality, rewarding good behaviour; and by giving divine reinforcement to moral imperatives by declaring them commands of God. But these 'supports' actually weaken morality, he contended, since the truly moral person will do the right thing irrespective of reward, and obey God only in so far as his command is judged to be right. McLagan therefore rejected the personal God of much Christian spirituality, and regarded God as essentially no more and no less than morality itself.

Meanwhile many (Cupitt, 1988) have argued that the emphasis on 'original sin' and human unworthiness in traditional Christianity detracts from responsible ethics, and leads to a despair about social improvement. And Richard Holloway has argued (1999) for 'keeping religion out of ethics' because appeals to divine authority by particular religions are destructive in a multicultural society.

Being Responsible about Being Responsible

But if amoral spirituality is suspect, unspiritual morality can be graceless and hypocritical. Macquarrie argues (1970) that sin and grace are common human experiences, and that all those who seek to lead good lives come across profound obstacles, some within themselves, some in society. Western theology, with its notions of original sin and the need for God's grace, is simply being realistic about people's frequent experience of moral failure.

In Chapter 11 we explored the psychological dimension of this failure, and the way people can only become responsible for what they do by taking some responsibility for who they are, as those who find themselves doing those actions. Morality requires, in Bly's terms, 'being active about the soul'. And a proper understanding of the 'soul' will take seriously the formation of the soul in family and society, and a whole host of complexes and a depth of unconscious motive, which cannot be changed without changing society.

In this sense, therefore, Christian spirituality, far from undermining moral responsibility through its talk of sin and salvation and the need for grace, may represent a struggle to create the preconditions for genuine moral responsibility. In that case it would be a 'second order' moral responsibility, taking responsibility for our degree of responsibility, which requires that people struggle in all seriousness, both within the soul and in society, with all that renders them irresponsible.

Three Ways of Doing Ethics and Spirituality

In this book it would not be appropriate to investigate exhaustively all the possible ways in which moral philosophers and theologians have understood the basis of ethics. Instead we will focus on three ways – obedience, fulfilment and virtue – because they are among the most significant in themselves, but also because of the ways in which they can be seen to interact with spirituality and with one another. After reflecting on these interactions we will suggest a broad model whereby spirituality provides a 'how', a way of freeing ourselves to become responsible, that incorporates all three ethical ways in a subtle and creative balance.

The Spirituality of Obedience

On one very ancient understanding, morality is a matter of obeying the rules. Philosophers call this framework of morality 'deontology', from the Greek *dei*, 'it is necessary'. Discussion within this framework centres on 'moral obligation' and what people 'ought' to do.

In ancient societies, moral laws were not clearly distinguished from ritual, national and natural laws. All were believed to be laws the gods had decreed, and humans obeyed their society's customs with the same 'necessity' as the sun and the stars were seen as 'obeying' theirs (Ps. 19).

In modern times this sense of universal necessity has unravelled, rendering the authority of all kinds of law problematic. That is why Kant and other Enlightenment thinkers sought to set law on a rational basis to which everyone could agree, and replace 'heteronomy', or rule by an alien power such as God, with 'autonomy', or free self-rule. And Protestant theologians in the liberal tradition, like Rudolf Bultmann, have tended to support this brave attempt.

More orthodox Protestant thinkers, however, have sought to support an ethic based on profoundly 'heteronomous' divine command rather than autonomous human reason. Emil Brunner wrote (1937, p. 59): 'Nothing is good save obedience to the commands of God, just because it is obedience . . . But to be obedient means, "love your neighbour".' And the Calvinist Gustafson (1981) argued for a theocentric ethic of obedience characterized by the sovereignty of God, the centrality of piety and the requirement to order society according to God's command.

Surrender

In the Bible the sense of sin, at its most intense, is often a response to the kind of theophany described in Chapter 1. The law itself is there described as given in theophany on Mount Sinai (Ex. 19—24), while Isaiah responded to the vision of God in the Temple with a sense of being 'a man of unclean lips' (Isa. 6.1–8). Encounter with the bright omnipotence of God casts a shadow, which is a sense of contrasting human finitude, frailty, unworthiness and shame. As Otto noted (Chapter 7), the holy fascinates and allures us, but makes us tremble with fear. Thus the spiritualities of obedience find their root in *doxa*, worship, where the *doxa* (glory and repute) of self is abandoned in favour of 'the greater glory of God'. As Calvin put it, humankind 'cannot, without sacrilege, claim for himself even a crumb of righteousness, for just so much is plucked and taken away from the glory of God's righteousness' (2001, 3.8.2).

This spirituality of glory doubtless lies behind the view that divine will simply overwhelms the human will: as Calvin's 'irresistible grace'; as the relentless love of the 'Hound of Heaven' so wonderfully depicted in Francis Thompson's poem of that name; or in the quietist annihilation of the human desire for its own good in the face of the divine will, even to the extent of willing one's own damnation if God wills it.

This is surely one basis of the 'indifference' and 'detachment' favoured by many mystics, which Belden Lane links with the encounter with the sublime otherness of God in the 'fierce landscapes' of the desert. There he discovered (1998), as Job discovered in his encounter with God in the whirlwind (Job 38ff.), that one's own life and fulfilment can come to seem terribly small and insignificant in a way that is strangely liberating. God's will, unfathomable to the intellect, boding one's potential destruction as well as salvation, is there accepted in all its sublime glory, generating a spirit of self-forgetful adoration. Simone Weil likewise declares (2002, pp. 44, 48):

> Obedience is the supreme virtue. We have to love necessity.
> Every creature which obtains perfect obedience constitutes a special, unique, irreplaceable form of the presence, knowledge and operation of God in the world.

Such a spirituality runs deep in all three monotheistic faiths, and is perhaps simplest and clearest in Islam, a religion whose very name means 'submission'. Nevertheless, Jesus is never recorded as advocating disinterested obedience. His parables and teachings characteristically promise an ultimate reward. They not only command, but persuade, inviting a free response to a glimpse of something better. So we move to consider the spirituality that speaks not of a divine overwhelming of the will, but of the synergy of divine and human wills.

Obedience and Creation

Robinson (1971) has argued that for writers like Brunner and Gustafson, obedience to God takes place in a 'mythological beyond' floating detached from our natural and historical existence. But God's will is not alien to the nature he has created. There is continuity between Saul and Paul, between people's unregenerate nature and the new self reborn to obedience to God.

> God and his will or command are *not* extra items within the created world but lie behind the whole creation . . . Moral obligation *is* the impact of the divine will on human life. (p. 87)

So Aquinas contrasted obedience coerced by another human being with obedience to God.

> God's goodness requires that whatever he brings into existence, he should also guide towards its goal . . . The determination a creature receives from God constitutes its nature, whereas what man artificially imposes on a natural thing is a coercion. (1989, p. 152 (I.103.1))

In direct contrast with Calvin as quoted above, 'to detract from the creature's perfection is to detract from the perfection of the divine power' (cited in Taylor, 2007, p. 91). If Calvin's God is in some ways like a pagan god who feeds on our sacrifices and grows the more we are diminished, on Aquinas's understanding, to obey God is to obey the giver of our own nature, the one whose grace is shown most clearly, in people's own most free and least compelled acts.

This position has been taken further by Esther Reed (2000) who argues that an ethic of obedience to God does not force a submission to an alien power, but rather, liberates us from such powers. God is *authoritative* in ethics because he alone is *author* of creation. Just as Mikhail Bakhtin (1984) has argued that an author like Dostoyevsky creates a genuine autonomy in his characters, so God's authorship must allow for freedom and autonomy in people. God's word in scripture is not a monologue of imperatives, but a polyphony of diverse voices that enters into dialogue with itself and with humankind. Obeying God, unlike obeying a human authority, demands that people enter creatively and innovatively into dialogue with scripture, and so realize themselves as God's creations.

And James Alison notes (2001) that to obey God is to enter into Jesus' free receiving of his obedient Sonship from his Father. If people are to obey God as the only one to be called 'father' (Matt. 23.9), they are radically free from obedience to all human fathers and patriarchal authorities, even projected, 'divine' ones.

If this is so, then neither Calvin's heteronomous surrender nor Kant's autonomy constitutes the moral ideal. Perhaps it would be helpful to draw on Paul

Tillich's notion of theonomy (1976) and see people as growing through four moral stages, which you might compare with those of Erikson and Fowler (Table 5):

- **Anomy** – the pre-moral stage of the baby, living by self-centred instinct.
- **Heteronomy** – living to please others – including a naïvely understood God – and avoid punishment and shame; characteristic of childhood and adolescence.
- **Autonomy** – living up to one's own standards of self-respect; avoiding guilt; the sign of responsible adulthood.
- **Theonomy** – living in God, as autonomy is united to its own ground in the One who is both other, and more inward, than the responsible self; characteristic of mid-life onwards, as ego and bodily strength wane, but conscience grows.

Conscience

In familiar Christian spirituality, the voice of God is described as coming to us through conscience, a word that originally meant simply consciousness or self-awareness. Some – like Freud – would regard conscience as the internalization of 'heteronomous' voices of our fathers and our social customs. But Macquarrie (1970) identifies a deeper understanding more closely linked with the term's original sense: conscience can be understood as the answer to the question 'how is it with you?'

People speak of having a 'clear' conscience, when there is nothing they want to obscure from themselves and others. But they also describe conscience as a 'voice' they have to obey, a voice that comes from 'inside' and is capable of over-riding the external voices and laws of society. Whereas sight communicates a spatial distance or externality in what we see, hearing communicates a voice that is that of the *other*, without necessarily being *external*. Intimate voices can seem to come from within, mingling with our own thoughts in the kind of dialogue Reed describes.

Wherein lies the 'otherness' here that would distinguish this process from an autonomous reasoning, and require talk of God and spirituality? We have already noted that morality is not always easy. People often find through bitter experience that they cannot clarify their consciences by their own lights and efforts. The self, as Freud and Jung have shown so well, contains too much that is excluded from the light, yet acts in us. The centre around which people seek integration is always another – parents, teachers, soul-friends – but God is the only other who is not in any way a rival other but, as we have seen, closer to people than anything, even themselves. We need to find 'the engagement [with God] which has been formed within us in spite of ourselves' (Weil, 2002, p. 44).

Of course conscience involves clarity about the external situation too. In traditional terms, conscience needs to be 'informed' with a rich and balanced view of the situations and choices it confronts. Consciences need educating well, since they are shaped by the society people live in and the company they keep. So conscience will involve an inter-illumination of external and internal clarities.

Conscience will not override the will or demand a complete surrender, but requires a laying aside both internal defences and compulsions and external prejudices. The parables of Jesus seem designed to set people working both on their perceptions of situations, and on their adequacy of response. And it was through parables, and other witty and pithy wise sayings, that Jesus summoned people to obedience to the kingship of God.

Obedience on this understanding requires both being 'informed' about the situation, and being 'well formed' and integrated oneself. The latter is the spiritual issue of becoming 'responsible for the soul' that we have already noted. And that issue links the spirituality of obedience with those of fulfilment and integration, to be considered next.

The Spirituality of Fulfilment

Having hinted that unlike 'surrender', the 'conscience' form of obedience throws us back on questions of what constitutes our self and its fulfilment, we turn to a form of ethics that relates to questions of what is 'good' and worth seeking as our future goal, rather than what we 'ought' to do in obedience to past law. An ethic that judges acts by the intended result is termed *teleological* (from the Greek for 'end' or 'purpose'); one that judges by actual consequences, whether intended or otherwise, is termed *consequential*.

The notion that we should judge ethics by the consequences they bring for ourselves and others is suggested in the Wisdom literature of the Bible (including Proverbs, Job, Ecclesiastes, parts of the Psalms, and the apocryphal Ecclesiasticus and Wisdom), which balances the emphasis on obedience in the Law and the Prophets.

What should we seek?

There have been many conflicting accounts of what the 'good' consists in. Here are the main accounts, moving from the most individual to the most cosmic:

1 **Becoming oneself.** The goal of each person's life is unique, and she must discover and pursue it for herself (Kierkegaard, Chapter 6).
2 **Order** triumphing over our inner chaos (Bertocci and Millard, 1963).
3 **Happiness.** The 'utilitarians' Jeremy Bentham and John Stuart Mill argued that happiness is the one thing we all in practice value. Mill saw it as the basis of Jesus' flexible, anti-legalistic ethics.
4 **Flourishing.** According to Aristotle, each species needs certain basic things to flourish. Humans, irrespective of race and class, all need food, shelter, education, society and so forth, without which they dwindle and fail to reach their potential. This became the basis for a 'natural law' understanding of ethics and human rights.
5 **The 'common good'.** Another factor in 'natural law' ethics: individual flourishing may have to be sacrificed to that of the majority, or society as a whole. However in a society of plural values the common good is proving ever harder to define.
6 **Global flourishing.** The flourishing of ecosystems, and non-human species, have come to matter to us. The notion of earth as 'Gaia', a self-regulating individual whole (Lovelock, 2000) enables us to apply the notion of flourishing to the whole earth; but so, arguably, does the notion of creation as something that God delights in and desires to see come to fulfilment and freedom through the Spirit (Bergmann, 2005). Many – though by no means all – Christians advocate a move in spirituality away from its earlier 'male' concern with the individual soul or citizen towards a 'feminine' embrace of the earth (Radford-Ruether, 1989; Primavesi, 2000).

Future Fulfilment and Present Obedience

There are huge problems as to how we balance such ends, and in particular how we decide when, if ever, a moral *end* can justify immoral *means*. Teleology sounds initially the most benign form of ethics, with its concern for people's flourishing rather than obedience to rigid laws; yet the tyrannies of the twentieth century in particular have been teleological tyrannies, in which a fixed and absolute ideal of future good has been used to justify terrible present harm: torture, genocide, the elimination of entire classes and races.

If, as we are suggesting, Christian obedience is essentially that of conscience rather than surrender, then it is inextricably linked with our own integration or 'coming to ourselves' (like the prodigal son, Luke 15.17). And this in turn cannot be divorced from the question of the other and her coming to be herself; so Christian fulfilment cannot be selfish or escapist; it can mean self-sacrifice, but can never sacrifice people as means to a utopian future goal. Whereas some secular notions of purpose defer the goal of life to some far off utopian future, the Christian goal is always embodied in the person in front of one, whom Jesus found – in Christian belief – a goal worth his own dying on the cross.

Christian spirituality needs constantly to replenish, with its end-time imagination, humanity's ever-weakening hold on the ultimate goals, but always and only in a way that sharpens, rather than (as it often has) escaping from, the sense of present opportunities and obligations to love.

And in practice an ethic that has to calculate all the possible effects of different actions, and weigh them up, before decision can be made, will defer infinitely any responsible action. In practice an ethic of fulfilment, of whatever kind, will need to learn and instil by repeated experience the habits that make for fulfilment in ourselves and others; so the ethic of fulfilment will unfold into one of virtue.

Spirituality and Virtue

In Aristotle's thought, a virtue is a disposition to do good. Virtues are created by good habits which 'engrave' themselves on the soul; his term for this process, *'character'*, literally meant engraving. Perhaps the main contribution behaviourist psychology can make to spirituality is its understanding of the way repeated responses form habits and dispositions.

Plato had linked four cardinal virtues with the right ordering of self and society.

- **Moderation**, ruling our animal nature, the virtue of the working classes.
- **Courage**, directing our energies and feelings, the virtue of warriors.
- **Wisdom**, guiding the mind, the virtue of philosophers and rulers.
- **Justice**, rightly ordering these three levels of the individual and society.

Aquinas added to these four virtues the three 'theological virtues' of *faith*, *hope* and *love*, making a somewhat mixed bag of seven (Macquarrie, 1970, p. 132).

Meanwhile in the ascetic traditions of the desert (Kirk, 1931) Evagrius had noted the eight *deadly sins* with which the monks experienced themselves as struggling. In order of increasing severity they were greed, lust, avarice, grief, anger, apathy, vanity and pride. In the West, Gregory the Great reduced the list to seven and began the tradition of ranking them according to the degree to which they offended against love, the scheme which informed Dante's imagination of the geography of purgatory (Figure 9, based on Dorothy Sayers, 1955, p. 62):

a **Love disordered**: divided further into:
   loving a secondary good excessively in place of the ultimate good which is God: desiring sex, food or possessions too much in lust, gluttony and avarice. These are placed at the top of the mountain within nearest reach of heaven.
   Loving the ultimate good deficiently: sloth, in the middle.
b **Love rejected or perverted**: anger, envy and pride, which actively seek to deprive others of the good, and even to harm them, are on the lower slopes.

The focus on virtues and vices declined with the Reformation. As dispositions in ourselves to 'good works', they seemed to compromise the need for obedient dependence on God. Only recently have they been rehabilitated to the centre of ethical debate, following Alistair Macintyre's argument (1981) that only a focus on the virtues could rescue ethics from its current relativism.

Figure 9: The Ethics of Mount Purgatory

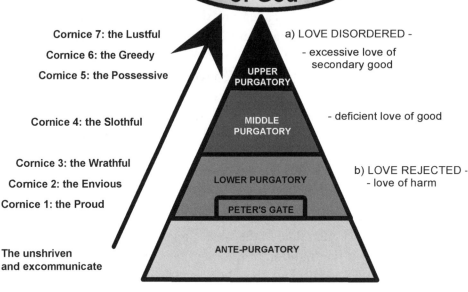

Education in Virtue

Spirituality itself might be conceived as the education of virtue, a schooling of sense and feeling so that we begin to desire what is good (Gorringe, 2001). But Christian understanding of such an education will differ in at least two ways from the classical Greek.

First, this will not be a spiritual athleticism or self-confident self-training. If the Holy Spirit, or grace, is for Christians the teacher of virtue, both humility and openness will be primary learning requirements. Jonathan Edwards (1989, Vol. 8, p. 254) believed that grace 'imparts humility and contrition to the moral struggle', and so 'restores an excellent enlargement and extensiveness to the soul'.

Virtue and Violence

Second, the classical virtues were obviously linked to classical culture. In Plato's scheme, they are based on power. Courage belongs to the violent warrior, justice maintains a threefold hierarchical order, moderation can do violence to legitimate bodily needs in the interests of a 'higher' mind, and wisdom is not balanced by compassion, which Aristotle regarded as a kind of weakness. The society to which Christian virtue relates will not be the hierarchical city state of Plato, but the kingdom of God, whose school is the Church.

René Girard (2001) argues that almost all societies base their systems of justice and morality on the violence of sacrifice, in which a scapegoat is cast out or slaughtered in order to make peace between people whose imitation of one another's values has locked in rivalry for the valued things. Law and conventional morality seem to be led by the hunger to apportion penalty and blame when things go wrong, and in our post-Christian society this is proving ever more the case. But in Christianity God moves from being the false God, who guarantees social order in return for sacrifice, to being the scapegoat sacrifice himself. 'The false God changes suffering into violence. The true God changes violence into suffering' (Weil, 2002, p. 73).

Virtues of the Peaceable Kingdom

In response, Christian life and spirituality need to be organized to develop virtues that are not just distinctive, but in many ways contrary, to what society conceives of as moral and just: virtues of participation in the free, peaceable and indifferent love of the Father, embracing those whom conventional justice and morality exclude. This is the constant theme of the writings of Girard's follower, James Alison (1996; 2001). It is perhaps the exclusive and judgemental kind of morality which Brunner provocatively, but rightly dubbed as 'evil', something Christian virtue must oppose with the divine embrace (Volf, 1996) of life in Christ, in whom there is 'no condemnation' (Rom. 8.1). Of course, Christians themselves have yet to construct an ethic wholly free from the concept of blame.

The instinct of Gregory (though questioned by Aquinas) to order the vices by the standard of love is therefore clearly right. As Edwards again argues, for

Christians 'true virtue most essentially consists in benevolence to being in general . . . and love to God, the being of beings' (1960, pp. 3 and 14.) The 'solar ethic' of Jesus (Cupitt, 1995) – whereby we are called to love like that of the sun that shines indifferently on good and bad alike (Matt. 5.45) – commands a kind of virtue radically opposed to the warrior and ruler virtues of Plato. Perhaps Christian virtue ethics would do better to look to the Beatitudes (Matt. 5.1–10) and the nine Pauline 'fruits of the spirit' (Gal. 5.22–23) as the foundation of a distinctive ethic of grace-based and non-violently generous virtues. And Jesus' parables express the profound difference of the kingdom and its virtues.

It is in this spirit that Stanley Hauerwas (1981; 1998) argues for the Church as the society that educates in the distinctive virtues of Christ's peaceable kingdom. Virtue ethics here relates to a community of obedience to Christ, requiring us to reintroduce our first ethical strand. James Childs (1992) makes this link very explicit, seeing the Church as community of formation of virtue in response to 'the ongoing experience of God's approach to us in law and gospel, God's word of judgment and grace' (p. 75).

Spirituality as the Transforming How of Ethics

The Scottish philosopher David Hume famously pointed out that logically it is invalid to argue for a moral statement on the basis of a factual one, or to derive a statement saying what ought to be done from one that describes what is the case. But what cannot be proven in logic is perhaps often achieved in actual lives. Whenever we base what we do and advise others to do on what we believe to be true, we are in fact doing this, and the process of doing it can be called spirituality in the broadest sense. *Spirituality is how 'is' becomes 'ought'*; how teaching, tradition and vision translate into desires and virtues and thence into life and action; how what we believe about the world becomes expressed in the way we live.

What philosophical logic cannot hold together, practice has to. Even a simple matter like driving a car requires obedience to the rules of the highway code, an idea of one's destination and how to get there, and the virtues of good driving. Any philosophical purist who advocated one of these at the expense of the other two would end up either crashing or getting lost! The practice of living according to one's beliefs is bound even more to hold together obedience, ends and virtues. We have seen how this is certainly the case with Christian spirituality.

Christianity as spirituality, not morality?

But we might go further, and suggest that perhaps Christianity is primarily a spirituality and only secondarily an ethic; that Jesus taught not a set of moral instructions, but a way of discovering and desiring the good life for ourselves. This is John Stuart Mill's point (2002, Chapter 2):

> Others beside utilitarians have been of the opinion that the Christian revelation was intended, and is fitted, to inform the hearts and minds of mankind with a spirit which should enable them to find for themselves what is right, and incline them to do it when found, rather than to tell them, except in a general way, what it is.

We have also noted that Christian spirituality presents a challenge to ethical systems. *It is and is not ethics*; it is a source of morality but more than just a morality. We have discussed three rival ways of deducing the content of ethics; but we also saw that in terms of Christian spirituality the three are interdependent rather than rivals. And this is because of the way Christian spirituality challenges each way and transforms it into something else, creating a circle of ethical dependences.

- **Obeying** God requires attention to conscience, for which God is not a distant alien but the inward voice of the author and fulfilment of our own being. Obedience in Christian spirituality challenges forms of obedience based on submission to alien power, and addresses our consciences, where the voice that calls us is the voice that is making us and leading us to our *fulfilment*.
- **Fulfilment** for Christian spirituality challenges both the selfish pursuit of individual fulfilment and the sacrifice of the individual in the present to any future corporate utopia. It opens an end-time imagination for possibilities outside the scope of the imagined projects of humanity, yet with us even now: the kingdom of God, an ultimate future that is 'presented' in the

corporate life of the Church where we are schooled in the Christian *virtues*.
- But these **virtues** are in many ways opposed to the violence behind the classical virtues, and find their context in a community formed by *obedience* to the peaceable Word of God, whose command to share his 'solar' generosity is without rivalry.

Spirituality, Ethics and Theology

Finally, it may be possible boldly to venture some parallels between the content of Christian faith, the stages of the spiritual journey, and the three theological virtues (see Table 7):

Table 7: Ethics, Spirituality and Theology

Ethics as . . .	Spiritual grounding of this ethic	Person of Trinity	Spiritual 'stage'	Virtue
obedience	God to be obeyed as author and fulfilment . . .	The only one to be obeyed as Father	Purification	Faith
fulfilment	Christ the embodiment of Christian virtue . . .	Christ in his life of goodness	Illumination	Hope
virtue	Learned through the community of obedience	Spirit as divine virtue in midst	Union	Love

- **Obedience** is owed solely to the only one to be called Father, the author and perfecter of being. It is expressed especially in the spiritual stage of purification, where false alternative idols are purged and obedience to God streamlined. The virtue required is faith – trust in God and faithfulness to divine command.
- **Fulfilment** of Christian life is in Christ, who embodies the goodness of God for Christians in his own obedience to the Father. In spiritual illumination the vision of God in Christ increases and shows Christians the true goals worth seeking and what to hope for as their end.

- **Virtue** is for Christians the life of the Holy Spirit – or 'grace' – the divine life in the midst of the Church, teaching all things and bringing about union with God, or *theosis*, expressed above all in the supreme virtue of love.

For Reflection and Discussion

1 Do you regard spirituality as transcending ethics or ethics as better off without spirituality? Which of the arguments in the opening sections do you find convincing, and which not?
2 Do you find it easy or hard to be good? Does spirituality make it easier or harder? How and why?
3 Is goodness something you encounter from outside or something that quietly stirs your conscience? Which arguments in this section do you resonate with most?
4 List the goals on p. 193 in your order of preference, and discuss or justify to yourself your reasons. What really matters to you?
5 List the virtues described in the Beatitudes and the Pauline gifts of the spirit. Compare them with the four classical virtues. Taking all three lists of virtues into account, which would you see as the three most important virtues of all? Do they all come from one list or an amalgam? Why would you say these virtues were so important to you?
6 Reflect on the model expressed in Table 7. What are its strengths and weaknesses? On balance in what ways do you think spirituality helps people lead a good life, or not?

Further Reading

James Alison, 2001, *Faith beyond Resentment,* London: DLT.

Stanley Hauerwas, 1998, *Sanctify Them in the Truth: Holiness Exemplified,* Edinburgh: T & T Clark.

Alasdair MacIntyre, 1981, *After Virtue, A Study in Moral Theory,* London: Duckworth.

Esther Reed, 2000, *The Genesis of Ethics: On the Authority of God as the Origin of Christian Ethics,* London: DLT.

Peter Vardy and Paul Grosch, 1999, *The Puzzle of Ethics,* London: Fount.

Miroslav Volf, 1996, *Exclusion and Embrace,* Nashville: Abingdon Press.

John Howard Yoder, 1994, *The Politics of Jesus,* Grand Rapids: Eerdmans.

13

Spiritual Space? Spirituality in a World of Difference

Many who lived through 1968 in their formative years will witness to the indelible spiritual mark it has left. After post-war austerity, and before the threats of ecological decline had come into view, people felt optimistic and generally materialistic. And a wave of protest swept the world, reducing venerated bastions of learning to chaos: in America, the anti-war demonstrations, in China, the devastating 'Cultural Revolution', in Paris and elsewhere the student 'sit ins', in Latin America, Medellín and the beginnings of liberation theology, and in Czechoslovakia a liberalization brutally crushed.

Everywhere the empires of reason were being contested. States that had been constructed in different ways – communist or liberal capitalist – to promote equality and freedom were under attack. Something vaguer was somehow 'in the air', an almost erotic longing – expressed in the hippies' 'flower power' and in the newly 'mystical', psychedelic cadences of pop music – for a world free from the rule of a cramped rationalism, brimming with spontaneity, innocence, free love and peace.

That world never came into being, and perhaps never could, but the longing has defined a spirituality that is with us still: global and yet suspicious of any universal claims, whether rationalist or religious, and seeing human difference as something to be celebrated rather than contained. 'Metanarratives' – all-embracing stories of how the world is or ought to be – are suspect. If the hopes of constructing a world by and for 'man' out of a universally applicable reason and good institutions was 'modern', we have become 'postmodern'. We are, or spiritually want to be, 'after' all that.

In this chapter we will examine the impact of this world of celebrated difference on Christian spirituality. We will look first at different spiritual responses to the many faiths which Christianity encountered first through the world empires, but now at home. Then we will look at the postmodern situation generally, finally putting forward the authors' own suggestions as to how the insights of postmodernism can be carried forward in spirituality without its potentially destructive effects.

Christianity and Different World Spiritualities

As Christianity encountered other faiths and cultures, overseas and at home, two kinds of issue arose with great implications for Christian spirituality. One concerned the spiritual status of those faiths themselves – whether they were valid spiritual paths, inspired by or leading to the same God or salvation. The other concerned whether the spiritualities, beliefs, worship and practices of those faiths and cultures should be incorporated in Christian worship and practice, especially if they were in tension with Christian tradition.

Exclusivism: One Way, One Christ

The mainstream approach of the Catholic Church from the time of Augustine, and declared as official teaching from the thirteenth century, was '*extra ecclesiam nulla salus*' – there is no salvation outside the (Catholic) Church. And the Protestant tradition with its emphasis on salvation by faith alone gave, if anything, even less scope for the notion that the good works of non-Christians could be a means of salvation (Netland, 1991).

In the twentieth century *Karl Barth*'s understanding of religion as a vain, faithless human striving for God had the effect of negating the value of non-Christian religions, along with Christianity itself when considered as a religion:

Religion is unbelief . . . From the standpoint of revelation religion is clearly seen to be a human attempt to anticipate what God in his revelation wills to do and does do. It is the attempted replacement of the divine work with a human manufacture. (1956, pp. 299–300)

So in one form or another, 'exclusivism' – the belief that Christ is the only way to salvation, and the Church the only way to Christ – has been the mainstream, consensus view for most of Christian history.

Inclusivism: Many Ways through One Christ

However, we have seen (p. 22) how Clement of Alexandria believed that God's Word was scattered like a seed throughout pagan culture, while Origen believed salvation in Christ was universal. Such beliefs formed a constant undertow to exclusivism, allowing the Church as it spread to 'inculturate' its own worship and teaching into the forms of local philosophy and spirituality.

In the twentieth century, a rationale for this approach was developed. *Karl Rahner* (1904–84) criticized the traditional Catholic separation of nature from grace or the supernatural, and argued that all creation is in a sense graced with Christ, who is the fulfilment of all human longings, including religious longings. Each religion must be a way to salvation because in some way it must point to Christ. Those who follow their own religion devoutly and faithfully are, in Rahner's well-known phrase, 'anonymous Christians'. In the 1960s the Roman Catholic bishops at Vatican II gave general approval to these ideas. *Jacques Dupuis* (1997) took a further step, arguing that the overflowing life of the Trinity means that salvation must exist in *different* forms outside the Church, so that those of other faiths will not necessarily be drawn into the Church when they encounter it.

'Inculturation' and dialogue rather than direct evangelism have come to characterize Catholic and many other churches' mission to those of other faiths. For example (Kuster, 2001), the Tanzanian Charles Nyamiti and the Zairean Bénézet Bujo adapted African notions of ancestor worship to present Jesus Christ as the brother-ancestor or first ancestor. M. M. Thomas and Stanley Samartha pioneered the presentation of Christ in terms of a Hindu framework; and Katzumi Takizawa and Seiichi Yagi have allowed the Buddhist doctrine of no-self to challenge traditional Christologies and suggest new ways of seeing the person of Christ.

Universalism: Many Ways to One Reality

It is often asserted that the mystical essence or goal of all religions is the same, and we noted in Chapter 7 how the 'perennial philosophy' takes such a stance, as does John Hick (p. 120). But we also saw that this position was vulnerable to the philosophical critique of Katz and Lindberg, who in their different ways question whether we can detach an experiential essence of religions from the concepts of a religious culture.

Ramon Panikkar (b.1918) however has sought to articulate this shared mystical core in a manner that does more justice to the diversity of faiths. Implicitly criticizing positions like Hick's, Panikkar transforms the notion of the many religious paths up to the one 'mountain' goal in a typically postmodern way:

> It is not simply that there are different ways leading to the peak, but that the summit itself would collapse if all the paths disappeared. The peak is in a certain sense the result of the slopes leading to it . . . It is not that this reality *has* many names as if there were a reality outside of the names. This reality *is* the many names, and each name is a new aspect. (1981, pp. 24 and 19)

Panikkar believes that the doctrine of the Trinity allows of this diversity in God, enabling us to do justice to the names of God in other faiths. For authentic faith in all traditions is at once prophetic, humane and mystical. But when people approach God exclusively through one 'person' of what Christianity terms the Trinity, distortion results, and God is lost in one of the following:

- **Nihilism**: when the transcendence of the Father becomes a total unknowability.
- **Humanism**: when the humanity of Christ eclipses the divinity and leaves merely 'human values'.
- **Angelism**: when spirituality seeks a disembodied and asexual purity.

Panikkar's understanding intriguingly combines aspects of universalism, inclusivism and pluralism, and is hard to pin down to any one of these.

Liberationism: All Ways in Question

Volker Kuster (2001, pp. 181–6) distinguishes two ways in which Christian spirituality can take genuine root in another culture. What he terms the 'cultural and religious' approach – which tends to presuppose inclusivism – emphasizes dialogue with the local culture and religion and adoption of appropriate elements from them. The 'socio-economic and political' approach, on the other hand, emphasizes the need for liberation from both Western and local culture. The liberation perspective sees Christianity not as a timeless 'essence' that can be translated into differing perspectives and cultures, but as a future and immanent end, a kingdom that challenges and transforms all perspectives and cultures, including Christian ones.

In Latin America, the home of liberation theology, in North American Black theology, Indian Dalit theology, Korean Minjung theology, and feminist, gay and other theologies of the oppressed, we therefore witness no peaceable and peacemaking dialogue between mainstream presentations of Christianity and other faiths and cultures. Rather we witness an interaction between the 'underbellies' of each that is subversive of the 'mainstream' understanding of both Christianity and the local culture. Such interaction can prove sharply critical of the exclusive claims of traditional Christianity, seeing them as supporting, or arising from, Western imperialism. Inclusive and universal approaches are often criticized, too, for 'including' all people in a Western Christian framework, or advancing a Western analysis as 'universal'.

Liberation and the Deconstructive Grin

This critique of knowledge as power can be very liberating for peoples who have hitherto thought in concepts inherited from alien and dominating civilizations. But there is liberation here only if such 'deconstruction' refrains from presenting itself as (paradoxically) a universal metanarrative of its own, to the effect that all knowledge is power and only power. The problem for the vulnerable then becomes, if there is no truth, how can truth ever be spoken to power? If there is only power pitted against power, surely the strong will always win?

Liberation theology has certainly helped us see the power and vested interest behind a great deal that passes for factual truth. But if we see *all* truth claims as power claims, the Cheshire cat of liberation disappears – as being just another metanarrative or universal story – leaving only the omni-critical grin of deconstruction. This is what we seem to find in the stronger forms of postmodernism.

Postmodern Spirituality?

Postmodernism is often identified with another approach to the many faiths which we shall discuss: pluralism. But if pluralism believes there are many paths to many goals, and no way of judging between them (in the jargon, they are 'incommensurable'), postmodernism in its more radical forms believes that there are no paths to anywhere, because all are judged wanting. The 'judge' is the deconstruction of all truth as power; the omni-critical grin.

We shall consider the possibility of a 'pluralist realism' at the end of the chapter, and focus now on postmodernism in this more radical sense.

Postmodernism is a tangled plant with many roots and shoots, which it is beyond the scope of this book to discuss, but any postmodern canon of scripture would have to include the German philosopher Friedrich Nietzsche (1844–1900), his French interpreter Michel Foucault (1926–84) and the 'father' of deconstruction, Jacques Derrida (1930–2004). All three argue that all claims to truth and knowledge can be deconstructed as serving the interests of power. Behind every argument is coercion, striving to force acceptance of what is in reality only a subjective viewpoint, in order to bring someone under the reign of another's influence.

Nietzsche's response was to celebrate the will to power, and urge people to use their imagination to enhance their power over weaker humans. Foucault and Derrida take the opposite line, suspecting all grand 'metanarratives' and seeking out the lost worlds of the powerless, or the hints of truth writers produce despite themselves, lost in unacknowledged interstices of their texts. The resulting 'deconstruction' is not critique, which presents arguments for truth alternative to what the author presents, thus prolonging the struggle for power. Rather it is a way of using the text against its author, to unsay the ideas he proclaimed, and say the truths he must have known, but did or could not acknowledge.

The other major postmodern 'testament' would include writers in the Anglo-Saxon tradition, such as Wittgenstein, Kuhn and Berger, and in theology, D. Z.

Phillips, Katz and Lindbeck – the constructivists discussed in Chapter 8, who argue that we cannot prize truth apart from culture.

We will now consider a 'deconstruction' of Christian spirituality, before looking at some moves towards a postmodern Christian spirituality.

Mysticism and Male Power: Jantzen

The feminist writer Grace Jantzen (1995) deconstructs successive definitions of mysticism as serving to enhance male, patriarchal power at the expense of women. Identifying many of the developments we have covered, she detects male bias in each:

1 **Pre- and early Christian**: mystics were defined as the 'mystical ones' of secret mystery cults. These cults celebrated the feminine, but identified it with the 'lower' realm of nature. Many of the cults were for men only.
2 **Neoplatonic:** the early 'Fathers' identified spirituality with the rational, which was seen as 'male' by contrast with the more emotional and passionate female. Women could become mystics only by renouncing their sexuality and becoming spiritually 'male' nuns.
3 **Mystical meanings** were discerned in the scriptures especially from Origen onward, and the mystic was defined as the one able to elucidate them. Christianity shifted to being a 'religion of the book' with great emphasis on scripture and doctrine, devaluing as we have seen (p. 36) the oral 'instruction of the mother'. Generally only men had the education to study such things.
4 **Affective mysticism** developed in the medieval West counterbalancing these rationalist strands. But only with female writers such as Hildegard, Julian and Hadewijch do we find a real celebration of the body, the sensual and the visionary. In time the Church came to suppress this and associate it with heresy and even witchcraft.
5 **Ineffability.** At best, mysticism was relegated to the realm of private, ineffable psychological experiences, which became the subject of much modern study of spirituality (Chapter 7). But it thereby became irrelevant to the realms of serious theology, let alone feminist and other issues of power.

Jantzen's represents one of very few serious and subtle attempts to deconstruct the Christian spiritual tradition, and she gives a plausible feminist spin to many of the developments we have considered. But an equally plausible and opposite account of mysticism and its relation to power is possible, as in the next two writers.

Mysticism as Unsaying: Sells

Rather than maintaining religious power, and so needing deconstruction, Michael Sells argues that mysticism deconstructs itself. In a careful study (1994) of several mystics he argues that they employ a 'language of unsaying' in which propositions cancel one another out and create an 'anarchic moment' which, despite its conceptual challenge, creates a powerful effect on the reader. He gives as examples (p. 209) Eriugena's nothingness of God, Porete's annihilation of the self and its will to do anything or refrain from doing anything for God, and Eckhart's letting go of God to find God.

Sells compares this mystical use of language to the joke, where again language subverts the very expectations it generates, creating an anarchic 'punchline' with a hilarious, dizzying effect on our customary perspectives.

Mysticism as Deconstruction: Cupitt

Don Cupitt uses postmodernism to effect a jubilant mysticism of endless ecstasy, in a way that reverses Jantzen's understanding. Far from consolidating male hierarchical and doctrinal power, for Cupitt (1998, pp. 43–4)

> The entire literature of mysticism and religious experience incorporates a feminine protest against . . . the dour alienated masculinism of official doctrine and of social authority . . . In its rapture the soul is dissolved, drowned . . . God pours out his Spirit. Grace erupts into the soul like a jet of warm liquid. It tastes sweet.

Whereas the careful hierarchical distinctions of institutional religion give men the advantage, mystical religion gives it to women, because it involves something akin to female orgasm (p.64): 'the basic religious act of cosmic, total, extravertive self-surrender into bliss is female, and in religious devotion every man has to become a woman' (p. 64).

Cupitt's own 'mysticism of the secondary' consists in just such a 'female' surrender to the fact that there is no 'primary' substantial enduring reality behind anything, but only chaos. He argues (p. 134) that we can come to this surrender through religious meditation, philosophical analysis, postmodern deconstruction, the physical or biological sciences, music, painting or the media. All mystical language aims to effect it.

So who is right – Jantzen when she argues that mysticism serves to maintain male order, or Cupitt when he argues that it seeks to effect a 'feminine' surrender? Perhaps it depends on which mysticism one is talking about. The tight yet 'ecstatic' hierarchy of Denys, and the 'epektasis' of Gregory of Nyssa, extending up into the womblike dark of God, seem 'male' and very different from the orgasmic surrender of many medieval Western and quietist mystics.

This suggests that both kinds of deconstructive approach to spirituality may be simplistic, and that between the extremes described there may be room for a spirituality that is neither a wielding of nor a surrender to power, but a balanced engagement with reality in its life-giving mystery.

God without Being: Marion

A subtler, but more difficult approach is Jean-Luc Marion's assimilation of the apophatic tradition of Denys, which, without denying God's existence, places God 'above being'. Marion's argument reaches a similar conclusion from a different approach, based on the distinction between the idol, which seeks by art to bring the god within the range of the visible by reflecting him in stone or paint, and the icon, which brings us within the gaze of the invisible God, which we ourselves begin to mirror. 'If man, by his gaze, renders the idol possible, in reverent contemplation of the icon, on the contrary, the gaze of the invisible, in person, aims at man' (1995, p. 19).

Idols, for Marion, seek to fix the god and pin him in our perspective, placing him as it were in our power. But (see p. 29) icons do not seek to place the *nature* of the historical Jesus before our eyes, but rather invoke the divine *person* who addresses us in the face of Jesus and the saints. We do not bring God into our horizons, but allow God to open our limited perspectives up to his divine perspective.

But Marion argues with the apophatic mystics that concepts can be idols. This happens when we construct theological and metaphysical systems, grand narratives of being of which God is a part, subject to our intellectual gaze like Plato's form of the Good. That is why Marion rejects all 'onto-theology' – theology based on general accounts of being – as idolatrous. Following the Jewish philosopher Emmanuel Levinas, he urges that God is love and goodness, but 'otherwise than being'.

Marion here gives the spiritual priority over the systematic in theology; indeed his own writing is full of 'unsaying' in Sells's sense. However, though he is clear about the 'idolatrous' metaphysical theology he rejects, he does not make it clear what it would mean to construct a truly 'iconic' theology.

Virtual Faith: Beaudoin

In a far more accessible and popular mode, Tim Beaudoin (1998; compare Lynch, 2002; Tracey, 2004; Heelas, 2004) assimilates postmodern insights into a discussion of the seeming continuation of a form of spirituality within a 'Generation X' that has largely rejected formal religion. He argues that we find in many today a 'virtual faith' that has no concern or understanding for the truth claims or moral demands of faith, but is fascinated by its imagery, and uses it intensively in art, film and other media. This approach, jettisoning the Christian metanarratives, and cleaving to what some would term a 'superficial', aesthetic excitement in religion, is typically postmodern. Beaudoin's point is not to evaluate, but to help us see where those who value Christian spirituality have now to begin.

Many Ways, Many-Sided Spiritual Reality?

Perhaps the key issue for spirituality 'after modernity' is whether one can create a meaningful life without either resorting or submitting to power and compulsion. Can we be free in our relationships with one another and with God, and yet make sense to one another and to ourselves? To respect one another's freedom, do we have to lock one another into incommensurable cultural boxes, and renounce communication? And another aspect of the same question: can we speak of meaning and reality without surreptitiously trying to impose on others, or subject ourselves to, some power-wielding 'metanarrative'? Can belief in a real world or a real God ever be innocent?

In harmony with the very points we are about to make, we shall offer, not solid proof, but attempts to persuade you that spirituality has a key role in the possibility of

- an 'innocent' encounter with reality;
- accepting uncertainty without giving up on reality;
- talking about this reality in non-coercive but persuasive ways;
- building together an understanding of reality that is both pluralist and realist.

Innocent Encounter

For hard-line postmodernism, freedom and a sense of objective reality vary *inversely*. The more we believe in objective reality outside us, the more our actions are constrained. The more we distrust one another's claims, the freer we shall be.

However, in our discussion of the practical basis of knowing, and our example of sailing the boat (pp. 149–50), we suggested in effect that freedom and a sense of reality vary in *direct* proportion. To be free to sail where he wishes is not possible to one who seeks absolute power over wind and wave. Freedom comes through humbly learning to respect the powers of boat and weather, interacting with them to move the boat where we wish to go. We become freer ourselves, as we acknowledge their reality over against us, and renounce fantasies of absolute power and absolute submission in favour of care-full interaction.

Spirituality might require a similar deepening of our sense of interaction with reality (Thompson, 1990). Authentic spirituality humbly acknowledges reality reaching far beyond our physical and conceptual grasp, without abasing itself in surrender to overwhelming powers. It patiently learns to dance in synergy with God.

So when do action and freedom degenerate into freedom-denying power? Surely when one side of this interaction gives way, so that we are either simply acting to overcome outside forces and persons, or letting ourselves be 'put upon' by them.

We argued (pp. 150–1) that the pastoral cycle shows how a spirituality can enhance our dialogue with reality through a cycle of action and experience resourced by tradition-catalysed reflection.

Uncertainty and Relativism

For the absolutist, truth is identified with sure and certain belief, belief that can be irrefutably proven from sure foundations on which everyone is agreed. For the postmodern relativist, there are no such agreed foundations, so nothing can ever be known for sure. There are no certainties, so there are no truths. What appears to be proof is therefore an exercise of power: one person or group trying to force their view on another.

But the move from uncertainty to a strong form of relativism is surely made too quickly here. A relativism that allows us to mean different things by the same words, and even a relativism that allows us to know things about the world in different ways, are possible without subscribing to the relativism that says we live in sealed, incommensurable 'worlds' so there is no 'real world' to be known at all (Thompson, 1989).

Indeed, we argued (pp. 131–2) that it is precisely the hunger for reality that makes both science and spirituality ready to jettison inadequate 'certainties'.

Persuasion and Emergent Truth

There are quite obviously middle options between proof and power. We are not always (or even usually) when we use language, trying either to demonstrate or command; we are often trying to persuade (Brummett in Buley-Meissner, 2000). Rather than logical argument, we may use language to stir feelings and paint verbal pictures so as to open eyes to the truth as we see it. There is often no agreed rational framework whereby speakers can prove their points to those who hold a different perspective. Nevertheless, as they try to persuade each other from their different perspectives, new truth upon which both sides agree may emerge.

As emergent, this truth may not be in competition with the truth that either side is holding to. So, 'Rhetoric is the flux that merges epistemologies. Argument is the secret passage connecting ways of knowing. Persuasion is the alembic that can transubstantiate the academic and the spiritual' (Brummett, p. 132).

Thus, as Cupitt also notes, it was not knock-down argument that convinced people, at a certain stage in history, that slavery, or the inequality of women, or (currently) condemning people for their sexuality, is wrong. Nobody has ever 'proven' those things to be wrong, but a lot of persuasion has gone on to effect a shift to a new perspective; so that what was once 'common sense' ('*of course* civilization rests on slavery . . . woman was made for man . . . homosexuality is unnatural') emerges as a ludicrous, primitive and offensive wielding of power.

If relativism were entirely true, this could not happen. The world of slavery and the world of freedom would be a matter for personal preference. When Thomas Kuhn (1996) spoke of the revolutions in science, like the Copernican revolution to a sun-centred world, he was pointing out that one could not prove the sun-centred world was true on the basis of the old system, or on the basis of any independent criteria. The new sun-centred universe had to argue its own merits rhetorically on its own new terms. One can never prove that the world is not earth-centred, but if we follow the invitation to see it as sun-centred, the facts fall into place much more beautifully, elegantly and simply than they did before.

The parts of religions that deal with proof and certainty are rather small, and probably bypass the spirituality of most of the faithful. Much more central is the rhetoric of liturgy and sermon, which seek to persuade and improve by appeal to both head and heart with the sheer dance and flow of words. This is language that does not demonstrate or command anything; rather, it *does* something to the hearers. It invites them to see the world anew, more beautifully and more challengingly, and so live differently.

Spiritual writing uses other forms also: the parable, the Zen *koan*, the witty story of the Sufis, the paradox-laden poetry of the Syrians and the Beguines. Here something of Sells's unsaying seems to be at work. The conceptual content actually eats itself up, as it were, leaving only the impact of something viscerally, not mentally understood. Such language stops our ordinary way of seeing things in its tracks, and invites, lures or sometimes threatens us into a new perspective. It is this *metanoia* (transformation of mind or intent) into the wider and deeper perspectives of God, that is arguably at the heart of spiritual writing and saying.

Pluralist Realism

Mark Heim (1995) argues that 'nirvana and communion with God are contradictory only if we assume that one or the other must be the sole fate of human beings' (p. 149). Heim proposes that we take seriously each faith's claims to take believers towards goals that are described in radically different ways: for the Muslim paradise, the Christian communion with God in the kingdom, Buddhist nirvana are not obviously just different ways of describing the same reality.

Heim draws back from the radical nature of this proposal, however, by describing the 'other faith' goals as 'penultimate religious fulfilment' whereas the Christian heaven and hell are 'ultimate'. We note that in Buddhism, on the contrary, heaven and hell are penultimate possible states on the way to ultimate Nirvana!

The possibility of many paths to many goals does not necessarily imply relativism and subjectivity, any more than the existence of many roads and destinations in England imply there is no objective England! It could be the case that there we inhabit a real 'spiritual space' of possible goals and paths in which, for any one person at any one time, some pathways are really more profitable to take than others; and the religions are there ultimately to enable us to discover the right path to take at each stage. The Enneagram (Table 6) is worth considering as a map of such space, suggesting as it does that there are nine kinds of idolatry, leading to eternal loss, to be overcome, and nine corresponding ultimate kinds of goal! Not that we should advocate the Enneagram as the ultimate metanarrative! Rather, the way it holds genuinely plural and perhaps incompatible journeys together in a single reality supplies a model for the kind of pluralist realism we have in mind.

Maybe, as Žižek argues (2005, pp. 214ff.), the otherness of the world is manifest not, as in much modern philosophy, an exact correspondence between our descriptions and reality (about which we should always be suspicious) but in the need for a 'parallax view' in which incompatible perspectives have to be held in tension. This tension in descriptions may derive, not from the lack of reality, but from its ineluctable, plural richness.

It is in the spirit of such a pluralist realism that Francis Clooney and James Fredericks have reconstructed the (originally nineteenth-century) notion of *'comparative theology'*. These writers believe that theology today must start not from a particular, Christian metanarrative, but from dialogue and interaction between faiths, writing our theology out of acceptance of and reflection on the difference of perspectives. Thus Clooney (1993) reads Aquinas's *Summa Theologica* in the contrasting light of Hindu Vedanta thought, and this he believes offers new insight into Aquinas's own vision of God, while Fredericks (2004) views Jesus' parable of the Prodigal alongside the story of Krishna and the Milkmaids, and approaches New Testament thought on the resurrection through the lens of Zen Buddhism.

Such an approach neither seeks to emphasize contrast, after the manner of exclusivism; nor does it seek to integrate the 'other' approach to a Christian perspective, like inclusivism; nor, again, does it seek to impose some third, wider understanding that embraces both, like universalism. Comparative theology is pluralist in that it accepts difference, but it refuses to put the religions in incommensurable compartments, or to surrender the ideal of truth. Rather, it allows sparks of insight to fly from real difference, suggesting that if we accept our difference and work with it, we may find ourselves inhabiting a shared spiritual world after all.

Spirituality, as we have seen, is not a 'super religion' – a core of 'perennial' independent truths which all religions share – but religions conceived of as bodies of transformative stories and practices of engaging with life and God. Perhaps then it is *as spiritualities* that religions will be able to interact and learn from one another, if they are able to do so at all, in the interactive dance of their rhetorics, hoping for sparks of new truth to fly.

If it turns out that the religions cannot do this, then possibly religions will turn out to be, after all, merely the kind of ideological power structures that postmodern thinkers have unmasked. For then our choice would be merely which religion to submit to, which religion we permit to rule our lives, without the questions an alternative faith might pose. Or alternatively, to submit to none of them, and go without those meanings, freedoms and disciplines of relating which spirituality can provide.

That might be a very profitable path for Christian spirituality to follow:

*seeking and not seeking unity; resting and rejoicing in difference, but not compla-
cently.* Not at any rate engaging in broad speculations, but familiarizing itself
with texts and ceremonies of other faiths, until the sparks fly and suggest, in
their momentary light, that shared world.

For Reflection and Discussion

1 Do you agree with Barth that 'religion is unbelief'? Describe what
 you feel are the risks and benefits of accepting non-Christian faiths as
 equal partners in the quest for spiritual truth.
2 Which faiths do you feel might fall prey to each of Panikkar's temptations? And can you think of three spiritual writers who risk falling
 into each respective temptation? What are the strengths and weaknesses you see in his Trinitarian approach to the world faiths?
3 Does all spirituality seem feminine in Cupitt's sense? Can you think
 of examples of masculine, feminine and balanced spirituality?
4 What evidence, if any, do you find of the developments described by Beaudoin? In what ways do you find them encouraging or discouraging?
5 Reflect on the Enneagram as a model for religious temptations and
 goals. Can you think of a faith, and a spiritual writer, corresponding
 to each of the nine points? Or do you find this model of 'nine paths,
 nine goals' unhelpful, and why?
6 Do you agree that it is as spiritualities that the faiths will have to
 interact in the future? Can you think of aspects of the religions which
 such interaction might be in danger of ignoring?

Further Reading

Tim Beaudoin, 1998, *Virtual Faith, The Irreverent Spiritual Quest of Generation X*,
 New York: Jossey-Bass.
Don Cupitt, 1998, *Mysticism after Modernity*, Oxford and Malden, MA: Blackwell.
Jacques Dupuis, 1997, *Toward a Christian Theology of Religious Pluralism*, Maryknoll,
 NY: Orbis.
Grace Jantzen, 1995, *Power, Gender and Christian Mysticism*, Cambridge, New York
 and Melbourne: Cambridge University Press.
Paul Knitter, 2002, *Introducing Theologies of Religions*, Maryknoll, NY, Orbis.

Volker Kuster, tr J. Bowden, 2001, *The Many Faces of Jesus Christ: Intercultural Christ-ology,* London: SCM Press.

Raimon Panikkar, 1973, *The Trinity and the Religious Experience of Man,* Maryknoll, NY: Orbis.

Ross Thompson, 1989, 'What Kind of Relativism?', *New Blackfriars,* April.

Conclusion

Writing this book has felt rather like painting an immense and awesome landscape on a minute canvas. Errors in the smallest verbal brushstroke may mean that infinite vistas have been wrongly depicted, and here we can only ask forgiveness! For the study of spirituality seems to recede into the infinite in seven dimensions: into the ineluctability of experience, the regress of scientific explanations, the transcendence of God, the mysteries of the body, the depths of the soul, the tangles of ethics, and the inexhaustible delight of human difference. A complete study of spirituality would require a complete study of everything!

But perhaps that elusiveness clarifies what spirituality is – not a 'something' whose essence we can define, more of what Schneiders has called a 'project of life-integration through self-transcendence towards the horizon of ultimate values one perceives' (1989, p. 266). This kind of horizon recedes in every human search, but it is what motivates the search and makes its unachievable object desirable. Spirituality just is what makes everything about our human condition so impossible to pin down, so tantalizingly ever-open to new approaches.

It is impossible to extract an 'essence' of spirituality from all this, not least because history has not come to an end. New challenges and new insights await, which we cannot predict. Only you can say whether our explorations have given you a sense of spirituality as a coherent yet living and evolving reality, or not.

Equally, we have not witnessed a historical progress, in which humanity has come ever closer to the 'best' form of spirituality, whatever that might be. There is no demonstrable sense in which Thomas Merton, say, represents an advance on Gregory of Nyssa or even the early cave dwellers. But if we do not forget or reject past spiritualities, we do witness (despite many setbacks and corruptions) an ongoing enrichment, an outpouring of ever new manifestations.

And we do witness one consistent trajectory in which Christian spirituality has moved in response to each historical challenge. Whether this trajectory is shared by all spiritualities or is specific to Christian spirituality, and whether it is a 'good thing', is beyond the scope of this book to say. But we have noted

- the shift in the Old Testament from specific theophanic encounters with God to a sense of God's universal reality even when absent from oneself;
- the turn from the esoteric to the mystical, in which secret teaching about the outer world became open teaching inwardly applied to the soul;
- the turn in Augustine to his inward autobiographical journey;
- the shift in medieval times to a greater emphasis on emotions and on the humanity of Christ;
- the move with the Reformation – both Catholic and Protestant – from intellectual vision to obedience of will and desire;
- the move 'through the looking glass' such that whereas before, inner realities mirrored the outer, now the outer world mirrored and provided images for the deepening understanding of inward, psychological reality.

At each step there is a move we could loosely describe as being from outward to inward, and this seems to be continuing apace in the interest in spirituality today.

'Inward' need not mean 'subjective', but those of us who wish to retain a sense of spirituality as engaging with the reality of God, and defend spirituality against the charges of self-delusion and escapism, will need to show a way in which the inward can nonetheless be rigorous and real. We hope this book has shown how spirituality can be so. In the second half we have argued in successive chapters as numbered here:

7 that spirituality is not primarily a matter of ineffable private experiences but a way of gleaning from a religious tradition a way of experiencing the world;

8 that in spirituality a religious tradition moves beyond dogmatic certainty to become vulnerable to the real in a way analogous to science;

9 that spirituality relates experience, faith and practice together in the kind of cycle in which we learn new truth;

10 that despite its bad historical witness, a spirituality of incarnation is

committed to a positive view of the body and the material realities it puts us in touch with;

11 and 12 that spirituality enables us to be 'serious about soul', and to become more capable of freely and ethically engaging with the world;

13 that Christianity is one of many paths in a 'spiritual space', one way of engaging with the real in its many-sidedness.

But before we become complacent we need to return to the point made above, that Christian spirituality never fastens upon a final reality. It is perhaps even definable as that in all reality – experience, knowledge, God, the body, the soul, the good life and human difference – which both motivates and eludes our desire. That is why we have frequently found it necessary to analogize Christian spirituality as a kind of being or life.

Christians need not balk at this, bearing in mind the hint to which we have returned time and again, that spirituality in the Christian sense has to do with God's knowing and loving of Godself in us; that is to say, the work of the Holy Spirit. But to say that is not to define Christian spirituality, simply to give its elusiveness a divine name.

Bibliography

Anthologies and Collections

M. Downey, ed., 2000, *Exploring Christian Spirituality: An Ecumenical Reader*, Grand Rapids, Baker Books.

Louis Dupré & James A. Wiseman, eds, 2001, *Light from Light: An Anthology of Christian Mysticism*, 2nd ed., Mahwah NY: Paulist Press.

Harvey Egan, ed., 1991, *An Anthology of Christian Mysticism*, Collegeville, MN: Liturgical Press.

Richard Foster and James Smith, eds, 2005, *Devotional Classics: Selected Readings for Individuals and Groups*, New York: HarperOne.

F. C. Happold, 1963, *Mysticism: A Study and an Anthology*, Harmondsworth: Penguin.

Felicity Leng, 2006, *Invincible Spirits – A Thousand Years of Women's Spiritual Writings*, Norwich: Canterbury Press.

Shawn Madigan, eds, 1998, *Mystics, Visionaries, and Prophets: A Historical Anthology of Women's Spiritual Writings*, Minneapolis: Fortress Press.

Bernard McGinn, ed., 1978–, *Classics of Western Spirituality*, New York: Paulist Press. Includes over 100 volumes of writings by individual mystics, many listed below under 'References and further study'.

John R. Tyson, ed., 1999, *Invitation to Christian Spirituality: An Ecumenical Anthology*, New York: Oxford University Press.

General Studies

Stephen Barton, ed., 2003, *Holiness Past and Present*, London and New York: T&T Clark.

Sister Wendy Beckett, 1992, *Art and the Sacred*, London: Rider Books.

Louis Bouyer, ed., 1978, *A History of Christian Spirituality*, 3 vols, New York: Seabury.

Lawrence Cunningham and Keith Egan, 1996, *Christian Spirituality: Themes from the Tradition*, Mahwah, NY: Paulist Press.

Steven Fanning, 2001, *Mystics of the Christian Tradition*, London and New York: Routledge.

Mark Holder, ed., 2005, *The Blackwell Companion to Christian Spirituality*, Oxford, Malden, Victoria: Blackwell.

William Johnston, 1996, *Mystical Theology: The Science of Love*, San Francisco: HarperCollins.

Cheslyn Jones, Geoffrey Wainwright and Edward Yarnold, eds, 1986, *The Study of Spirituality*, London: SPCK.

Vladimir Lossky, 1957, *The Mystical Theology of the Eastern Church*, Cambridge and London: Clarke.

Bernard McGinn, 1991–, *The Presence of God, A History of Western Christian Mysticism*, New York: Crossroad. Vol. 1 (1991): *The Foundations of Mysticism*; Vol. 2: (1994): *The Growth of Mysticism*; Vol. 3 (1998): *The Flowering of Mysticism*. Vol. 4: (2006) *The Harvest of Mysticism*. To be continued . . .

Alister McGrath, 1999, *Christian Spirituality*, Oxford: Blackwell.

Mark McIntosh, 1998, *Mystical Theology*, Oxford: Blackwell.

Gordon Mursell, ed., 2001, *The Story of Christian Spirituality: Two Thousand Years, from East to West*, Oxford: Lion Books.

David Runcorn, 2006, *Spirituality Workbook: A Guide for Explorers, Pilgrims and Seekers*, London: SPCK.

Philip Sheldrake, ed., 2005, *The New SCM Dictionary of Christian Spirituality*, London: SCM Press.

Philip Sheldrake, ed., 2005, *The New Westminster Dictionary of Christian Spirituality*, Louisville, KY: Westminster John Knox.

Philip Sheldrake, 2006, *A Brief History of Spirituality*, Oxford: Blackwell.

Karen Smith, 2007, *SCM Core Text: Christian Spirituality*, London: SCM Press.

Evelyn Underhill, 1999, *Mysticism: The Nature and Development of Spiritual Consciousness*, Oxford: Oneworld Publications.

Rowan Williams, 1979, *The Wound of Knowledge*, London: DLT.

Richard Woods, 2006, *Christian Spirituality: God's Presence through the Ages*, Maryknoll, NY: Orbis.

References and Further Study

Introduction

Tim Beaudoin, 1998, *Virtual Faith, The Irreverent Spiritual Quest of Generation X*, New York: Jossey-Bass.

Elizabeth Dreyer and Mark Burrows, 2005, *Minding the Spirit: The Study of Christian Spirituality*, Baltimore: Johns Hopkins University Press.

Daniel Helminiak, 1998, *Religion and the Human Sciences: An Approach via Spirituality*, New York: State University of New York Press.

Bruce Lescher and Elizabeth Liebert, eds, 2006, *Exploring Christian Spirituality*, New York/Mahwah, NJ: Paulist Press.

George Lindbeck, 1984, *The Nature of Doctrine: Religion and Theology in a Postliberal Age*, Philadelphia: Westminster Press.

Bernard McGinn, 1991–, *The Presence of God, A History of Western Christian Mysticism*, New York: Crossroad. See General Studies, above, for details.

Bernard McGinn, 1998, 'Quo Vadis? Reflections on the Current Study of Mysticism', *Christian Spirituality Bulletin* (Spring) 13–21.

Alister McGrath, 1999, *Christian Spirituality*, Oxford: Blackwell.

Mark McIntosh, 1998, *Mystical Theology*, Oxford: Blackwell.

W. Roof, 1993, *A Generation of Seekers*, New York: HarperSanFrancisco.

Sandra Schneiders, 1989, 'Spirituality in the Academy', *Theological Studies* 50: 676–97.

Philip Sheldrake, 1991, *Spirituality and History: Questions of Interpretation and Method*, London: SPCK.

Ross Thompson, 2006, *SCM Studyguide: The Sacraments*, London: SCM Press.

Chapter 1: Appearance and Abandonment: Biblical Spirituality

Rob Bell, 2006, *Velvet Elvis: Repainting the Christian Faith*, Grand Rapids: Zondervan.

Charles Causley, 1975, *Collected Poems 1951–1975*, London: Macmillan.

J. D. Crossan, 1992, *The Historical Jesus. The Life of a Mediterranean Jewish Peasant*, London: HarperCollins.

Trevor Dennis, 1991, *Lo and Behold! – The Power of Old Testament Storytelling*, London: SPCK.

Elizabeth Schussler Fiorenza, ed., 1994, *Searching the Scriptures, Volume Two: A Feminist Commentary*, London: SCM Press.

Elizabeth Schussler Fiorenza, 1995, *Jesus: Miriam's Child, Sophia's Prophet: Issues in Feminist Christology*, London: SCM Press.

Reuven Hammer, 1995 *Classic Midrash: Tannaitic Commentaries on the Bible*, Mahwah, NJ: Paulist Press.

Wilfrid Harrington, 1975, *Key to the Bible*, New York: Alba House.

Moshe Idel & Bernard McGinn, eds, 1996, *Mystical Union in Judaism, Christianity, and Islam: An Ecumenical Dialogue*, London and New York: Continuum.

Margaret Magdalen, 1994, *The Hidden Face of Jesus: Reflections on the Emotional Life of Christ*, London: DLT.

Melvyn Matthews, 1992, *The Hidden Word: Your Story in Scripture*, London: DLT.

Bernard McGinn & John Meyendorff, eds, 1985, *Christian Spirituality I: Origins to the Twelfth Century*. New York: Crossroad/Herder & Herder.

Jack Miles, 1996, *God, a Biography*, London: Vintage Books.

Jack Miles, 2001, *Christ, a Crisis in the Life of God*, London: Heinemann.

William Morrice, 1997, *Hidden Sayings of Jesus: Words Attributed to Jesus outside the Four Gospels,* London: SPCK.

Gordon Oliver, 2006, *Holy Bible, Human Bible,* London: DLT.

Elaine Pagels, 1979, *The Gnostic Gospels*, New York: Random House; also 1982, Harmondsworth: Penguin.

James Robinson, ed., 1990, *The Nag Hammadi Library*, San Francisco: Harper-Collins.

E. P. Sanders, 1985, *Jesus and Judaism*, Philadelphia: Fortress Press.

Sandra Schneiders, 1999, *The revelatory Text: Interpreting the New Testament As Sacred Scripture,* Collegeville: Liturgical Press.

Alan Segal, 1990, *Paul the Convert: The Apostolate and Apostasy of Saul the Pharisee,* New Haven: Yale University Press.

R. S. Thomas, 1995, *Collected Poems 1945–1990,* London: Phoenix.

Ross Thompson, 2006, *SCM Studyguide: The Sacraments,* London: SCM Press.

Walter Wink, 2002, *The Human Being. Jesus and the Enigma of the Son of Man,* Minneapolis: Fortress Press.

N. T. Wright, 1996, *Jesus and the Victory of God*, London: SPCK.

N. T. Wright and M. Borg, 1999, *The Meaning of Jesus*, London: SPCK.

John H. Yoder, 1994, *The Politics of Jesus*, Grand Rapids: Eerdmans.

Chapter 2: Struggle and Synthesis: Patristic Spirituality

Louis Bouyer, tr. Illtyd Trethowen, 1990, *The Christian Mystery: From Pagan Myth to Christian Mysticism.* Edinburgh: T & T Clark.

David Brakke, 1998, *Athanasius and Asceticism*, Baltimore: Johns Hopkins Press.

Sebastian Brock, 1992, *The Luminous Eye: The Spiritual Vision of Ephrem the Syrian*, Kalamazoo, MI: Cistercian Publications.

Ephrem the Syrian, ed. Kathleen McVeigh, 1990, *Ephrem the Syrian: Hymns*, Mahwah, NJ: Paulist Press.

Gregory of Nyssa, tr. A. J. Malherbe and E. Ferguson, 1978, *The Life of Moses*, Mahwah, NJ: Paulist Press.

Gregory of Nyssa, tr. Casimir McCambley, 1987, *Commentary on the Song of Songs*, Brookline, MA: Hellenic College Press.

Friedrich Heiler, 1997, *Prayer: A Study in the History and Psychology of Religion*, Oxford: Oneworld Publications.

John Hick, ed., 1977, *The Myth of God Incarnate*, London: SCM Press.

John Hick, 2007, *Evil and the God of Love*, London: Palgrave Macmillan.

W. R. Inge, 1959, *The Awakening of the Soul*, London: Mowbray.

John Peter Kenney, 2005, *The Mysticism of Saint Augustine: Rereading the Confessions*, London and New York: Routledge.

Michael Kessler and Christian Sheppard, eds, 2003, *Mystics: Presence and Aporia*, Chicago and London: University of Chicago Press.

Christopher King, 2005, *Origen on the Song of Songs as the Spirit of Scripture: The Bridegroom's Perfect Marriage-Song.* Oxford and New York: Oxford University Press.

K.E. Kirk, 1931, *The Vision of God: The Christian Doctrine of the Summum Bonum*, London: Longmans.

Vladimir Lossky, 1957, *The Mystical Theology of the Eastern Church*, Cambridge and London: Clarke.

Vladimir Lossky, 1984, *The Vision of God*, New York: St Vladimir's Seminary Press.

Andrew Louth, 2002, *Denys the Areopagite*, London and New York: Continuum.

Arthur Lovejoy, 1972, *The Great Chain of Being*, Cambridge, MA: Harvard University Press.

Maximus the Confessor, 2005, *St Maximus the Confessor*, Mahwah, NJ: Paulist Press.

Bernard McGinn, 2006, 'How Augustine Shaped Mysticism', *Augustinian Studies* 37, no. 1.

Bernard McGinn & John Meyendorff, eds, 1985, *Christian Spirituality I: Origins to the Twelfth Century.* New York: Crossroad/Herder & Herder.

Anders Nygren, P. Watson, tr., 1953, *Agapé and Eros*, London: SPCK.

Origen, 1979, *Exhortation to Martyrdom, Prayer*, Mahwah, NJ: Paulist Press.

Plato, tr. H. D. P. Lee, 1955, *The Republic*, Harmondsworth: Penguin.

Albrecht Ritschl, 2005, *Three Essays*, Eugene, OR: Wipf and Stock.

Charles Taylor, 2007, *A Secular Age*, Cambridge, MA and London: Harvard University Press.

Denys Turner, 1998, *The Darkness of God: Negativity in Christian Mysticism*, Cambridge, Cambridge University Press.

Rowan Williams, 1979, *The Wound of Knowledge*, London: DLT.

Chapter 3: Monastery and Mystery: Spirituality through the 'Dark Ages'

Anselm, ed. Benedicta Ward, 1973, *The Prayers and Meditations of Saint Anselm*, Harmondsworth: Penguin.

Athanasius, 1980, *The Life of St Anthony*, Mahwah, NJ: Paulist Press.

Peter-Damian Belisle, 2003, *The Language of Silence: the Changing Face of Monastic Solitude*, Maryknoll, NY: Orbis.

Bernard of Clairvaux, ed. G. R. Evans, 2000, *Selected Writings*, Mahwah, NJ: Paulist Press.

Jane Bobko, 1995, *Vision: The Life and Music of Hildegard of Bingen*, New York: Penguin Books USA.

Robert Boenig, ed., 2001, *Anglo-Saxon Spirituality*, Mahwah, NJ: Paulist Press.

Louis Bouyer, tr. Illtyd Trethowen, 1990, *The Christian Mystery: From Pagan Myth to Christian Mysticism*. Edinburgh: T & T Clark.

Odo Brooke, 1980, *Studies in Monastic Theology*, Kalamazoo: Cistercian Publications.

David Brown and Ann Loades, eds, 1996, *Christ the Sacramental Word*, London: SPCK.

Peter Brown, 1990, *The Body and Society: Men, Women and Sexual Renunciation in Early Christianity*, London: Faber and Columbia: Columbia University Press.

Steven Chase, 2003, *Contemplation and Compassion: The Victorine Tradition*, Maryknoll, NY: Orbis.

Adam Cooper, 2005, *The Body in St. Maximus the Confessor: Holy Flesh, Wholly Deified*, Oxford and New York: Oxford University Press.

'Denys the Areopagite', 1993, *Pseudo-Dionysius: the Complete Works*, Mahwah, NJ: Paulist Press.

Elizabeth Dreyer and Mark Burrows, 2005, *Minding the Spirit: The Study of Christian Spirituality*, Baltimore: Johns Hopkins University Press.

Evagrius Ponticus, tr. J. Bamburger, 1978, *The Praktikos and Chapters on Prayer*, Kalamazoo, MI: Cistercian Publications.

David Foster, 2005, *Reading with God: Lectio Divina*, London: Continuum.

Etienne Gilson, 1990, *The Mystical Theology of Bernard of Clairvaux*, Kalamazoo: Cistercian Publications.

Robert Graves, 1999, *The White Goddess,* London: Faber.

Guigo II, ed. E. College and J. Walsh, 1978, *Guigo II: The Ladder of Monks and Twelve Meditations,* New York: Doubleday Image.

Hildegard of Bingen, eds C. Hart and J. Bishop, 1990, *Scivias,* Mahwah, NJ: Paulist Press.

John the Scot Eriugena, tr. I. P. Sheldon-Williams and J. J. O'Meara, 1987, *Periphyseon (the Division of Nature),* Montreal/Paris: Bellarmin.

E. Kadloubovsky and G. E. H. Palmer, eds, 1954, *Early Fathers from the Philokalia,* London: Faber.

E. Kadloubovsky and G. E. H. Palmer, eds, 1992, *Writings from the Philokalia on Prayer of the Heart,* London: Faber.

Belden Lane, 1998, *The Solace of Fierce Landscapes,* Oxford and New York: Oxford University Press.

C. S. Lewis, 1977, *The Allegory of Love,* Oxford: Oxford Paperbacks.

Andrew Louth, 1996, *Maximus the Confessor,* London: Routledge.

Makarios, 1989, *Pseudo-Macarius,* Mahwah NJ: Paulist Press.

Bernard McGinn, 1994, *The Growth of Mysticism,* New York: Crossroad.

Bernard McGinn & John Meyendorff, eds, 1985, *Christian Spirituality I: Origins to the Twelfth Century,* New York: Crossroad/Herder & Herder.

P. Murray, ed., 1986, *The Deer's Cry: A Treasury of Irish Religious Verse,* Dublin: Four Courts.

Barbara Newman, ed., 1998, *Voice of the Living Light: Hildegard of Bingen and Her World,* Berkeley: University of California Press.

Richard of St Victor, tr. G. A. Zinn, 1979, *Twelve Patriarchs,* Mahwah, NJ: Paulist Press.

Alexander Schmemann, 2002, *For the Life of the World: Sacraments and Orthodoxy,* New York: St Vladimir's Seminary.

Guy Stroumsa, 2005, *Hidden Wisdom: Esoteric Traditions and the Roots of Christian Mysticism,* Leiden and Boston: Brill.

Ross Thompson, 2006, *SCM Studyguide: The Sacraments,* London: SCM Press.

Esther de Waal, 1999, *Seeking God: The Way of St Benedict,* Norwich: Canterbury Press.

Benedicta Ward, tr., 1984 *The Sayings of the Desert Fathers,* Kalamazoo, WI: Cistercian Publications.

Rowan Williams, 2004, *Silence and Honey Cakes,* Oxford: Lion Hudson.

Chapter 4: Hierarchy and Heresy: Medieval Spirituality

Thomas Aquinas, ed. T. McDermott, 1989, *Summa Theologiae, A Concise Translation,* London: Methuen.

Iulia de Beausobre, 1979, *Flame in the Snow: A Russian Legend* (St Seraphim of Sarov), London: Fount.

Bonaventure, tr. E. Cousins, 1978, *The Soul's Journey into God,* Mahwah, NJ: Paulist Press.

Louis Bouyer, 1968, *Orthodox Spirituality and Protestant and Anglican Spirituality,* London: Burns and Oates. (Vol. 3 in *A History of Christian Spirituality*).

Louis Bouyer, tr. Illtyd Trethowen, 1990, *The Christian Mystery: From Pagan Myth to Christian Mysticism.* Edinburgh: T & T Clark.

Caroline Bynum, 1984, *Jesus As Mother: Studies in the Spirituality of the High Middle Ages,* Berkeley: University of California Press.

Caroline Bynum, 1988, *Holy Feast and Holy Fast,* Berkeley: University of California Press.

Catherine of Genoa, tr. S. Noffke, 1990, *The Dialogue,* Mahwah, NJ: Paulist Press.

Catherine of Siena, tr. S. Hughes, 1979, *Purgation and Purgatory,* Mahwah, NJ: Paulist Press.

Common Worship: Daily Prayer, 2005: London: Church House Publishing.

Catherine de Hueck Doherty, 1977, *Poustinia,* London: Fount.

Eamon Duffey, 2003, *Voices of Morebath,* London and New Haven: Yale University Press.

John van Engen, ed., 2004, *Devotio Moderna: Basic Writings,* Mahwah, NJ: Paulist Press.

Matthew Fox, 1992, *Sheer Joy: Conversations with Thomas Aquinas on Creation Spirituality,* New York: HarperCollins.

Etienne Gilson, 1965, *The Philosophy of St. Bonaventure,* Patterson, NY: St. Anthony Guild Press.

Hadewijch, tr. Columba Hart, 1980, *The Complete Works,* London: SPCK; New York: Paulist Press.

Kerrie Hide, 2001, *Gifted Origins to Graced Fulfilment: The Soteriology of Julian of Norwich,* Collegeville, MN: Liturgical Press.

Mark Holder, ed., 2005, *The Blackwell Companion to Christian Spirituality,* Oxford, Malden, Victoria: Blackwell.

Johan Huizinga, 1965, *The Waning of the Middle Ages,* Harmondsworth: Penguin.

Grace Jantzen, 1995, *Power, Gender and Christian Mysticism,* Cambridge, New York and Melbourne: Cambridge University Press.

Julian of Norwich, ed. Edmund Colledge, 1990, *The Showings*, Mahwah, NJ: Paulist Press.

Thomas à Kempis, 1973, *The Imitation of Christ*, Harmondsworth: Penguin.

Michael Kessler and Christian Sheppard, eds, 2003, *Mystics: Presence and Aporia*, Chicago and London: University of Chicago Press.

William Langland, 2000, *Piers Plowman*, Oxford and New York: Oxford University Press.

Gordon Leff, 1967, *Heresy in the Later Middle Ages: The Relation of Heterodoxy to Dissent, 1250–1450*, 2 vols, New York: Barnes & Noble.

Vladimir Lossky, 1957, *The Mystical Theology of the Eastern Church*, Cambridge and London: Clarke.

Mother Maria, Sister Thekla and Sister Katherine, 1973, *Orthodox Potential: Collected Essays*, Newport Pagnell: Greek Orthodox Monastery of the Assumption.

Bernard McGinn, ed., 1994, *Meister Eckhart and the Beguine Mystics*, London and New York: Continuum.

Bernard McGinn, 2001, *The Mystical Theology of Meister Eckhart*: New York: Herder/Crossroad.

Mechthild of Magdeburg, tr. F. Tobin, 1998, *The Flowing Light of the Godhead*, Mahwah, NJ: Paulist Press.

Gordon Mursell, 2001, *English Spirituality: From the Early Days to 1700*, London: SPCK.

Nicholas of Cusa, tr. G. Heron, 1954, *Of Learned Ignorance*, London: Routledge.

Rik van Nieuwenhove, 2003, *Jan van Ruusbroec, Mystical Theologian of the Trinity*, Notre Dame: University of Notre Dame Press.

Kenan Osborne, ed., 1994, *The History of Franciscan Theology*, St. Bonaventure, NY: Franciscan Institute.

Gregory Palamas, 1983, *Triads*, Mahwah, NY: Paulist Press.

Elizabeth Petroff, 1994, *Body and Soul: Essays on Medieval Women and Mysticism*, Oxford and New York: Oxford University Press.

Marguerite Porete, ed. E. Babinsky, 1993, *The Mirror of Simple Souls*, Mahwah, NJ: Paulist Press.

John Ruusbroeck, ed. J. Wiseman, 1993, *Spiritual Espousals and other Works*, Mahwah, NJ: Paulist Press.

Alexander Schmemann, 1981, *The Historical Road of Eastern Orthodoxy*, New York, St Vladimir's Seminary Press.

Nil Sorsky, tr. G. Maloney, 1999, *The Complete Writings*, Mahwah, NJ: Paulist Press.

Symeon the New Theologian, tr. G. A. Maloney, 1975, *Hymns of Divine Love*, Denville, NJ: Dimension Books.

Paul Szarmach, ed., 1984, *An Introduction to the Medieval Mystics of Europe: Fourteen Original Essays,* Albany, NY: State University of New York Press.

Denys Turner, 1998, *The Darkness of God: Negativity in Christian Mysticism,* Cambridge, Cambridge University Press.

Ulrike Wiethaus, 1992, *Maps of Flesh and Light: the Religious Experience of Medieval Women Mystics,* Syracuse, NY: Syracuse University Press.

Ulrike Wiethaus, 1996, *Ecstatic Transformation: Transpersonal Psychology in the Work of Mechthild,* Syracuse, NY: Syracuse University Press.

Richard Woods, 1998, *Mysticism and Prophecy: The Dominican Tradition,* Maryknoll, NY: Orbis.

Chapter 5: Foundations for Faith: Reformation Spirituality

Johann Arndt, 1979, tr. P. C. Erb, 1979, *True Christianity,* Mahwah, NJ: Paulist Press.

Hans urs von Balthasar, tr. D. Nichol, 1954, *Thérèse of Lisieux: the Story of a Mission,* New York: Sheed and Ward.

Michael Birkel, 2004, *Silence and Witness: The Quaker Tradition,* Maryknoll: Orbis.

Jakob Boehme, ed. P. C. Erb, 1990, *The Way to Christ,* Mahwah, NJ: Paulist Press.

Louis Bouyer, 1968, *Orthodox Spirituality and Protestant and Anglican Spirituality,* London: Burns and Oates.

Louis Bouyer, tr. Illtyd Trethowen, 1990, *The Christian Mystery: From Pagan Myth to Christian Mysticism.* Edinburgh: T & T Clark.

Michel de Certeau, 1995, *The Mystic Fable, Vol. I, The Sixteenth and Seventeenth Centuries,* Chicago: University of Chicago Press.

William Countryman, 2000, *The Poetic Imagination: An Anglican Tradition,* Maryknoll, NY: Orbis.

John Donne, ed. J. Hayward, 1929, *Complete Verse and Selected Prose,* London: Nonesuch Press.

Eamon Duffy, 2001, *The Stripping of the Altars: Traditional Religion in England, c.1400–c.1580,* New Haven: Yale University Press.

Louis Dupré & Don E. Saliers, eds, 1989, *Christian Spirituality III: Post-Reformation and Modern,* New York: Crossroad/Herder & Herder.

Christopher Durston and Jacqueline Eales, eds, 1996, *The Culture of English Puritanism 1560–1700,* London: Palgrave Macmillan.

K. Dyckman, M. Garvin and E. Leibert, *The Spiritual Exercises Reclaimed,* Mahwah, NY: Paulist.

Harvey Egan, 1991, *Ignatius the Mystic,* Collegeville: Liturgical Press.

George Fox, 1997, *Journal*, Philadelphia: Quaker Books.

Paul Handley et al., eds, 1987, *The English Spirit: The Little Gidding Anthology of English Spirituality*, London: DLT.

Edward Howells, 2002, *John of the Cross & Teresa of Avila: Mystical Knowing and Self-hood*, New York: Herder & Herder.

John of the Cross, 1997, *Selected Writings*, Mahwah, NJ: Paulist Press.

Cheslyn Jones, Geoffrey Wainwright and Edward Yarnold, eds, 1986, *The Study of Spirituality*, London: SPCK.

Michael Kessler and Christian Sheppard, eds, 2003, *Mystics: Presence and Aporia*, Chicago and London: University of Chicago Press.

Raymond Lawrence, 1989, *The Poisoning of Eros: Sexual Values in Conflict*, New York: Augustine Moore Press.

Martin Luther, tr. B. Hoffman, 1992, *Theologica Germanica*, Mahwah, NJ: Paulist Press.

Richard Marius, 1999, *Martin Luther: The Christian Between God and Death*, Cambridge, MA: Belknap.

Alister McGrath, 1990, *A Life of John Calvin: A Study in the Shaping of Western Culture*, Oxford: Blackwell.

Gordon Mursell, ed., 2001, *The Story of Christian Spirituality: Two Thousand Years, from East to West*, Oxford: Lion Books.

Vincent de Paul, F. Ryan, ed., 1996, *Vincent de Paul and Louise de Marillac*, Mahwah, NJ: Paulist Press.

William Perkins, ed. Ian Breward, 1970, *The Works of William Perkins*, Sutton Courtenay.

Jill Raitt, ed., 1987, *Christian Spirituality II: High Middle Ages and Reformation*, New York: Crossroad/Herder & Herder.

Michael Ramsay, 1991, *The Anglican Spirit*, London: SPCK.

Francis de Sales and Jeanne de Chantal, tr. P. M. Thibert, 2005, *Letters of Spiritual Direction*, Mahwah, NJ: Paulist Press.

John Smith, 2007, *Select Discourses, to which is added a Sermon preached at the Author's Funeral*, Whitefish MT: Kessinger.

John Spurr, 1998, *English Puritanism 1603–1689*, London: Palgrave Macmillan.

Douglas Steere, ed., 1995, *Quaker Spirituality: Selected Writings*, Mahwah, NJ: Paulist Press.

Peter Sterry, 1683, *The Rise, Race and Royalty of the Kingdom of God in the Soul of Man*, in 1994, *Peter Sterry, Select Writings*, New York: P. Lang.

Charles Taliaferro, ed., 2004, *Cambridge Platonist Spirituality*, Mahwah, NJ: Paulist Press.

Charles Taylor, 2007, *A Secular Age*, Cambridge, MA and London: Harvard University Press.

Jeremy Taylor, ed., 1990, *Selected Works*, Mahwah, NJ: Paulist Press.

Teresa of Avila, tr. K. Kavanaugh and O. Rodriguez, 1979, *The Interior Castle*, Mahwah, NJ: Paulist Press.

Sister Thekla, 1974, *George Herbert: Idea and Image*, Normanby: Greek Orthodox Monastery of the Assumption.

Colin P. Thompson, 2003, *St. John of the Cross: Songs in the Night*, Washington: Catholic University of America Press.

Thomas Traherne, 1960, *Centuries*, Oxford: Clarendon.

Denys Turner, 1998, *The Darkness of God: Negativity in Christian Mysticism*, Cambridge: Cambridge University Press.

Rowan Williams, 1979, *The Wound of Knowledge*, London: DLT.

Rowan Williams, 1991, *Teresa of Avila*, London: Chapman.

Chapter 6: Revival or Retreat? Spirituality after the Enlightenment

James Alison, 1996, *Raising Abel: The Recovery of the Eschatological Imagination*, New York: Crossroad; also published as 1997, *Living in the End Times: The Last Things Reconsidered*, London: SPCK.

Karl Barth, 1985, *Prayer*, Louisville, KY: Westminster John Knox.

D. M. Bell, 2001, *Liberation Theology after the End of History: The Refusal to Cease Suffering*, London and New York: Routledge.

William Blake, 1971, *Complete Writings*, Oxford: Oxford University Press.

Dietrich Bonhoeffer, 1981, *Letters and Papers from Prison*, London: SCM Press.

Dietrich Bonhoeffer, 2001, *The Cost of Discipleship*, London: SCM Press.

Louis Bouyer, 1968, *Orthodox Spirituality and Protestant and Anglican Spirituality*, London: Burns and Oates.

Richard Brantley, 1984, *Locke, Wesley, and the Method of English Romanticism*, Gainesville: University of Florida Press.

Widson Bridges, 2001, *Resurrection Song: African American Spirituality*, New York: Orbis.

Callum Brown, 2001, *The Death of Christian Britain*, London and New York: Routledge.

Jean-Pierre Caussade, tr. J. Beever, 1992, *Abandonment to Divine Providence*, New York: Image.

Raymond Chapman, 2006, *Firmly I Believe: An Oxford Movement Reader*, Norwich: Canterbury Press.

D. Crowner and G. Christianson, eds, 2003, *The Spirituality of the German Awakening*, Mahwah, NJ: Paulist Press.

Dorothy Day, 1999, *On Pilgrimage*, Grand Rapids, MI: Eerdmans.

Louis Dupré & Don E. Saliers, eds, 1989, *Christian Spirituality III: Post-Reformation and Modern*, New York: Crossroad/Herder & Herder.

Peter Erb, ed., 2003, *The Pietists: Selected Writings*, Mahwah, NJ: Paulist Press.

C. Brad Faught, 2003, *The Oxford Movement: A Thematic History of the Tractarians and Their Times*, Pennsylvania: Penn State University Press.

Peter Fuller, 1988, *Theoria: Art, and the Absence of Grace*, London: Chatto and Windus.

Gustavo Gutierrez, 1984, *We Drink from Our Own Wells: The Spiritual Journey of a People*, Maryknoll, NY: Orbis.

Paul Heelas, Scott Lash and Paul Morris, eds, 1996, *Detraditionalisation*, Oxford: Blackwell.

Søren Kierkegaard, 1968, *Fear and Trembling and The Sickness unto Death*, Princeton: Princeton University Press.

William Law, 2001, *The Spirit of Prayer* Part I, in *The Works of William Law*, Eugene, OR: Wipf and Stock.

Gerald McDermott, 1996, *Seeing God: Jonathan Edwards and Spiritual Discernment*, Vancouver: Regent College.

Thomas Merton, 1974, *New Seeds of Contemplation*, New York: Norton.

Blaise Pascal, tr. A. J. Krailsheimer, 1995, *Pensées*, London: Penguin.

Ina Randall, 2005, *What a Friend We Have in Jesus: The Evangelical Tradition*, Maryknoll, NY: Orbis.

Walter Rauschenbusch, ed. W. S. Hudson, 1984, *Walter Rauschenbusch: Selected Writings*, Mahwah, NY: Paulist Press.

Robert Rix, 2007, *William Blake and the Cultures of Radical Christianity*, Aldershot: Ashgate.

Friedrich Schleiermacher, 1999, *The Christian Faith*, Edinburgh: T & T Clark.

Jon Sobrino, 1987, *The Spirituality of Liberation: Toward Political Holiness*, Maryknoll, NY: Orbis.

Francis Sullivan, 1986, *Pentecostalism and the Charismatic Movement*, Dublin: Veritas.

Charles Taylor, 2007, *A Secular Age*, Cambridge MA and London: Harvard University Press.

Simone Weil, 2001, *Waiting for God*, London: HarperCollins.

Simone Weil, 2002, *Gravity and Grace*, London and New York: Routledge.

John and Charles Wesley, ed. F. Whaling, 1981, *Selected Writings and Hymns*, Mahwah, NJ: Paulist Press.

Richard White, 1997, 'The Sublime and the Other', *Heythrop Journal* 38 (2): 125–43.

Walter Wink, 1998, *The Powers That Be: Theology for a New Millennium*, London and New York: Continuum.

William Wordsworth and S. T. Coleridge, 1965, *Lyrical Ballads*, London: Methuen.

John Howard Yoder, 1994, *The Politics of Jesus*, Grand Rapids: Eerdmans.

Chapter 7: Encounter or Escapism? Spirituality and Experience

Martin Buber, 1976, *I and Thou*, Edinburgh: T&T Clark.

E. Canda, 1988, 'Spirituality, Religious Diversity, and Social Work Practice', in *Social Casework* no. 69.

Robert Forman, 1999, *Mysticism, Mind and Consciousness*, Albany: State University of New York Press.

F. C. Happold, 1963, *Mysticism, A Study and an Anthology*, Harmondsworth: Penguin.

John Hick, 1989, *An Interpretation of Religion: Human Responses to the Transcendent*, New Haven: Yale University Press.

John Hick, 2006, *The New Frontier of Religion and Science: Religious Experience, Neuroscience and the Transcendent*, Basingstoke: Palgrave Macmillan.

Freidrich von Hügel, 1999, *The Mystical Element of Religion*, New York: Crossroad.

Aldous Huxley, 1954, *The Doors of Perception*, New York: Harper.

William James, 1983, *The Varieties of Religious Experience*, Harmondsworth: Penguin.

Steven Katz, ed., 1978, *Mysticism and Philosophical Analysis*, London: Sheldon.

George Lindbeck, 1984, *The Nature of Doctrine: Religion and Theology in a Postliberal Age*, Philadelphia: Westminster Press.

Rudolf Otto, 1958, *The Idea of the Holy*, Oxford and New York: Oxford University Press.

W. Roof, 1993, *A Generation of Seekers*, New York: HarperSanFrancisco.

Ninian Smart, 1976, *The Religious Experience of Mankind*, 2nd ed., New York: Scribner.

Ninian Smart, 1998, *The World's Religions*, Cambridge: Cambridge University Press.

Walter Stace, 1960, *The Teaching of the Mystics*, New York: New American Library.

Walter Stace, 1961, *Mysticism and Philosophy*, London: Macmillan.

Denys Turner, 1998, *The Darkness of God: Negativity in Christian Mysticism*, Cambridge, Cambridge University Press.

Evelyn Underhill, 1937, *The Spiritual Life*, London: Hodder and Stoughton.

Evelyn Underhill, 1999, *Mysticism: The Nature and Development of Spiritual Consciousness*, Oxford: Oneworld Publications.

William Wainwright, 1981, *Mysticism, A Study of Its Nature, Cognitive Value and Moral Implications*, Wisconsin: Wisconsin University Press.

Brian Wicker, 1975, *The Story Shaped World, Fiction and Metaphysics*, Notre Dame, IN: University of Notre Dame Press.

Ken Wilber, 2006, *Integral Spirituality: A Startling New Role for Religion in the Modern and Postmodern World*, Boston: Shambhala.

Rowan Williams, 1979, *The Wound of Knowledge*, London: DLT.

Ludwig Wittgenstein, 1973, *Philosophical Investigations*, Oxford: Blackwell.

Richard Woods, ed., 1980, *Understanding Mysticism*, New York: Image/Doubleday.

R. C. Zaehner, 1969, *Mysticism, Sacred and Profane*, Oxford: Oxford University Press.

Chapter 8: Contemplative Questioning? Spirituality and Science

Gregory Bateson, 2000, *Steps to an Ecology of Mind*, Chicago: University of Chicago Press.

John Bowker, 2005, *The Sacred Neuron: Extraordinary New Discoveries Linking Science and Religion*, London: I.B. Tauris.

Lorraine Daston and Peter Galison, 2007, *Objectivity*, New York: Zone Books.

John Davies, 1992, *The Mind of God: Science and the Search for Ultimate Meaning*, Harmondsworth: Penguin.

Richard Dawkins, 2006, *The Blind Watchmaker*, Harmondsworth: Penguin.

Jeffrey Goldstein, 1999, 'Emergence as a Construct: history and issues', in *Emergence, Complexity and Organization* 1: 49–72.

Douglas Hofstadter 1980, *Gödel, Escher, Bach: An Eternal Golden Braid*, Harmondsworth: Penguin.

Douglas Hofstadter and Daniel Dennett, 1982, *The Mind's I: Fantasies and Reflections on Self and Soul*, Harmondsworth: Penguin.

W. R. Inge, 1959, *The Awakening of the Soul*, London: Mowbray.

Stanley Jaki, 1986, *Creation and Science*, Edinburgh: Scottish Academic Press.

Grace Jantzen, 1984, *God's World, God's Body*, Kentucky: Westminster John Knox Press.

Steven Johnson, 2001, *Emergence: The Connected Lives of Ants, Brains, Cities, and Software*, New York: Scribners.

Julian of Norwich, 1952, *Revelations of Divine Love*, London: Burns and Oates.

E. Kadloubovsky and G. E. H. Palmer, eds, 1954, *Early Fathers from the Philokalia*, London: Faber.

Steven Katz, ed., 1978, *Mysticism and Philosophical Analysis*, London: Sheldon.

Stuart Kauffman, 1995, *At Home in the Universe: The Search for Laws of Self-Organisation and Complexity,* Harmondsworth: Penguin.

Ursula King, 2002, *Spirituality and Postmodernism,* Framlington Papers PR11, Oxford: Framlington Institute for Christian Studies.

Sara Maitland, 1995, *A Big Enough God: Artful Theology,* London and New York: Mowbray.

Maximus the Confessor, *Contemplative and Active Texts,* in Kadloubovsky and Palmer, 1954.

Harold Morowitz, 2002, *The Emergence of Everything: How the World Became Complex*, Oxford and New York: Oxford University Press.

Nancey Murphy and George Ellis, 1996, *On the Moral Nature of the Universe: Theology, Cosmology and Ethics,* Minneapolis: Augsburg Fortress.

David Peat, 1988 and 1992, *Superstrings and the Search for the Theory of Everything,* Chicago: Contemporary Books and London: Abacus.

Roger Penrose, 1994, *Shadows of the Mind: A Search for the Missing Science of Consciousness,* Oxford and New York: Oxford University Press.

Plato, tr. H. D. P. Lee, 1955, *The Republic*, Harmondsworth: Penguin.

Michael Polanyi, 1974, *Personal Knowledge*, Chicago: University of Chicago Press.

John Polkinghorne, 2007, *One World: The Interaction of Science and Theology,* W. Consohocken: Templeton Foundation Press.

Karl Popper, 1972, *Objective Knowledge: An Evolutionary Approach*, Oxford: Oxford University Press.

Karl Popper, 2002, *Conjectures and Refutations,* London and New York: Routledge.

Rudy Rucker, 1984, *Infinity and the Mind: The Science and Philosophy of the Infinite,* London: Paladin.

Rudy Rucker, 1988, *Mind Tools: The Five Levels of Mathematical Reality*, Harmondsworth: Penguin.

Ross Thompson, 1990, *Holy Ground: The Spirituality of Matter,* London: SPCK.

Ross Thompson, 1992, 'Scientific and Religious Understanding', *The Way*, October.

Ross Thompson, 2002, 'Postmodernism and the Trinity – How to Be Postmodern and Post-Barthian Too', *New Blackfriars* May.

E. O. Wilson, 1986, *Biophilia: The Human Bond with Other Species,* Cambridge, MA: Harvard University Press.

Ludwig Wittgenstein, 1961, *Tractatus Logico-Philosophicus,* London and New York: RKP.

Chapter 9: A Kind of Knowing? Spirituality and Theology

H. Anderson and E. Foley, 1998, *Mighty Stories, Dangerous Ritual: Weaving Together the Human and Divine*, San Francisco: Jossey Bass.

S. Bevans, 2002, *Models of Contextual Theology*, New York: Orbis.

P. Bourdieu, 1998, *Practical Reason, or the Theory of Practice*, Cambridge: Polity.

Mary Buley-Meissner, Mary Thompson and Elizabeth Tan, eds, 2000, *The Academy and the Possibility of Belief: Essays on Intellectual and Spiritual Life*. Cresskill, NJ: Hampton Press.

Elaine Graham, Heather Walton and Frances Ward, 2005, *Theological Reflection: Methods*, London: SCM Press.

Laurie Green, 2002, *Let's do Theology*, London and New York: Continuum.

Stanley Hauerwas, Nancey Murphy, and Mark Nation, eds, 1994, *Theology Without Foundations: Religious Practice and the Future of Theological Truth*, Nashville: Abingdon.

Paul Heelas, Linda Woodhead, Benjamin Steel, Karin Tusting and Bron Szerszynski, 2004, *The Spiritual Revolution: Why Religion Is Giving Way to Spirituality*, Oxford: Blackwell.

Patricia O'Connell Killen and John de Beer, 1994, *The Art of Theological Reflection*, New York: Crossroad.

D. Kolb, 1984, *Experiential Learning: Experience As the Source of Learning and Development*, New Jersey: Prentice Hall.

Elizabeth Liebert, 'The Role of Practice in the Study of Christian Spirituality', in Elizabeth Dreyer and Mark Burrows, 2005, *Minding the Spirit*, Baltimore: Johns Hopkins University Press, pp. 79–99.

Bernard Lonergan, 1973, *Method in Theology*, London: DLT.

Vladimir Lossky, 1957, *The Mystical Theology of the Eastern Church*, Cambridge and London: Clarke.

Andrew Louth, 1981, *The Origins of the Christian Mystical Tradition: From Plato to Denys*, Oxford: Clarendon Press,

Mark McIntosh, 1998, *Mystical Theology*, Oxford: Blackwell.

Anthony de Mello, 1983, *The Song of the Bird*, Anand: Gujerat Sahitya Prakash.

Jennifer Moon, 2004, *A Handbook of Reflective and Experiential Learning: Theory and Practice*, London, Routledge Falmer.

Judith Thompson with Stephen Pattison and Ross Thompson, 2008, *Studyguide to Theological Reflection*, London: SCM Press.

Ross Thompson, 1990, *Holy Ground: The Spirituality of Matter*, London: SPCK.

Ross Thompson, 2004, 'Academic Learning and Ministerial Formation: Toward a Contemplative Approach', *Theology*, July–August.

Andrew Todd, Michael West and Graham Noble, 1999, *Living Theology*, London: DLT.

Simone Weil, 2001, 'Reflections on the Right Use of School Studies with a View to the Love of God', in *Waiting for God*, London: HarperCollins.

Chapter 10: Temple or Temptation? Spirituality and the Body

Athanasius, 1980, *The Life of St Anthony*, Mahwah: Paulist Press.

Rob Bell, 2007, *Sex God: Exploring the Endless Connections Between Sexuality and Spirituality*, Grand Rapids: Zondervan.

Peter Brown, 1988, *The Body and Society: Men, Women, and Sexual Renunciation in Early Christianity*, New York: Columbia University Press.

Walter Brueggemann, 1997, *Cadences of Home: Preaching Among Exiles*, Kentucky: Westminster John Knox Press.

Caroline Bynum, 1988, *Holy Feast and Holy Fast*, Berkeley: University of California Press.

L. W. Countryman, 1989, *Dirt, Greed and Sex*, London: SCM Press.

Nancy Eiesland, 1994, *The disabled God: Toward a Liberatory Theology of Disability*, Nashville: Abingdon Press.

Oliver Frieberger, ed., 2006, *Asceticism and Its Critics: Historical Accounts and Comparative Perspectives*, Oxford and New York: Oxford University Press.

Lisa Isherwood and Elizabeth Stuart, 1998, *Introducing Body Theology*, Sheffield: Sheffield Academic Press.

Julian of Norwich, 2004, *The Showings of Julian of Norwich*, New York: Norton.

Raymond Lawrence, 1989, *The Poisoning of Eros: Sexual Values in Conflict*, New York: Augustine Moore Press.

Gerald Loughlin, 2007, *Queer Theology: Rethinking the Western Body*, London: Blackwell.

M. R. Miles, 1888, *Practicing Christianity: Critical Perspectives for an Embodied Spirituality*, New York: Crossroad.

James Morrow, 1994, *Towing Jehovah*, London and New York: Harcourt.

Edwin Muir, 1960, *Collected Poems*, London: Faber.

James B. Nelson, 1988, *The Intimate Connection: Male Sexuality, Masculine Spirituality*, Philadelphia: Westminster Press.

James B. Nelson, 1996, *Reuniting Sexuality and Spirituality*, in Thatcher and Stuart.

Philo, tr. C. D. Yonge, 1993, *The Works of Philo*, Peabody, MA: Hendrickson.

Richard Price, 1996, *The Distinctiveness of Early Christian Sexual Ethics*, in Thatcher and Stuart.

Paul Ricoeur, 1979, 'Wonder, Eroticism and Enigma', in Hendrick Ruitenbeek, ed., *Sexuality and Identity*, New York: Dell.

Thomas Ryan, ed., 2004, *Reclaiming the Body in Christian Spirituality*, New York: Paulist.

Gilbert Ryle, 1970, *The Concept of Mind*, Harmondsworth: Penguin.

Peter Singer, ed., 1996, *A Companion to Ethics*, Oxford: Blackwell.

Elizabeth Stuart and Adrian Thatcher, eds, 1996, *Christian Perspectives on Sexuality and Gender*, Leominster: Gracewing.

Peter Swaesey, 1997, *From Queer to Eternity: Spirituality in the Lives of Gay, Lesbian and Bisexual People*, London: Cassell.

Charles Taylor, 2007, *A Secular Age*, Cambridge, MA and London: Harvard University Press.

Vincent L. Wimbush & Richard Valantasis, eds, 1995, *Asceticism*, New York: Oxford University Press.

Chapter 11: Serious about Soul? Spirituality and the Psyche

Richard Appignanesi and Oscar Zarate, 2004, *Introducing Freud*, Cambridge: Icon.

Robert Assagioli, 1974, *Psychosynthesis, A Manual of Principles and Techniques*, Winnipeg: Turnstone.

Eilis Bergin and Eddie Fitzgerald, 1993, *An Enneagram Guide: A Spirituality of Love and Brokenness*. Dublin: SDB Media.

Peter Bertocci and Richard Millard, 1963, *Personality and the Good: Psychological and Ethical Perspectives*, New York: David McKay.

Dan Blazer, 1998, *Freud vs. God: How Psychiatry Lost Its Soul and Christianity Lost Its Mind*, Downers Grove, Ill: InterVarsity Press.

Robert Bly, 1990, *Iron John*, Shaftesbury: Element.

Louis Bouyer, 1968, *Orthodox Spirituality and Protestant and Anglican Spirituality*, London: Burns and Oates.

Ronald Bullis, 1996, *Spirituality in Social Work Practice*, Washington: Taylor and Francis.

Ruth Burrows, 2007, *Guidelines for Mystical Prayer*, London: Burns and Oates.

Michel de Certeau, 1995, *The Mystic Fable, Vol. I, The Sixteenth and Seventeenth Centuries*, Chicago: University of Chicago Press.

Bruce Duncan, 1993, *Pray your Way: Your Personality and God*, London: DLT.

James Fowler, 1981, *Stages of Faith: The Psychology of Human Development and the Quest for Meaning*, San Francisco: Harper and Row.

Friedrich Heiler, 1997, *Prayer: A Study in the History and Psychology of Religion,* Oxford: Oneworld Publications.

Sandra Hirsh, 2006, *Soultypes: Matching Your Personality and Spiritual Path,* Minneapolis: Augsburg Fortress.

Maggie Hyde and Michael McGuinness, 1999, *Introducing Jung,* Cambridge: Icon.

Carl Gustav Jung, 1961, *Modern Man in Search of a Soul,* London: RKP.

Joel Kovel, 1978, *A Complete Guide to Therapy: From Psychoanalysis to Behaviour Modification,* Harmondsworth: Penguin.

Frank Lake (abridged by Martin Yeomans), 1986, *Clinical Theology: A Typological and Psychological Basis to Clinical Pastoral Care,* London: DLT.

Darian Leader and Judy Groves, 2000, *Introducing Lacan,* Cambridge: Icon.

R. S. Lee, 1967, *Freud and Christianity,* Harmondsworth: Penguin.

Andrew Louth, 1981, *The Origins of the Christian Mystical Tradition: from Plato to Denys,* Oxford: Clarendon Press.

Joseph Maréchal, tr. Algar Thorold, 1964, *Studies in the Psychology of the Mystics,* Albany, NY: Magi.

Jeffrey Masson, 1990, *Against Therapy,* London: Fontana.

John Peters, 1989, *Frank Lake: The Man and His Work,* London: DLT.

Richard Rohr and Andreas Ebert, 1994, *Discovering the Enneagram: an ancient tool for a new spiritual journey,* North Blackburn, Australia: CollinsDove.

Anthony Stevens, 1991, *On Jung,* Harmondsworth: Penguin.

Charles Taylor, 2007, *A Secular Age,* Cambridge, MA and London: Harvard University Press.

Fraser Watts, 2002, *Theology and Psychology,* Aldershot and Burlington VT: Ashgate.

Fraser Watts, ed., 2007, *Jesus and Psychology,* London: DLT.

Slavoj Žižek, 2001, *On Belief,* London and New York: Routledge.

Chapter 12: Training in Transformation? Spirituality and Ethics

Bernard Aleney, 1995, *Strange Virtues: Ethics in a Multicultural World,* Downers Grove, Illinois: IVP.

James Alison, 1996, *Raising Abel: The Recovery of the Eschatological Imagination,* New York: Crossroad; also published as 1997, *Living in the End Times: The Last Things Reconsidered,* London: SPCK.

James Alison, 2001, *Faith beyond Resentment,* London: DLT.

Thomas Aquinas, ed. T. McDermott, 1989, *Summa Theologiae, A Concise Translation,* London: Methuen.

Mikhail Bakhtin, tr. C. Emerson, 1984, *Problems of Dostoevski's Poetics*, Minnesota: University of Minnesota Press.

Sigurd Bergmann, 2005, *Creation set Free: The Spirit As Liberator of Nature*, Grand Rapids and Cambridge: Eerdmans.

Peter Bertocci and Richard Millard, 1963, *Personality and the Good: Psychological and Ethical Perspectives*. New York: David McKay.

Emil Brunner, 1937, *The Divine Imperative*, London: Lutterworth.

John Calvin, 2001, *Institutes of the Christian Religion*, 2 vols, Louisville KY: Westminster John Knox Press.

James Childs, 1992, *Faith, Formation and Decision: Ethics in the Community of Promise,* Minneapolis: Fortress.

Don Cupitt, 1988, *The New Christian Ethics*, London: SCM Press.

Don Cupitt, 1995, *Solar Ethics*, London: SCM Press.

Celia Deane-Drummond, 2003, *The Ethics of Nature,* Oxford: Blackwell.

Jonathan Edwards, 1960, *The Nature of True Virtue*, Ann Arbor: University of Michigan Press.

Jonathan Edwards, 1989, *The Works of Jonathan Edwards,* New Haven, CT: Yale University Press.

Rene Girard, 2001, *I see Satan fall like Lightning*, New York: Orbis.

T. J. Gorringe, 2001, *The Education of Desire: Towards a Theology of the Senses,* London: SCM Press.

J. M. Gustafson, 1981, *Theology and Ethics*, Oxford: Blackwell.

Stanley Hauerwas, 1981, *A Community of Character,* Notre Dame, IN: Notre Dame.

Stanley Hauerwas, 1998, *Sanctify them in the Truth: Holiness Exemplified,* Edinburgh: T & T Clark.

Richard Holloway, 1999, *Godless Morality: Keeping Religion out of Ethics,* Edinburgh: Canongate.

Søren Kierkegaard, 1968, *Fear and Trembling and The Sickness unto Death*, 1954: Princeton NJ: Princeton University Press.

K. E. Kirk, 1931, *The Vision of God: The Christian Doctrine of the Summum Bonum,* London: Longmans.

Belden Lane, 1998, *The Solace of Fierce Landscapes*, Oxford and New York: Oxford University Press.

Arthur Lovelock, 2000, *Gaia, A New Look at Life on Earth*, Oxford: Oxford Paperbacks.

Martin Luther, tr. J. Pelikan and H. T. Lehmann, 1955–, *Luther's Works*, 55 vols, St Louis, Concordia and Philadelphia: Fortress.

Alasdair MacIntyre, 1981, *After Virtue, A Study in Moral Theory*, London: Duckworth.

John Macquarrie, 1970, *Three Issues in Ethics*, London: SCM Press.

Herbert McCabe, 1968, *Law, Love and Language*, London and Sydney: Sheed and Ward.

W. G. McLagan, 1961, *The Theological Frontier of Ethics*, London: Allen and Unwin.

Mary Midgley, 2001, *Wickedness*, London and New York: Routledge.

John Stuart Mill, 2002, *Utilitarianism*, Indianapolis: Hackett.

Iris Murdoch, 1979, *The Sovereignty of Good*, London and New York: Routledge.

Anne Primavesi, 2000, *Sacred Gaia*, London and New York: Routledge.

Rosemary Radford Ruether, 1989, *Gaia and God: An Ecofeminist Theology of Earth Healing*, London: SCM Press.

Esther Reed, 2000, *The Genesis of Ethics: On the Authority of God as the Origin of Christian Ethics*, London: DLT.

Norman Robinson, 1971, *Groundwork of Christian Ethics*, London: Collins.

Dorothy Sayers, tr., 1955, *Dante, The Divine Comedy 2: Purgatory*, Harmondsworth: Penguin.

Robert Solomon, 1999, *Wicked Pleasures: Meditations on the Seven Deadly Sins*, New York and Oxford: Rowman and Littlefield.

Charles Taylor, 2007, *A Secular Age*, Cambridge MA: Harvard University Press.

Paul Tillich, 1976, *Systematic Theology* Vol. 3: *Life and the Spirit; History and the Kingdom of God*, Chicago: University of Chicago Press.

Miroslav Volf, 1996, *Exclusion and Embrace*, Nashville: Abingdon Press.

Simone Weil, 2002, *Gravity and Grace*, London and New York: Routledge.

Rowan Williams, 2000, *Lost Icons*, Edinburgh: T&T Clark.

Walter Wink, 1992, *Engaging the Powers: Discernment & Resistance in a World of Domination*, Minneapolis: Fortress.

Chapter 13: Spiritual Space? Spirituality in a World of Difference

Karl Barth, 1956, *Church Dogmatics*, Volume I, Part 2, Edinburgh: T&T Clark.

Tim Beaudoin, 1998, *Virtual Faith, the Irreverent Spiritual Quest of Generation X*, New York: Jossey-Bass.

Mary Buley-Meissner, Mary Thompson and Elizabeth Tan, eds, 2000, *The Academy and the Possibility of Belief: Essays on Intellectual and Spiritual Life*, Cresskill, NJ: Hampton Press.

Francis Clooney, 1993, *Theology after Vedanta: An Experiment in Comparative Theology*, Albany, NY: State University of New York Press.

Don Cupitt, 1986, *Life Lines*, London: SCM Press.

Don Cupitt, 1998, *Mysticism after Modernity*, Oxford and Malden, MA: Blackwell.

Don Cupitt, 2001, *Taking Leave of God*, London: SCM Press.

Oliver Davies & Denys Turner, eds, 2002, *Silence and the Word: Negative Theology and Incarnation*, Cambridge and New York: Cambridge University Press.

Gavin D'Costa, 1990, *Christian Uniqueness Reconsidered: The Myth of a Pluralistic Theology of Religions*, Maryknoll, NY: Orbis.

Gavin D'Costa, 2000, *The Meeting of Religions and the Trinity*, Maryknoll, NY: Orbis.

Jacques Dupuis, 1997, *Toward a Christian Theology of Religious Pluralism*, Maryknoll, NY: Orbis.

James Fredericks, 2004, *Buddhists and Christians: Through Comparative Theology to Solidarity*, Maryknoll NY: Orbis.

Paul Heelas, Linda Woodhead, Benjamin Steel, Karin Tusting and Bron Szerszynski, 2004, *The Spiritual Revolution: Why Religion Is Giving Way to Spirituality*, Oxford: Blackwell.

Mark Heim, 1995, *Salvations: Truth and Difference in Religions*, Maryknoll, NY, Orbis.

John Hick, 1989, *An Interpretation of Religion: Human Responses to the Transcendent*, New Haven: Yale University Press.

John Hick, 2006, *The New Frontier of Religion and Science: Religious Experience, Neuroscience and the Transcendent*, Basingstoke: Palgrave Macmillan.

E. Jameson, 1991, *Postmodernism: or The Cultural Logic of Late Capitalism*, Durham, NC: Duke University Press.

Grace Jantzen, 1995, *Power, Gender and Christian Mysticism*, Cambridge, New York and Melbourne: Cambridge University Press.

Thomas Kuhn, 1996, *The Structure of Scientific Revolutions*, Chicago: University of Chicago Press.

Volker Kuster, tr. J. Bowden, 2001, *The Many Faces of Jesus Christ: Intercultural Christology*, London: SCM Press.

George Lindbeck, 1984, *The Nature of Doctrine: Religion and Theology in a Postliberal Age*, Philadelphia: Westminster Press.

Gordon Lynch, 2002, *After Religion: Generation X and the Search for Meaning*, London: DLT.

Jean-Luc Marion, tr, T. A. Carlson, 1995, *God without Being*, Chicago and London: University of Chicago Press.

Declan Marmion, 2005, *Christian Identity in a Postmodern Age: Celebrating the Legacies of Karl Rahner and Bernard Lonergan*, Rockwall, Texas: Veritas.

Harold Netland, 1991, *Dissonant Voices: Religious Pluralism and the Question of Truth*, Grand Rapids: Eerdmans.

Lesslie Newbigin, 1989, *The Gospel in a Pluralist Society*, Grand Rapids: Eerdmans.

Friedrich Nietzsche, 1998, *On the Genealogy of Morals: A Polemic*, Oxford: Oxford Paperbacks.

Raimon Panikkar, 1981, *The Unknown Christ of Hinduism*, Maryknoll, NY: Orbis.

Raimon Panikkar, 2004, *Chistophany: The Fullness of Man*, Maryknoll, NY: Orbis.

Aloysius Pieris, 2000, *Christ beyond Dogma: Doing Theology in the Context of the Religions of the Poor*, Louvain Studies 25.

Peter Rollins, 2006, *How (not) to Speak of God*, London: SPCK.

Rosemary Radford Ruether, 1981, *To Change the World: Christianity and cultural Criticism*, New York: Crossroad.

Robert Scott, 1967, 'On Viewing Rhetoric As Epistemic', *Central States Speech Journal*, 17: 9–16.

Michael Sells, 1994, *Mystical Languages of Unsaying*, Chicago and London: University of Chicago Press.

George Steiner, 1991, *Real Presences*, London: Faber.

David Tracy, 1998, *The Analogical Imagination, Christian Theology and the Culture of Pluralism*, London: SCM Press.

David Tracy, 2004, *The Spirituality Revolution: The Emergence of Contemporary Spirituality*, Hove: Brunner-Routledge.

Ross Thompson, 1989, 'What Kind of Relativism?' *New Blackfriars*, April.

Ross Thompson, 1990, *Holy Ground: The Spirituality of Matter.* London: SPCK.

Slavoj Žižek, 2005, *Interrogating the Real*, London and New York: Continuum.

Conclusion

Sandra Schneiders, 1989, 'Spirituality in the Academy', *Theological Studies* 50: 676–97.

Index of Subjects and Key Names

Index covers main text, not questions and references. Names are given for mystics and writers referred to widely throughout the book, or with significant quotation. Bold type represents major or defining entries.

Index of Biblical References